From Icons to Idols

From Icons to Idols

Documents on the Image Debate
in Reformation England

DAVID J. DAVIS

◆PICKWICK *Publications* • Eugene, Oregon

FROM ICONS TO IDOLS
Documents on the Image Debate in Reformation England

Copyright © 2016 David J. Davis. All rights reserved. Except for brief quotations in critical publications or reviews, no part of this book may be reproduced in any manner without prior written permission from the publisher. Write: Permissions, Wipf and Stock Publishers, 199 W. 8th Ave., Suite 3, Eugene, OR 97401.

Pickwick Publications
An Imprint of Wipf and Stock Publishers
199 W. 8th Ave., Suite 3
Eugene, OR 97401

www.wipfandstock.com

PAPERBACK ISBN 13: 978-1-62564-685-9
HARDCOVER ISBN 13: 978-1-4982-8548-3

Cataloguing-in-Publication Data

Davis, David J. (David Jonathan)

    From icons to idols : documents on the image debate in Reformation England / David J. Davis

    xii + 212 p. ; 23 cm. Includes bibliographical references and index.

    ISBN: 978-1-62564-685-9 (paperback) | ISBN: 978-1-4982-8548-3 (hardback)

    1. Reformation and art—England. 2. Reformation—Great Britain. 3. Iconoclasm—Europe. 4. Protestantism—England—History—16th century. 5. Protestantism—England—History—17th century. I. Title.

BV153.G7 D38 2016

Manufactured in the U.S.A.   02/25/2016

To my parents, who exemplify that wonderful alchemy
of truth blended with love.

Contents

List of Illustrations | x
Acknowledgements | xi
*Abbreviation*s | xii

General Introduction | 1

PART 1: THE EARLY REFORMATION | 15

DOCUMENT 1
John Ryckes, *The Image of Love* | 19
(London, 1525)

DOCUMENT 2
William Tyndale, *An Answer unto Sir Thomas More's Dialogue* | 24
(London, 1532)

DOCUMENT 3
Martin Bucer, *A Treatise Declaring and Showing that Images Are Not to be Suffered in Churches* | 35
(London, 1535)

DOCUMENT 4
Woodcut title-page, *The Great Bible* | 43
(London, 1539)

DOCUMENT 5
John Calvin, *The Sermons of M. John Calvin upon the Fifth Book of Moses called Deuteronomy* | 47
(London, 1583)

DOCUMENT 6
Roger Edgeworth, *Sermons, Very Fruitful, Godly, and Learned* | 56
(London, 1557)

DOCUMENT 7
John Hooper, *A Declaration of the Holy Ten Commandments* | 64
(London, 1549)

PART 2: THE ELIZABETHAN REFORMATION | 71

DOCUMENT 8
Woodcut of Ezekiel's Vision of Heaven, *Geneva Bible* | 74
(Geneva, 1560)

DOCUMENT 9
Woodcut of Isaiah's Vision of Heaven, *Bishops Bible* | 77
(London, 1568)

DOCUMENT 10
Marcus Gheeraerts the Elder, *The Allegory of Iconoclasm* | 79
(London, 1566–1568)

DOCUMENT 11
Heinrich Bullinger, *Fifty Godly Sermons* | 82
(London, 1577)

DOCUMENT 12
John Jewel, "Homily Against the Peril of Idolatry
and Superfluous Decking of Churches" | 89
(London, 1571)

DOCUMENT 13
John Martiall, *A Treatise of the Cross* | 98
(Antwerp, 1564)

DOCUMENT 14
Nicholas Sander, *A Treatise of the Images of Christ* | 109
(Louvain, 1567)

DOCUMENT 15
Peter Vermigli, *The Common Places of the Most Famous and Renowned
Divine Doctor Peter Martyr* | 118
(London, 1583)

DOCUMENT 16
Gregory Martin, *A Discovery of the Manifold Corruptions of the Holy Scripture by the Heretics of Our Days* | 135
(Rheims, 1582)

PART 3: THE POST-REFORMATION | 145

DOCUMENT 17
William Perkins Two Documents | 147

DOCUMENT 18
William Bishop, *A Reformation of a Catholic Deformed* | 161
(English Secret Press, 1604)

DOCUMENT 19
Robert Bellarmine, *An Ample Declaration of the Christian Doctrine* | 169
(English Secret Press, 1604)

DOCUMENT 20
John Heigham, *The Touchstone of the Reformed Gospel* | 174
(St. Omer's Press, 1652)

DOCUMENT 21
Richard Montagu, *A Gag for the New Gospel?: No, a New Gag for an Old Goose* | 179
(London, 1624)

DOCUMENT 22
Anonymous, "Controversii et compendium Becari" | 188
(1625)

Bibliography | 199
General Index | 209

Illustrations

Figure 1 Woodcut: "Title-page," *The Great Bible* (London: R. Grafton & E. Whitchurch, 1541), frontispiece. Reproduced by permission of the Dunham Bible Museum | 46

Figure 2 Woodcut: "Vision of Ezekiel," *The Geneva Bible* (Geneva: R. Hall, 1560), sig. 3N3v. Reproduced by permission of the Dunham Bible Museum | 76

Figure 3 Woodcut: "Vision of Isaiah," *The Bishops Bible* (London: R. Jugge, 1572), sig. 3K3v. Reproduced by permission of the Dunham Bible Museum | 78

Figure 4 Woodcut: Marcus Gheeraerts the Elder, *The Allegory of Iconoclasm* (London, 1566–1568). Reproduced by permission of the Trustees of the British Museum | 81

Acknowledgements

THIS BOOK HAS BEEN over ten years in the making. Much of that time I did not even realize that it was quietly gestating. A full acknowledgement, then, of everyone who had a hand in the making of this book would itself be a chapter, as it represents much of my own study on the Reformation since I was an undergraduate student. Profs. Alexandra Walsham, Peter Marshall, and Margaret Aston are the most important among those many scholars that I have relied upon for insight and guidance. Also, I have been blessed by my associations and interactions with other members of the Tyndale Society and the Sixteenth Century Studies Society. Toward the end of the writing process, Adam Morton and John Mack provided excellent critiques and suggestions that proved invaluable to the final volume. Once again, as in the past, Diana Severance and the Dunham Bible Museum have been more than generous with the use of their illustrations and their reading room. Also, I am indebted to the assistance of the Department of Prints and Drawings at the British Museum.

Finally, in the earliest stages of writing, my good friend Micah Mattix provided encouragement during numerous cycling outings, and throughout the entire process, my wife Lisa was more patient than I will ever deserve.

Abbreviations

ANF *Ante-Nicene Fathers: The Writings of the Fathers Down to A.D. 325*, edited by Rev. Alexander Roberts and James Donaldson (London: T. & T. Clark, 1867–73)

NPNF *Nicene and Post-Nicene Fathers of the Christian Church*, edited by Philip Schaff and Henry Wace (London: T. & T. Clark, 1886–1900)

ODNB *Oxford Dictionary of National Biography*, edited by H. C. G. Matthew and Brian Harrison (Oxford: Oxford University Press, 2004); an online, updated version is available to subscribers at www.oxforddnb.com

VAI *Visitation Articles and Injunctions of the Period of the Reformation*, 3 vols., edited by Walter Howard Frere (London: Longmans, 1910)

General Introduction

ICONOCLASM IN REFORMATION ENGLAND

In 1547, the young King Edward VI issued a series of religious injunctions intending to reform the churches in England. Among the targets of these injunctions were icons and other religious imagery, about which he commanded his clergy and royal officials:

> Take away, utterly extinct, and destroy all shrines, covering of shrines, all tables, candle-sticks, trindals, and rolls of wax, pictures, paintings, and all other monuments of feigned miracles, pilgrimages, idolatry, and superstition, so that there remain no memory of the same in walls, glasses, windows, or elsewhere with their churches and houses, preserving nevertheless or repairing both the walls and glass windows. And they shall exhort all their parishioners to do the like within their several houses.[1]

England, in the 1540s, was already a doctrinal battlefield littered with the wreckage of religious images. Henry VIII had instituted a series of religious changes, particularly the dissolution of over 800 monasteries and nunneries, condemning large swathes of traditional Catholic religious practice and iconography. His son Edward and Edward's counsellors followed the even more iconoclastic example of the reform movements in Switzerland and Germany.[2] Images—statuaries, murals, stained glass, rood screens, altars, paintings, carvings, roadside crosses, and many other sorts—were the most public displays of Catholicism in the sixteenth century. Unlike other points of theological dispute, religious imagery was a tangible and permanent aspect of the landscape, both inside and outside the churches.

1. VAI, II, 126.
2. Wandel, *Voracious Idols*; Eire, *War Against the Idols*.

For many people, it was one of the first aspects of the church to be reformed, and the degree to which it was reformed often was indicative of an individual's or community's theological leanings.

Behind this destruction was a longstanding debate over the nature, purpose, and appropriate uses of images, particularly in relation to worship and devotion. The Reformation was not the first period in church history where Christians asked questions about images and art. Nor were Protestant reformers the first to seize the hammers of iconoclasm. Destroying would-be idols had marked strong religious sentiment since the early church, and both Catholics and Protestants employed the examples and arguments of earlier movements in their debates.[3] Reformers found inspiration from precedents like the Byzantine iconoclasm of the eighth century and from biblical models like the Old Testament King Josiah.[4]

The Reformation lines between icon and idol, however, are much more difficult to identify than any single debate, event, or royal injunction would suggest. One of the oftentimes overlooked aspects of the debates during the Reformation was how much the issues surrounding idolatry changed over time, not only as lines of demarcation shifted but also as certain points of emphasis arose as others fell away. This volume tracks the image debate—from the perspectives of both Protestants and Catholics—across the period of religious change in England from 1525 to 1625. England offers the most useful context for seeing this kind of diversity and change, as arguments and discourse in England evolved in different directions over the century. Unlike the reformations in Germany, France, and elsewhere, the image debate in England continued to play a major role in the theological discourse well into the seventeenth century. Also, England, while maintaining an official Protestant confession, played host to a variety of religious confessions and perspectives (some of which originated in continental Europe), including: pre- and post-Tridentine Catholicism, church papism (Catholics who conformed to the Book of Common Prayer), puritanism, Lutheranism, evangelical Protestantism, Anglicanism, and conforming Calvinism. Taken together, these different viewpoints demonstrate the richness and complexity of ideas that were on offer, each helping to shape one of the most

---

3. Van Asselt et al., eds, *Iconoclasm and Iconoclash*; Kitzinger, *The Cult of Images*; Belting, *Likeness and Presence*.

4. Aston, *King's Bedpost*, 26–36. In this regard, the Byzantine iconoclastic controversy stands out among the rest. Unfortunately, it has historically been woefully oversimplified and misunderstood. See Brubaker, *Inventing Byzantine Iconoclasm*; Giakalis, *Images of the Divine*; Parry, *Depicting the Word*. Perhaps the most thorough study of Carolingian iconoclasm and art is Noble, *Images, Iconoclasm*.

longstanding religious questions of the Reformation: what makes an image idolatrous?

Iconoclasm has been sifted thoroughly by historians, theologians, and literary experts over the past four decades. It is not my purpose here to retread what is already a well-paved road, but a few comments about this scholarship is useful. The English context has been examined particularly by John Philips and Margaret Aston. Aston's work has proven to be the most formative, outlining the intellectual and theological underpinnings of Protestant iconoclasm in England. Also, she demonstrated the importance of iconoclasm in the Reformation, as something that was more than simply the removal of visual religion:

> It was ... quite as momentous as the removal of the monasteries. In some ways it was more so. Iconoclasm affected the whole fabric of worship and the ways in which people believed. It bore upon the making of the whole Reformation settlement. It contributed to the continuously recurring violence of the Reformation years a form of disturbance that led straight into the troubles of the Interregnum. Also, more theoretically, the switch from an imaging to an imageless church seems relevant to some of the major shifts in seventeenth-century thought.[5]

For scholars of the English Reformation, iconoclasm has played a major role in the historiographical disputes over the nature, length, and efficacy of Protestant reform. Since Eamon Duffy's revisionist work *The Stripping of the Altars*, which argued against a traditional understanding of the English Reformation as a revival of sincere religion, Protestant iconoclasm has become a necessary talking point when discussing the Reformation in England.[6] Iconoclasm mattered not only for the religion that it was destroying but also for the religion it was helping to create.

While there was a tradition of iconoclasm in England stemming back to the Lollard heresy of the fifteenth century, the English reformers took their lead in iconoclasm from the Lutheran and Swiss reformers who were already instituting different policies of iconoclasm on the continent in the 1520s.[7] The work of Carlos Eire, Lee Palmer Wandel, Sergiusz Michalski, and others have shaped our understanding of continental iconoclasm, and

---

5. Aston, *England's Iconoclasts*, 16.

6. Duffy, *Stripping of the Altars*. The debate over the English Reformation has become something of a quagmire of academic wrangling, summarized in Marshall, "(Re)defining the English Reformation," 564–86.

7. On Lollard iconoclasm see Aston, *Lollards and Reformers*.

these will be referenced throughout this book in order to connect the continental and English reformations.[8]

Several key points arise from these works about the general nature of Reformation iconoclasm that are important to mention here. First, even in Protestant regions, not all destruction was legal, and civil authorities (regardless of their beliefs) generally frowned upon non-official destruction.[9] Simply because city officials were removing and burning images did not permit everyone to rush pell-mell into the churches, ripping and destroying as they went. Second, the emphasis that reformers placed upon the act of destroying images could fluctuate dramatically, so that a single year could contain most of the iconoclasm in a region for that decade. Third, few reformers agreed completely with one another about the theological motivation behind iconoclasm or what should be destroyed and by whom.[10]

Since the late 1980s, many historians have seen the Protestant church in England as an iconophobic institution after the year 1580. This thesis, which was first put forward by the late Patrick Collinson, has been heavily criticized over the last twenty years.[11] At the same time, there is a growing recognition that very few Protestants ever denounced all visual images, even all religious images. There has been for some time a silent admission that the relationship between the visual arts and the Reformation movements across Europe is much more subtle and complex than previously assumed. Protestants regularly failed to find consensus on many basic questions surrounding iconoclasm and image use. What constituted an idol? Should they be defaced or completely annihilated? Could legitimate images become idols? Could idols be reformed? Were there degrees of reverence/respect that someone could give to an image without committing idolatry? What degrees were appropriate? There are no cut-and-dry answers to these questions from the Protestant position in England.

IMAGES AND THE ENGLISH REFORMATION

Alongside the destruction that has come to characterize the Protestant relationship with religious imagery, recent studies highlight the various

---

8. The Dutch Reformation's waves of iconoclasm, and the Calvinist theology behind these waves, has been studied by Crew, *Calvinist Preaching*.

9. Eire, *War Against the Idols*, 151–65.

10. Michalski still has the most thorough reading of the major continental Protestant positions on images, though he wrongly lumps John Calvin in with Andreas Karlstadt as an iconophobe: Michalski, *Reformation and the Visual* Arts, 1–74.

11. Collinson, "From Iconoclasm." For one of the earliest challenges to the iconophobia thesis see Watt, *Cheap Print*, 136–9.

ways that Protestants—from across the confessional spectrum—used images. The uses that Protestants in England found for images varies strikingly, undermining any strict, simplistic icon/idol paradigm. First and foremost, Protestants continued to employ images as works of art. Recent works on visual culture and art history have begun to balance out the long-held, oversimplified paradigm of Protestants being inherently iconoclastic. Art historical studies by scholars like Carl Christensen drew attention to the extensive use Lutherans made of certain art forms, particularly in the works of artists like Lucas Cranach and Albrecht Durer. Christensen writes, "Luther's theology . . . called for a somewhat more discriminating use of religious imagery than had characterized the Roman Catholic Church . . . . Yet it is equally clear that the reformer by no means intended to eliminate the contribution of the artist to the worship and teaching of Christendom."[12] This seems to hold true, though to a lesser degree, in the Calvinist reformation in the Dutch Republic, which was perhaps the most iconoclastic of the reform movements. Recent examinations of both painting and printed images have revealed a robust religious art culture.[13] Similarly, scholarship of early modern England demonstrates a burgeoning art culture that proudly displayed religious themes in paintings and interior decor.[14]

A second use that Protestants found for images were as tools in propaganda.[15] The anti-Catholic propaganda of Lutheranism in the 1520s, expertly analyzed by Robert Scribner, influenced Protestant visual culture in England, providing it certain visual tropes to excoriate Catholicism and positively depict things like justification by faith and the preaching of the Word.[16] The pope and the clergy were regularly depicted as the antichrist, the whore of Babylon, and the spawn of devils, and his disciples and followers were portrayed as dupes, idolaters, and fools.

A third use for images in Protestant England was book illustration. As I have demonstrated elsewhere, many of the woodcuts and engravings in Protestant books were quite similar to images that were being ripped from the churches, but this did not strike Protestant readers as duplicitous or hypocritical.[17] Protestants, both in England and continental Europe, often used pictures of Christ, God the Father, the Virgin, biblical events,

---

12. Christensen, *Art and the Reformation*, 65.

13. Works on the visual culture of the Dutch Republic include: Vanhaelen, *Wake of Iconoclasm*; Stronks, *Negotiating Differences*.

14. Hamling and Williams, eds, *Art Re-formed*; Hunter, ed., *Printed Images in Early Modern Britain*; Davis, *Seeing Faith*; Morton, "Images and the Senses."

15. For an overview of visual propaganda see Pettegree, *Reformation*, 102–27.

16. Scribner, *For the Sake of the Simple Folk*.

17. Davis, *Seeing Faith*.

and portraits of Protestant clergy to illustrate their books. The pictures of martyrs and heroic clergy in John Foxe's *Actes and Monuments* (popularly known as the *Book of Martyrs*) is perhaps the most obvious example in England. The 1570 edition contained over one hundred woodcuts, depicting the deaths of saints from the early church to the reign of Queen Mary in the 1550s.[18] However, Bibles, prayer books, devotionals, theological tomes, and many other texts were illustrated with a variety of religious images. While some Protestants voiced concerns over particular illustrations—a few Puritans even condemned the 1568 Bishops Bible (see document 9) for some of its illustrations—on the whole, there was more acceptance than distaste for religious images in books.[19]

Finally, we must not neglect the fact that Protestants used images for devotional purposes. Although it may seem counterintuitive, and it runs in the face of a great deal of Protestant polemic, it is clear that Protestants employed visual images in specific contexts to aid in spiritual devotion and understanding. Both Joseph Koerner and Robert Scribner have studied how Lutherans put images to use in devotional contexts, and recent studies on late sixteenth- and early seventeenth-century church altars indicates that the visual was not insignificant to devotion.[20] Most of the printed images in English Bibles were intended to inspire and aid in devotional reading. The preface to the Geneva Bible, which was the most Calvinist of English translations, specifically states this as their purpose. Furthermore, one of the most popular ways of depicting biblical saints in Protestant prayer books was to have them kneeling in supplication before a symbol of God (usually the Tetragrammaton).[21]

THE REFORMATION IMAGE DEBATE

Iconoclasm shaped the English Reformation in many ways. Religious images played an important role in the culture of late medieval Catholic devotion, and they became a lightning rod for acts of reformed violence, perpetrated by both the monarchy and the populace, from the pre-Reformation Lollard movement and the Dissolution of the Monasteries to the Puritan movement

---

18. Luborsky and Ingram, *A Guide to English Illustrated Books*, I.365–82; King, *Foxe's Book of Martyrs*, 162–95; Aston, "The Iconography."

19. Margaret Aston has analyzed the debate over pictures of godly churchmen, including Theodore Beze's approval of such images in Aston, "Gods, Saints, and Reformers."

20. Koerner, *Reformation of the Image*; Scribner, *Religion and Culture*, 104–28; Fincham and Tyacke, *Altars Restored*.

21. Ryrie, *Being Protestant*, 183; Davis, *Seeing Faith*, 206–10.

and the English Civil War.[22] Religious images were never simply pictures and statues, nor were they, as reformers would have us believe, only materialistic remnants of a corrupt Roman Catholic faith that had succumb to the allure of idolatry. Religious imagery came to be a marker of religious identity and confession, for both the Catholic Church and the various Protestant churches. What a person did to, or with, an image was also a profession of their own religious views on larger questions of faith and practice. People knelt before images, prayed to them, performed pilgrimages to them, burned candles before them, broke them, burned them, kissed them, bowed to them with reverence (with and without worshipful intent), ignored them, printed them in books, defended them as things indifferent, and used them to mock their religious opponents.

Images served as markers of religious identity during the sixteenth and seventeenth centuries. A person's inclination, or lack thereof, toward image use in religious devotion went a long way in announcing their own doctrinal and confessional positions. Even among different Protestant groups, a person's opinion of what images were tolerable, how they could be used in devotion (if at all), and the possibility of idolatrous worship provided a good indicator of the person's broader theology. These distinctions were not without meaning, and they are important to understand in order to fully comprehend the scope and complexity of the reformed movements.

Before we go any further, it is worthwhile addressing a common misconception about images in the Reformation. It is important to avoid the overly simplistic paradigm that sets Protestants opposing images and Catholics defending them. John Dillenberger exemplifies this egregious generalization when he writes, "By definition, the Reformed tradition kept the verbal modalities so central that the visual was rejected ... the sight lines of worship were different, all looking at one point, with attention only on hearing. Other sensibilities—seeing, tasting, smelling—had no place. Concentration must be on the Word alone in the medium of words, not the medium of sight."[23] Certainly, many Protestants destroyed or advocated the destruction of images that they considered idolatrous, and Catholics revered the same images as icons. However, treating either group as a homogenous whole is erroneous, as both Protestants and Catholics could vary in their beliefs about images from other individuals of the same creed. At certain times and places, Protestants also reverenced particular kinds of images, and Catholics were not above destroying, or even banning, choice

---

22. Duffy, *Voices of Morebath*; Duffy, *Stripping of the Altars*; Aston, *England's Iconoclasts*; Phillips, *Reformation of Images*.

23. Dillenberger, *Images and Relics*, 190. For an excellent reevaluation of this view, see Milner, *The Senses*.

depictions and representations, such as certain representations of the Trinity.[24] Part of the reason that oversimplifications, like Dillenberger's, continue to hold intellectual traction is that many of the sources that speak to the debate over images are difficult to access. While scholarship on iconoclasm and the image debate has teased out many of the nuanced relations between early modern Christians and religious images, primary sources like John Martiall's *A Treatise of the Cross* or William Perkins's *A Golden Chain* remain largely in the hands of the specialist academic. The purpose of this volume is to take a step in the direction of remedying this deficiency by providing a selection of different works from various authorities in the sixteenth-century debate. The documents in this volume represent a variety of positions on religious images, from a multitude of arguments and lines of reasoning.

Although it would not be unfruitful to identify every individual argument, it is sufficient for our purposes here to identify four major categories of the debate that all of the arguments fall into. First, many of the debates centered on the use and interpretation of particular biblical passages. All sides found scriptural justification for their views. Those who defended the use of images in religious devotion turned to the examples of the Old Testament temple in 2 Chronicles 3, which describes how Solomon was ordered to build statues of the cherubim. Also, the veneration of angels and divine visions (e.g., Genesis 18, Joshua 5, and Daniel 9) are identified as examples of appropriate forms of veneration. On the opposite side of the debate, iconoclasts martial verses that command and give examples of the destruction of images in the Old Testament (e.g., Deuteronomy 4, Isaiah 30, and 1 Kings 15). Also, the lists of sins in the New Testament that identify idolatry among them are often noted (e.g., 1 Corinthians 6, Galatians 5, Ephesians 5, and Colossians 3). Of course, the most important scriptural reference was the commandment against idolatry in Exodus 20. Iconoclasts noted this as irrefutable evidence against image veneration, whereas those who reverenced images believed it was directed only at images that were truly idols, which they defined in two ways. First, idols could only be representations of pagan gods that were being used in divine worship. Or, second, idols were images that had suffered idolatrous abuse, by being treated as God.

Second, the Reformation image debates were linguistic disputes. In particular, the authors focused on the distinction between Latin words meaning images (*imago* and *idolum*) and the distinction between types of worship (*dulia* and *latria*). Concerning the first distinction, a great deal of ink was spilled explaining, as Catholic writers will say, that while the Latin

---

24. Hallebeek, "Papal Prohibitions," in van Asselt, et al., eds, *Iconoclasm and Iconoclash*, 353–86.

words are used for two words in Greek (*eikon* and *eidolon*), Protestants conflate their meaning to mean only idol in their condemnation of idolatry, when they argue that all images are potentially idols. This, for Protestants, will take a dangerous turn at the end of the sixteenth century, when Catholic writers raised the question of how Protestants determined when this conflation is not appropriate. The distinction between *dulia* and *latria* was as equally influential, as Catholic writers distinguished between types of veneration, a lesser kind offered to saints and kings (*dulia*) and a greater kind offered only to God (*latria*). While Protestants will initially dismiss this distinction as mere dissimulation, they will develop their own distinctions to separate kinds of honor that they pay to representations of the monarchy, the Bible, and God.

Third, the image debates employed historical arguments, drawn from patristic texts, church history, and church tradition. Both Catholics and Protestants pulled passages (regularly out of context) from a variety of church fathers, including: Cyprian, Tertullian, Origen, Lactantius, Athanasius, Jerome, Augustine, Gregory of Nazianzus, Eusebius of Caeasaria, and John Chrysostom. For Catholic writers, most influential were the eighth-century treatises on images by John of Damascus. His arguments were regularly employed by Catholic authors, from the defense of laymen's books and historical examples of Christians using images for different kinds of veneration.[25] For iconoclastic Protestants, however, a letter from Pope Gregory the Great to Serenus, Bishop of Marseilles, was among the most popular sources. In the letter, Gregory condemned the iconoclasm of saints' statues. Protestants pointed to this letter as the beginning of illicit image worship.[26] Although these precedents were never considered sufficient on their own to warrant image veneration or condemnation, both Protestants and Catholics were careful to address them and to contest the other's use of particular sources.

Fourth, and finally, the debates stressed the distinctions between kinds of images and kinds of image veneration. The debates emphasized the practical use and/or abuse of images as a demarcation between image and idol. There was no consensus among Protestants as to the exact line separating the use and abuse of images, making this one of the more ambiguous—and thus hotly contested—topics of the debates. Since most Protestants considered images, themselves divorced from any context, to be *adiaphora* (things indifferent), images were neither essentially virtuous nor essentially corrupt and could potentially be used for either purpose. Determining when idolatry

---

25. Louth, ed. *Three Treatises.*
26. Gregory, "Epistle XIII," in NPNF, 2nd Series, vol. XIII, II.297–98.

occurred became a key issue. For the early reformer Martin Bucer (document 3), idolatry happened when images were brought into the churches, and many English Protestants followed this line of reasoning. Others, even Puritans like William Fulke, deviated from Bucer, stressing instead the ways that images were used in churches (i.e., an image of the queen could be set up without fear of idolatry).[27] Multiple factors could play into this question: location, historical use/abuse, popular appeal, color, size, dimensions, and what was represented. However, there was not ever any precise litmus test, short of devotees kneeling before an image and calling it God, that all Protestants agreed upon that could distinguish an image from an idol.[28] On the other hand, Catholic defenders of image veneration stressed that images of biblical and Christian figures could not be mistaken for idols, nor abused as idols were abused. However, they are not all in agreement here. Some, following the example of Thomas More, refused to admit the possibility that an icon could be corrupted, whereas others like Nicholas Sander (document 14) conceded the point, at least theoretically. Nevertheless, Catholics argued that, whatever the potential for idolatrous abuse, images continued to be valuable, as reminders of scriptural events and truths, as foci of reverence, and as laymen's books for those who could not read the scriptures.[29]

ABOUT THE DOCUMENTS

The documents that I have brought together for this volume are intended to be representative and indicative, rather than a comprehensive compilation of everything written on the subject. That being said, this book suffers from the shortcomings of all such collections. There are many sources that have not been included that arguably could have been, as the debate on images was taken up by many polemicists and theologians. What *From Icons to Idols* lacks in its exhaustiveness, I trust it will make up for in the authority and variety of its selections. Here, we have selections by writers from all walks of life: leading Protestant and Catholic theologians, Protestant bishops, Catholic cardinals, linguists, polemicists, printers, noblemen, and commoners. The types of texts from which these selections derive are no less diverse. Some are polemical works dripping with venom, others are careful theological tomes, as well as collected sermons. There are sermons intended as rote homilies, a catechism for those with limited education, and a private letter between cousins on opposites sides of the Reformation divide. What

27. Fulke, *A Defence*, 204.
28. Davis, *Seeing Faith*, 45–60.
29. Aston, *England's Iconoclasts*, 130–32; Wandel, *Voracious Idols*, 49–51

is most interesting in all of this diversity of writer and text is that on the one hand the major arguments, sources, and ideas remain relatively consistent. As we noted above, most of the arguments for or against images fall fairly comfortably into four categories, with much of the material being reused across several decades. On the other hand, there is a great deal of evolution as well. Different arguments and lines of reasoning are given more attention at certain times. The earlier arguments never fully evaporate, but later writers build upon aspects of them, abandon some parts, and place new issues at the forefront of debate.

The documents in the first part of this book represent the period of the Early Reformation, from before Henry VIII's break with Rome in the early 1530s until the reign of his daughter Queen Mary in the 1550s. This period contains perhaps the greatest variety of opinions on religious images, reflecting the fluctuating state of the English church.[30] Most importantly, it is clear in this section that images faced challenges from within and without Catholic orthodoxy (document 1) and that there is no Protestant consensus on images. William Tyndale (document 2) voices a more tolerant view of images than Martin Bucer (document 3) or John Calvin (document 5), but none of them completely condemned visual arts.

The second part of this book looks at the image debate in the Elizabethan years (1558–1603). Although two of the documents (documents 11, 15) were written before this period, the authors' influence in England became most profound in the latter half of the sixteenth century as a new generation of English Protestant clergy, who had cut their teeth on the writings of the continental reformers, took the reins of the church. The 1560s were a critical decade in the image debate of this period. Not only were two substantial Catholic apologies on image veneration (documents 13 and 14) written in these years, but also there were several conflicts within the Church of England dealing with imagery (see the introductions of documents 8, 9, and 12). While Queen Elizabeth's royal injunctions against images echoed her brother Edward's in many respects, there is clearly a shift toward a moderate view of iconoclasm. Not only did the queen keep a golden cross in her private chapel, and defend public monuments like the Cheapside Cross, which stood in the center of London, but she also insisted that stained glass windows be spared and that her bishops don the appropriate vestments during church service.[31]

---

30. For more on the English official religion during this period see Ryrie, *The Gospel*; MacCulloch, *The Boy King*.

31. Budd, "Rethinking Iconoclasm."

The third and final part of this book, which deals with the post-Reformation years during the reign of James I (1603–25), demonstrates the continued importance of the image debate to English religion. It begins with a debate between the Calvinist theologian William Perkins and the future Catholic bishop William Bishop. Perhaps most significantly in this section, it is evident that Protestant views on images have not fused together, as there is still a great difference between the modifying language of Richard Montagu (document 21) and Perkins's assault on Catholic idolatry (document 17). The debate is also part of the larger Catholic polemics and apologies of the day (documents 18 and 20), as well as the more accessible statements of catechetical dogma (document 19). Finally, document 22 offers a fitting conclusion to this collection, summarizing and echoing many of the essential debates surrounding images and placing the image debate in a context (a private letter) in which it is rarely seen.

NOTES ON THE TRANSCRIPTION

Any transcription or translation work must balance faithfulness to the original texts alongside the need to communicate clearly with the modern reader. Here, I have erred on the side of communication when necessary. The documents in this collection have been modernized as much as possible without clouding the meaning of the original. Thus, spellings (e.g., hath, doeth, iustice, etc.) have been updated, but arcane words (e.g., cavillation) have been retained, and a note on the meaning included when necessary. Likewise comma usage has been modernized and standardized. Slashes (/), which were common elements of grammar in the sixteenth century, have been replaced with semicolons or commas where appropriate. Colons have been replaced by periods when they clearly indicate the end of an independent clause. Inconsistent capitalization of the first letter of certain words (e.g., images, reformers, etc.) has been modernized when it is appropriate and not indicating a proper noun. "God" has been capitalized throughout, when it is a reference to the Christian God, and "Church" has been capitalized when it is a reference to the universal body of Christ.

Most of documents are presented here as large excerpts from the originals, and some are complete translations. However, several of them, because of space constraints and the length of the original, have been limited. Whenever text has been removed from the transcription, ellipses have been used to indicate it. When a portion of removed text is substantial (more than one paragraph), then the ellipses is preceded and followed by a paragraph break.

Greek and Hebrew fonts have been retained whenever they are employed, and likewise for any time an author places Greek script into Latin font. Quotes from foreign languages have been set off in italics, whereas quotations in English have been placed within quotations marks. Quotes from scripture have been transcribed as they are given in the original, which were often translations of the author's own making; however, when an established translation is used, it is identified in the notes. Also, while modern translations and editions of classical and patristic sources are provided in the notes, all quotes taken from these documents (unless otherwise indicated) have been retained as they were quoted. Finally, when a footnote begins "Margin note," this indicates a note from the original author. All other notes are mine.

PART 1

THE EARLY REFORMATION

HISTORICAL OVERVIEW

The first part of this collection covers the reigns of three monarchs, who each brought with them different kinds of religious changes to England. When Henry VIII broke from the Roman Catholic Church in the early 1530s, iconoclasm was already well trodden religious terrain. The heretical group known as the Lollards were well known for their hatred of abused images, attacking shrines and other images in the fifteenth and early sixteenth centuries. In the 1520s, other people in England, influenced by the Lutheran reforms and local reformers like William Tyndale, were outspoken in their hatred of idolatry.[32] Also, devotional works that spoke to the question of images began circulating. Some like John Ryckes's *The Image of Love* (1525 and 1531) (document 1) and the anonymous *The Mirror or the Looking Glass of Life* (1532) were critical of image worship. Others like Robert Barnes's *A Supplication* (1531) were openly antagonistic.[33]

As tensions between the king and the papacy reached their breaking point, acts of iconoclasm became much more public and brazen. In 1533 alone, the well-known Highway Cross of Coggeshall was torn down, along with several crosses in Stoke. Also, the image of St. Christopher was removed from the church in Sudbury, along with St. Petronella in Ipswich and

---

32. Aston, *Lollards and Reformers*, 135–92; Duffy, *Stripping of the Altars*, 2–6.
33. Aston, *England's Iconoclasts*, 174–94.

St. Anne in Buxton.³⁴ In London, similar outbreaks occurred throughout the early 1530s. One man named William Collins reportedly shot arrows at the image of St. Margaret at the church St. Margaret Pattens in London, "challenging it to defend itself and punish him, if it were able." According to Susan Brigden, "Some Londoners even pricked the fallen images mockingly to see whether they would bleed."³⁵ Although it was in the 1540s under the reign of Edward VI that iconoclasm would become, as Eamon Duffy states, "a central sacrament of the reform," its popularity was evident even before Henry broke with Catholicism.³⁶

Henry's official policy tended to err on the side of order and stability, condemning random acts of violence; however, he increasingly permitted the destruction of abused images, particularly those associated with the monasteries that were being dissolved between 1536 and 1540. The Ten Articles of 1536 offered a qualified permission for image use, reflecting the spirit and language of *adiaphora* that we will see in document 2. His injunctions issued in 1536 and 1538, on the other hand, dealt more censoriously with images, particularly targeting Thomas Becket's shrine in Canterbury Cathedral and certain images of the Virgin.³⁷

Images also played a role in the Catholic response to reform in the 1530s and 1540s. The 1536 uprising in the north of England, known as the Pilgrimage of Grace, opposed Henry's reforms, and many rebels raised banners with the five wounds of Christ on them.³⁸ Then, after 1539, when Henry backtracked on many of his reformed policies, iconoclasm became a crime across the realm. Patrick Collinson explains, "When Henry VIII swung the Church back to a conservatively defined Catholicism in the early 1540s, the city authorities in London clamped down on the hardcore protestant population, those who despised holy bread and holy water, read the Bible in church and were anticlerical and iconoclastic."³⁹ Although there was not a great host of prosecutions for iconoclasm, they do exist. In 1542, John Toftes of Canterbury was arrested and prosecuted because he had pulled down an image of the Virgin and "did hew her all in pieces." In 1543, a band of English soldiers in Flanders was arrested by their general Sir John Wallop for "pulling down, despitefully handling and burning of images."⁴⁰

34. Duffy, *Stripping of the Altars*, 385.
35. Ibid., 288; Brigden, *London and the Reformation*, 273.
36. Duffy, *Stripping of the Altars*, 480.
37. Spraggon, *Puritan Iconoclasm*, 3–4.
38. Bush, *The Pilgrimage of Grace*.
39. Collinson, *Birthpangs*, 40.
40. Cited in Shagan, *Popular Politics*, 218; Brewer et al., eds, *Letters and Papers*,

When Henry's young son Edward ascended the throne in 1547, his coronation was "greeted" with acts of iconoclasm around London, as more virulent reformers anticipated a sudden increase in reformed policies.[41] The individuals who executed these preemptive strikes were not disappointed. Edward's reign represents not only a return to a more coherent Protestant Church but also the establishment of an overtly reformed liturgy, where the theology coming out of Zurich and Geneva were given precedence. Edward was hailed as a King Josiah by preachers and counselors, and one of the expectations foisted upon Edward was that he would accelerate the pace of reform. His injunctions, quoted in the general introduction to this book, were the most adamant and thorough condemnation of religious images by any English monarch. In the late 1540s and early 1550s, waves of royal officials swept through the realm, cataloging and destroying images that were deemed idolatrous, as iconoclasm was made "law by statute" by Edward's Privy Council.[42] Michael O'Connell asserts that because of the extensive and sustained destruction, "In some respects, the royal directive of iconoclasm ... went beyond Zwingli's Zurich."[43] The reforms were most evident in London and southeast England. Indeed, in one example, Nicholas Ridley, bishop of London, ordered all altars removed, and personally attacked the tomb of John of Gaunt (father of King Henry IV) in St. Paul's Cathedral.[44] The verve of the reforms, however, was accompanied by increasing divisions within English Protestantism. There were internal disputes about how far the destruction and erasure of Catholic tradition should go. The most evident of these disputes was the quarrel between England's leading reformers over clerical vestments. Bishop of Gloucester John Hooper (document 7) was at the centered of this debate, as he denounced the wearing of clerical vestments, because they were material trappings of Catholic superstition. The vestments controversy highlights the spectrum of theological opinion about material religion, even among figures that were, in all other respects, in agreement.

When Edward died in the summer of 1553 and his half-sister Mary Tudor ascended the throne, the swift return to the Roman Catholic Church drastically changed the place of images in English religion. Of course, those who had remained loyal to Catholic tradition and practice welcomed the changes that Mary's reign brought to religion. Aided by bishops like

---

XVIII.i.420.

41. Spraggon, *Puritan Iconoclasm*, 4.
42. Phillips, *Reformation of Images*, 96–97.
43. Aston, *England's Iconoclasts*, 255; O'Connell, *The Idolatrous Eye*, 56.
44. VAI, II.276–77 (cited in Spraggon, *Puritan Iconoclasm*, 5).

Archbishop Reginald Pole and Bishop of London Edmund Bonner, Mary implemented a series of injunctions to restore and recover as much of the traditional iconography as possible. It was during this period of Catholic restoration that Roger Edgeworth's sermons (document 6) received their greatest airing in print. Around the kingdom, silver plate, pyxes, rood screens, jewels, vestments, altars, baptismal fonts, and tombstones—not to mention statues, windows, and other more overt images—had gone missing or been destroyed. Some of the missing items were returned by parishioners who had kept them safe, whereas other people proved "uncooperative," needing to be compelled to return things like candlesticks and roodscreens.[45] However, Mary's reign did a great deal, unintentionally, to strengthen the Protestant views about the relationship between Catholic corruption and image devotion. As we will see in Part 2, many of the Protestant reformers, like John Jewel (document 12), who spent the Marian period in exile, would return to England with a mind to redouble the efforts at reform and the removal of idolatry.

---

45. Aston, *England's Iconoclasts*, 283–87.

DOCUMENT 1

John Ryckes,
The Image of Love
(London, 1525)

INTRODUCTION

We know very little about the author John Ryckes. He claims, in the text, to be an Observant Franciscan friar who is writing to a community of nuns. Possibly the community was the Syon Abbey nuns, who subsequently purchased at least sixty copies of his book *The Image of Love*.[1] A devotional allegory, *The Image* exposits the various kinds of human love, which are echoes and/or corruptions of the true image of love found in God. While the text is "for the most part, from inside the institutional church," it was investigated on accusations of heresy in the late 1520s, and Thomas More targeted it in his polemics at the end of the decade.[2]

The ambiguity surrounding its acceptance within Catholic orthodoxy is significant as a starting point for the image debate in England. By 1525, Lutheranism was already considered a threat by the Tudor monarchy. Henry VIII had Protestant books burned, and Protestant preachers were hunted down and arrested. However, this is clearly not a Lutheran book. Instead, the tone and theology of *The Image* inhabit an often overlooked realm of orthodoxy that was critical of certain lavish practices and embellishments

---

1. Grise, "Moche profitable unto religious persones," in Jones and Walsham, eds, *Syon Abbey*, 139–40.
2. Erler, *Women, Reading, and Piety*, 107.

of ceremony. *The Image* echoed the Franciscan critique of clerical affluence, which had become a commonplace challenge found in the teachings of communities like the Brotherhood of the Common Life and Erasmian humanism.[3] *The Image* presents an internal challenge—as opposed to the Protestant external challenge—to things like the adornment of images and the costly displays of shrines and altars, at the expense of more basic needs like caring for the poor, sick, and otherwise helpless. However, this does not make *The Image* any less attractive to a Protestant audience. As Margaret Aston has pointed out, this "critique of ceremonialism could be assimilated . . . with a Protestant rejection of externals."[4] In 1532 and then again in 1587, *The Image* was reprinted by Protestants. The repackaged 1587 edition, completed by Anthony Munday, was amended with distinctly Protestant margin notes to make explicit things that a Protestant reader might see implicitly.[5]

The Image's message about religious icons and images is twofold. First, they are not worth the money that is spent upon them. This seems to be the main critique levelled at the culture of icons. The use of "godly" in the first portion of the excerpt should not be mistaken for a blanket affirmation. Instead, the word, here, is used to suggest that the images under discussion were intended to be employed in a religious context. While the text does not condemn the making of religious images, it certainly diminishes their importance in relation to other matters (e.g., the poor and needy). Second, *The Image* makes it clear that religious images cannot lead a person to the image of love in God, for the latter image "cannot be seen of the bodily eyes." *The Image* concedes that religious icons can aid in worship, for they can "for a time" move a person "unto religion." However, charity—the ultimate image of love—cannot be found in them.

TEXT[6]

Ch. 4 The Image of Artificers Be Not the Very Images of Love Nor But Little Conducing to Pity and Charity

Then leaving these perilous images, I went to the artificers that make marvelous godly images and diverse matters as in metal, stone, timber, and cloth diverse ways. But the very image of love was not there. Nevertheless there

---

3. Fuller, *Brotherhood of the Common Life*, 77–79.
4. Aston, *England's Iconoclasts*, 182.
5. These margin notes have been provided below from John Ryckes, *The True Image of Christian Love* (London, 1587).
6. Ryckes, *The Image of Love*, sigs. B2r–B8v.

was many godly images, which I thought should steer a man to devotion and to the love of God. And because it was hard to find the very true image, I set my mind to buy one of these and as I was choosing out one of the godliest there came to me a holy, devout doctor rebuking me greatly and said, "Why do you cast away your money upon these corruptible and vain things, your goods were not given to you for that intent, you are much to blame, see not how the godly living image of God most pitiful fades and decays every day in great multitude and yet you will bestow your money upon these. If you having wordly substance see your brother has need and you spare from him your treasure of mercy and pity in your heart, how is the charity of God in you."[7]

"Why sir," said I, "may not I spend mine own good as I will, so then I spend it not in sin. And poor people were in extreme necessity, I should sin deadly if I should see them be lost, having more than is necessary for me, but I know none such and there be many that will and be more able than I to help them, nor I am not bound to seek where such be that be in extreme necessity." Thus we fell into a long disputation and at the last he concluded thus. That not only extreme necessity does bind us to give alms but also when we have more than is necessary to our state and he alleged for him the gospel of Christ . . . . Giving alms of that then is superfluous. It is to be thought that there shall be no little company on the left hand of Christ, where he shall give sentence of damnation upon them rehearsing the lack of alms doing as principal cause in manner.

. . .

I break not nor take away none other men's goods but keep what is mine own . . . . It is rather to show the experience of this gentleness that you should have the greater merit for the well bestowing of your goods unto the poor. And for that the poor might be as well rewarded for his patience and thus he did conclude. It is the bread and sustenance for the hungry that you retain with thee, . . . it is the clothing of naked men that you spare up in your presses, it is the redemption and relief of them that be in thralldom and prison, the money that you hide in the ground.

. . .

"Beware, sir, what you say. Your opinion condemns the doing of many good men that be nowadays, which honor the temples of God with many godly images of great cost, of silver and of gold, set with pearls and stones,

---

7. Margin Note, 1587 edition: "A notable lesson for the Papists, the vain worshippers of stocks and stones."

great plenty of copes and vestments of tissue and cloth of gold and marvelous riches in plate, as crosses, candlesticks, censors, chalices, with many other things, which be greatly to the honor of God." "Aha," says he, "I see it is but vain to preach and teach men to learn and take example of Sts. Ambrose, Augustine, Gregory, Exupery, Nicholas, Martin—holy bishops and such others in whose time were but little of such things they would have all things that belonged to the church (and specially to the sacraments) honest, pure, and clean, but not costly nor curious.[8] Then were treen[9] chalices and golden priests, now be golden chalices and treen priests, or rather earthen priests. Then were religious clad with hair and sack cloth, and now they disdain or grudge to wear woolen cloth. Then were monasteries hospices for poor men and now they be palaces for lords and states than they were appareled with meekness, poverty, chastity, and charity now with silks, cloths of gold, pomp, and vanity, yet if there were no poor people, I might yet somewhat hold wall. But Christ says we shall ever have poor men among us. Also St. Paul says, *Templum enim dei sanctum est, quod estis vos.*[10] The temple of God is a holy thing that is none other but yourself. The temple of stone is not holy but by reason of the living temple therefore that is more holy and needs more to be maintained and enourned.[11] Should we then go lay up or spend our riches in the stony temple and suffer the quick temple to perish either bodily or ghostly.[12] We find not that Christ commanded to have so costly paraments[13] in his church, but commanded many times to nourish his poor people. And now men leave the commandments of God for their own traditions and ceremonies as the scribes and Pharisees did. . . . But some lay against me, Moses yet made the tabernacle of God with great sumptuousness of silver and gold and precious stones. And Solomon likewise the temple but that makes not with them but rather more against them. For all such things were but figures and shadows as St. Paul says unto us under Christ's law that is the very spiritual and profit law, therefore we should leave the shadow and follow the truth, avoiding that yet is imperfect and take that that is perfect."[14]

. . .

8. Margin note, 1587 edition: "Let the Papists mark this place well."
9. Wooden
10. 1 Cor 3:17.
11. Adorned
12. Spiritually
13. Ecclesiastical robe
14. Col 2:17.

Ch. 5 Where the True Image Is Found and What It Is

Then as I stood conjecturing what I might do, scripture spoke to me and said, "O foolish man. Why do you seek a living thing among dead things, light in darkness, a ghostly thing among earthly things, incorruptible among corruptible. It is not there, it is marvelous, godly, and wonderful to behold. The image that you seek, it cannot be seen of the bodily eyes but only with angels' eyes and pure with them that be dead from this world, living with Christ"; and, he said also all you ever I had was nothing to the price thereof. Nevertheless I would fain have had it for though I saw it never, I remember that a shadow I saw thereof in a glass, which passed by me suddenly without any tarrying and delighted me so that if ever I have such a desire to it that I would be glad to give all that I have for a little sight of it.

. . .

I went to a place of religion and took a ghostly father, showing him my intent that I came to clarify my sight that I might at least once see this image.[15] There, I thought, it should be for there were yet most godly appareled alters with tabernacles subtly carven and costly gilded. There was the sweetest harmony of songs and organs and godly devout observances that ever I saw or heard in so much that it moved me for a time unto religion there. Wherein I asked counsel of my ghostly father, but he persuaded me that contrary saying it is not all gold that shines as gold. There is one thing that destroys much goodness: the inordinate love to oneself, which is the cause of much ill as St. Paul prophesied to his disciple Timothy, saying that at the last end of the world there shall come perilous seasons, men shall have inordinate love to themselves, that shall cause them to be covetous, high minded, disdainful, proud, blasphemous, disobedient to their parents, cruel and unkind, without inward love or affection, without peace.[16] . . . Thus I prayed that charity might lack for all these gay outward things and observances, for all the gay singing and playing or multiplying of horizons, nor yet they be not evident proofs of love and charity, but sometimes some of them let or hinder charity and contemplation, stirring the mind to elation and vainglory, but charity, says St. Paul, is to edify our neighbor, to think of ourselves as one body, and so to use ourselves one to another, as the members naturally do in the body.[17]

15. Margin note, 1587 edition: "See here how frailty makes him fall again after the manner and custom of the Papists."

16. 2 Tim 3.

17. Margin note, 1587 edition: "A special note for the Papists."

DOCUMENT 2

William Tyndale,
An Answer unto Sir Thomas More's Dialogue
(London, 1532)

INTRODUCTION

William Tyndale (c.1494–1536) is a name that needs very little introduction. His translation of scripture, betrayal by Henry Phillips, and execution at Vilvorde Castle near Brussels at the hands of imperial authorities have been well memorialized by John Foxe and others. However, Tyndale's translation and martyrdom have eclipsed his role as a Protestant polemicist, particularly in his debates with Sir Thomas More in the late 1520s and early 1530s.[1] Even though Tyndale fled into exile on the European continent in 1524, he remained acutely aware of the religious life of England, becoming one of the most vocal critics of Henry VIII's divorce proceedings from Katherine of Aragon. Along with his Bible translation, Tyndale was prolific at writing some of the earliest Protestant theology in English, often drawing directly from Luther and other German reformers. Thomas More penned *Dialogue Concerning Heresies* (1529) to refute several of Tyndale's recent polemical writings, and Tyndale quickly fired back with his *Answer to Sir Thomas More's Dialogue* (1531).[2]

1. See Daniell, *William Tyndale*; Werrell, *Theology of William Tyndale*.
2. Aston, *England's Iconoclasts*, 183–86; Daniell, *William Tyndale*, 261–72.

In the *Answer*, Tyndale initially sounds Lutheran, or even Erasmian, in his tolerance for religious images that were not abused by idolatrous practices.³ Here, there are echoes of the tradition that Ryckes (document 1) is part of; however, Tyndale's permissiveness hinges upon how images were treated, and in this regard, he has a more narrow perspective on the purity of worship than his Lutheran and Erasmian counterparts. Margaret Aston explains that Tyndale's criticisms opened the door for more radical views, saying, "Images were abused and where there were such abuses images must go. The implication of the argument was, however, more radical than this, for since all images were seen as potential idols they ought all to be put down."⁴

While it is unclear how far Tyndale would have taken his views if put into practice, his *Answer* is important to the image debates, because it exemplifies the tension that was latent within the Protestant attack on visual religion. Tyndale raised several key criticisms of images that Protestants maintained across the sixteenth century: that they were too expensive, that most people did not understand their true (godly) purpose and so became slaves to the images, and that the potential for abuse and superstition was too high. Ultimately, images were not dangerous inherently, but instead were dangerous because of what they depicted (e.g., a statue of the pagan god Dagon) or became so through corrupt uses (e.g., unlawful worship and adoration). At the same time, Tyndale is able to write, "to kneel before the cross unto the Word of God which the cross preaches is not evil," permitting images of crosses, saints, and other religious figures without reproach, at least in some contexts. This level of ambiguity toward image reverence is akin to Lutheran theology, but it will quickly fade among many English reformers as a stauncher Calvinist line is established in the 1540s.

TEXT⁵

Now let us come to the worshipping or honoring of sacraments, ceremonies, images, and relics. First images are not god, and therefore no confidence is

---

3. For more on the Lutheran theology of images see Dyrness, *Reformed Theology*, 49–55.

4. Aston, *England's Iconoclasts*, 185.

5. The following excerpt is from: Tyndale, *An Answer*, E3v–F1v. The original was written in gothic font, creating unique challenges to transcription. An earlier transcription (edited by Henry Walter, 59–68) has provided a useful model, however, it is not consistent in its modernizations (e.g., changing the spelling of "Steven" to "Stephen" while keeping the spelling of "Salomon" the same). Also, Henry Craik produced a portion of this passage for *English Prose*, I.185–89.

to be given them.⁶ They are not made after the image of God nor are they the price of Christ's blood, but the workmanship of the craftsmen and the price of money and therefore inferior to man.

Wherefore of all right man is lord over them and the honor of them is to do man service and man's dishonor it is to do them honorable service, as unto his better. Images, then, and relics also and, as Christ says, the holy day too are servants unto man. And therefore it follows, that we cannot, but unto our damnation, put on a coat worth a hundred coats upon a post's back and let the image of God and the price of Christ's blood go up and down thereby naked. For if we care more to clothe the dead image made by man and the price of silver, than the lively image of God and price of Christ's blood, then we dishonor the image of God and him that made him the price of Christ's blood and him that bought him.

Wherefore the right use, office, and honor of all inferior creatures unto man is to do man service, whether they be images, relics, ornaments, signs or sacraments, holidays, ceremonies, or sacrifices. And that may be on this manner, and no doubt it so once was.⁷ If (for an example) I take a piece of the cross of Christ and make a little cross thereof and bare it about me, to look thereon with a repenting heart,⁸ at times when I am moved thereto, to put me in remembrance that the body of Christ was broken and his blood shed thereon for my sins and believe steadfastly that the merciful truth of God shall forgive the sins of all that repent for his death's sake and never think on the more, than it serves me and I not it and does me that same service as if I read that testament in a book or as if the preacher preached it unto me. And in like manner if I make a cross in my forehead as a remembrance that God has promised assistance unto all that believe in him for his sake that died on the cross, then does that cross serve me and I not it. And in like manner if I bear on me or look upon a cross of whatsoever matter it be or make a cross upon me in remembrance that whosoever will be Christ's disciple must suffer a cross of adversity, tribulations, and persecution, so does the cross serve me and I not it. And this was the use of that cross once, and for this cause it was at the beginning set up in the churches.

And so if I make an image of Christ or of anything that Christ has done for me in a memory it is good and not evil until it be abused.⁹

And even so if I take that true likeness of a saint and cause it to be painted or carved to put me in remembrance of the saint's life to follow the

---

6. Margin note: "Images."
7. Margin note: "The use of creatures inferior to men."
8. Margin note: "The worshipping of the cross."
9. Margin note: "The worshipping of images."

saint as the saint did Christ and to put me in remembrance of the great faith of the saint of God and how true God was to help him out of all tribulation and to see the saint's love toward his neighbor in that he so patiently suffered so painful a death and so cruel martyrdom to testify the truth for to save others and all to strengthen my soul with all and my faith to God and love to my neighbor then does the image serve me and I not it. And this was the use of images at the beginning and of relics also.

And to kneel before the cross unto the Word of God which the cross preaches is not evil. Neither to kneel down before an image, in a man's meditations to call the living of that saint to mind for to desire God of like grace to follow that example is not evil.[10] But the abuse of that thing is evil and to have a false faith. As to bear a piece of the cross about a man thinking that so long as that is about him spirits shall not come at him, his enemies shall do him no bodily harm, all causes shall go on his side even for bearing it about him, and to think that if it were not about him it would not be so, and to think if any misfortune chance that it came for leaving it off or because this or that ceremony was left undone and not rather because we have broken God's commandments or that God tempts to prove our patience.[11] This is plain idolatry and here a man is captive, bound, and a servant unto a false faith and a false imagination that is neither God nor his Word. Now am I God's only and ought to serve nothing but God and his Word. My body must serve the rulers of this world and my neighbor (as God has appointed it) and so must all my goods; but my soul must serve God only, to love his law and to trust in his promises of mercy in all my needs. And in like manner it is that thousands, while the priest patereth[12] St. John's gospel in Latin over their heads, cross themselves with, I trust, a legion of crosses, behind and before; and with reverence on the very asses[13] and (as Jack-of-napes when he claws himself) pluck up their legs and cross so much as their heels and the very soles of their feet, and believe that if it be done in the time that he reads the gospel (and else not) that there shall no mischance happen to them that day, because only of those crosses. And where he should cross himself, to be armed and to make himself strong to bear that cross with Christ, he crosses himself to drive the cross from him and blesses himself with a cross from the cross. And if he leaves it undone, he thinks it no small sin, and that God is highly displeased with him and if any misfortune chance thinks it is therefore which is also idolatry and not

---

10. Margin note: "False worshipping."
11. Duffy, *Stripping of the Altars*, 490.
12. To recite something, a prayer, esp. in a rapid, mechanical fashion.
13. Margin note: "S. John's gospel." Walter's edition leaves off this "coarse expression."

God's Word. And such is the confidence in the place or image or whatsoever bodily observance it be. Such is St. Agathe's letter written in the gospel time. And such are the crosses on Palm Sunday made in the passion time.[14] And such is the bearing of holy wax about a man. And such is that some hang a piece of St. John's gospel about their necks.[15] And such is to bear the names of God with crosses between each name about them. Such is that saying of gospels unto women in childbed. Such is the limiter's way of saying *in principio erat verbum* from house to house.[16] Such is the saying of gospels to the corn in the field in the procession week that it should the better grow. And such is holy bread, holy water, and serving of all ceremonies and sacraments in general without signification. And I pray you how is it possible that the people can worship images, relics, ceremonies, and sacraments, save superstitiously, so long as they know not the true meaning, neither will the prelates suffer any man to tell them? Yea, and the very meaning of some and right use, no man can tell.

And as for the riches that are bestowed on images and relics they cannot prove but that it is abominable, as long as the poor are despised and uncared for and not first served, for whose sake and to find preachers, offerings, tithes, land rents, and all that they have was given the spirituality.[17] They will say we may do both. May or may not. I see that the one most necessary of both is not done. But the poor are bereaved of that spirituality of all that was in time passed offered unto them. Moreover though both were done they shall never prove that the sight of gold and silver and of precious stones should move a man's heart to despise such things after the doctrine of Christ. Neither can the rich coat help to move thy mind to follow the example as he suffered in the most ungodly ways. Which thing taken away that such things with all other service, as sticking up candles, move not thy mind to follow the example of the saint, nor teach thy soul any godly learning, then the image serves not thee, but thou the image; and so art thou an idolater, that is to say, in English, a serve-image. And thus it appears that your ungodly and belly doctrine, wherewith you so magnify the deeds of your ceremonies, and of your pilgrimages, and offering, for the deed itself, to please God, and to obtain the favor of dead saints (and not

---

14. Margin note: "Superstitiousness." Agatha (Agathe) was part of a larger panorama of virgin saints that were highly cherished in late medieval England (Duffy, *Stripping of the Altars*, 171–72).

15. Watson, "Some Non-Textual Use of Books," 483.

16. John 1:1. Apparently, this phrase, taken from the first chapter of John's gospel, was a kind of salutation used by friars when entering or leaving a house: Pancoast and Spaeth, *Early English Poems*, 475.

17. Margin note: "Riches bestowed on images or relics."

to move you, and to put you in remembrance of the law of God, and of the promises which are in his Son, and to follow the example of the saint), is but an exhorting to serve images; and so are you image-servers, that is, idolaters. And finally the more devotion men have unto such deeds, the less they have unto God's commandment; insomuch that they which be most wont[18] to offer to images, and to show them, be so cold in offering to the poor, that they will scarce give them the scraps which must else be given dogs, or their old shoes, if they may have new brooms for them.

Pilgrimages

To speak of pilgrimages, I say, that a Christian man, so that he leave nothing undone at home that he is bound to do, is free to wither he will; only after the doctrine of the Lord, whose servant he is, and not his own. If he goes and visits the poor, the sick, and the prisoner, it is well done, and a work that God commands. If he goes to this or that place, to hear a sermon, or because his mind is not quiet at home; or if, because his heart is too much occupied on his worldly businesses, by the reason of occasions at home, he get himself into a more quiet and still place, where his mind is more abstract, and pulled from worldly thought, it is well done. And in all these places, if whatsoever it be, whether lively preaching, ceremony, relic, or image, stir up his heart to God, and preach the Word of God, and the example of our Savior Jesus, more in one place than in another; that he thither goes, I am content. And yet he bids a lord, and the things serve him, and he not them. Now whether his intent be so or no, his deeds will testify; as his virtuous governing of his house, and loving demeanor toward his neighbors. Yea, and God's Word will be always in his heart, and in his mouth, and he every day more perfect than other. For there can nothing edify man's soul, save that which preaches him God's Word. Only the Word of God works the health of the soul. And whatsoever preaches him, that cannot but make him more perfect.

But to believe that God will be sought more in one place than in another, or that God will hear you more in one place than in another, or more where the image is than where it is not, is a false faith, and idolatry, or image-service. For first, God dwells not in temples made with hands, Acts 17. Item, Stephen died for the contrary, and proved it by the prophets, Acts 7.[19] And Solomon, in the eighth of the first of the Kings, when he had built his temple, testified the same, and that he had not built it for God to dwell in; yea, and that God dwells not in the earth; but that he should out of

18. Customary behavior
19. Margin note: "God dwells not in any place. Acts 7." Acts 7:48; 17:24.

heaven hear the prayers of them that prayed there.[20] And the prophets did often testify unto the people, that had such a false faith that God dwelled in the temple, that he dwelled not there. Moreover, God in his testament binds himself unto no place, nor yet you, but speaks generally (concerning where and when), saying Psalm 49, "in the day of the tribulation you shall call on me, and I will deliver you, and you shall glorify me."[21] He sets neither place nor time; but wherever and whenever; so that the prayer of Job upon the dunghill was as good as Paul's in the temple. And when our Savior says in John 16, "Whatsoever you ask my father in my name, I will give it you."[22] He says not in this or that place or this or that day; but wherever or whenever, as well in the fields as in the town, and on the Monday, as on the Sunday. God is a spirit, and will be worshipped in the spirit, John 4.[23] That is, though, he be present everywhere, yet he dwells lively and gloriously in the minds of angels only, and hearts of men that love his laws and trust in his promises. And wherever God finds such a heart, there he hears the prayer, in all places and times indifferently. So that the outward place neither helps nor hinders, except (as I said) that a man's mind be more quiet and still from the rage of worldly businesses, or that something stir up the Word of God and example of our Savior more in one place than in another.

Whence Idolatry, or Image-service, Springs

Now that you may see whence all this idolatry or image-service is sprung; mark a little, and then I will answer unto the arguments which these image-servers make against the open truth. All the ceremonies, ornaments, and sacrifices of the Old Testament were sacraments. That is, to wit, signs preaching unto the people one thing or another.[24] As circumcision preached unto them, that God had chosen them to be his people, and that he would be their God, and defend them, and increase and multiply them, and keep them in that land, and bless the fruits of the earth, and all their possessions; and on the other side it preached, how that they had promised God again to keep his commandments, ceremonies, and ordinances. Now when they saw their young children circumcised, if they consented unto the appointment

20. 1 Kgs 8.

21. Margin note: "Psalm 49." Ps 50:15. Since Tyndale is translating his passages directly from the Vulgate, the numerical order of the Psalms is different from other translations taken from the Hebrew and Greek.

22. Margin note: "John 16." John 16:23.

23. Margin note: "John 4." John 4:24.

24. Margin note: "Sacraments. Circumcision."

made between God and them, moved by the preaching of that same, then they were justified thereby. Howbeit, the deed in itself, the cutting off the foreskin of the manchild's privy member, justified them not, nor was a satisfaction for the child's sins; but the preaching only did justify them that received the faith thereof. For it was a badge given indifferently, as well unto them that never consented in their hearts unto God's law, as unto the elect in whose hearts the law is written. And that this was the meaning of circumcision may be proved many ways. But namely by Paul, Romans 2, where he says, "circumcision is much worth, if you keep the law (whose sign it was)" and else not. And Romans 2, where he says that, "God did justify the circumcised of faith (whose sign it was on the other side)" and else not.[25]

And the Paschal lamb was a memorial of their deliverance out of Egypt only, and no satisfaction or offering for sin.[26]

And the offering of their first-fruits preached how they had received all such fruits of the hand of God, and that it was God that gave them that land, and that kept them in it, and that did bless and make their fruits grow.[27] In token whereof as unto a lord royal, they brought him the first ripe fruits of their harvest. Which remembrance, as long as it abode in their hearts, it moved them to love God again, and their neighbor for his sake, as he so often desired them. And out of this ceremony was fetched the blessing of our new ripe fruits, for like purpose, though we have lost the signification.

And their other offerings, as the sacrifices of doves, turtles, lambs, kids, sheep, calves, goats, and oxen, were no satisfactions for sin, but only a sign and token, that at the repentance of the heart, through an offering to come, and for that seed's sake that was promised Abraham, their sins were forgiven them.[28]

And in like manner, the ornaments, and all other ceremonies were either an open preaching, or secret prophecies, and not satisfactions or justifyings.[29] And thus the works did serve them and preach unto them, and they not the works, nor put any confidence therein.

False Worshipping

But what did the children of Israel and the Jews? They let the significations of their ceremonies go, and lost the meaning of them and turned them unto

25. Rom 2:25.
26. Margin Note: "Pascal lamb."
27. Margin Note: "First fruits."
28. Margin Note: "Sacrifice."
29. Margin Note: "Ornaments."

the works to serve them, saying that they were holy works commanded of God, and the offerers were thereby justified and obtained forgiveness of sins and thereby became good. As the parable of the Pharisee and the publican declares, Luke 18, and as it is to see in Paul, and throughout all the Bible and became captive to serve and put their trust in that which was neither God nor his Word.[30] And so the better creature, against nature, did serve the worse. Where of all likelihood God should have accepted their work by the reason of them, if their hearts had been right and not have accepted their souls for the blood's sake of a calf or sheep, forasmuch as a man is much better than a calf or sheep, as Christ testifies, Matthew 12. For what pleasure should God have in the blood of calves, or in the light of our candles? His pleasure is only in the hearts of them that love his commandments.[31]

Then they went further in the imagination of their blind reason, saying, "Inasmuch as God accepts these holy works, that we be made righteous thereby, then it follows that he which offered most is most righteous, and the best man; yea, and it is better to offer an ox than a sheep, because it is more costly." And so they strove who might offer most, and the priests were well paid. Then went they further in their fleshly wisdom, saying: "If I be good for the offering of a dove, and better for a sheep, and yet, better for an ox and so ever better thing I offer, the better I am. Oh how accepted should I be if I offered a man, and namely him that I most loved?" And upon that imagination they offered their own children, and burned them to ashes before images that they had imagined.[32]

And to confirm their blindness they laid for them, no doubt, the example of Abraham, which offered his son Isaac, and was so accepted, that God had promised him how that in his seed all the world should be blessed. Hereof ye see unto what abomination blind reason brings a man, when she[33] is destitute of God's Word.

And to speak of the Sabbath (which was ordained to be their servant and to preach and to be a sign unto them that God through his Holy Spirit and Word did sanctify them, in that they obeyed his commandments, and believed and trusted in his promises, and therefore were charged to leave working, and to come on the holy day, and hear the Word of God, by which they were sanctified) unto it also they became captive and bond to serve

---

30. Margin Note: "Luke 18." Luke 18:9–14.
31. Although he does not reference it, Tyndale is reciting Isa 1:11.
32. Lev 20:2–5.
33. The use of the feminine pronoun here is seemingly a misprint. It is the only use of the feminine, as a universal reference to humanity, in Tyndale's entire work; however, it could be that Tyndale is here expressing a common medieval and early modern trope of describing reason as a woman or lady.

it, saying that they were justified by abstaining from bodily labor (as ours think also), insomuch that though they bestowed not the holy day in virtue, prayer, and hearing the Word of God, in alms-deed, in visiting the sick, the needy and comfortless, and so forth, but went up and down idly; yet, whatever need his neighbor had, he would not have helped him on the Sabbath day, as you may see by the ruler of the synagogue, which rebuked Christ for healing the people on the holy day, Luke 13.[34]

And of like blindness they went and set out the brazen serpent, which Moses commanded to be kept in the ark for a memory, and offered before it; thinking (no doubt) that God must be there present, for else how could it have healed the people that came not nigh it, but stood afar off, and beheld it only.[35] And a thousand such madnesses did they.

And of the temple they thought that God heard them there better than anywhere else; yea, and he heard them nowhere save there.[36] And therefore they could not pray but there, as ours can nowhere but at church, and before an image. For what prayer can a man pray when the Word of God is not in the temple of his heart; yea, and when such come to church, what is their prayer, and what is their devotion, save the blind image-service of their hearts.

But the prophets ever rebuked them for such faithless works, and for such false faith in their works.[37] In the forty-ninth Psalm, the prophet says, "I will receive no calves of your houses, nor goats out of your folds; think you that I will eat the flesh of oxen or drink the blood of goats?"[38] And Isaiah says in his first chapter, "What care I for the multitude of your sacrifices? says the Lord. I am full. I have no lust in the burnt offerings of your rams, or in the fat of the fat beasts, or blood of calves, lambs, or goats; offer me no more such false sacrifice." And thereto, "Your sweet incense is an abomination unto me."[39] And thus he said, because of the false faith, and perverting the right use of them.

And for their false fasting,[40] not referring their fast unto the taming and subduing of their flesh unto the spirit, when they complained unto God, justifying themselves, and saying, "How did it happen that we have fasted, and you would not look upon it? We have humbled our souls, and

---

34. Luke 13:10–17.
35. Margin Note: "The brazen serpents."
36. Margin Note: "The temple."
37. Margin Note: "Psalm 46."
38. Ps 50:9.
39. Isa 1:11.
40. Margin Note: "Fasting."

you would not know it?" God answered them by the prophet Isaiah, in the fifty-eighth chapter, "Behold, in the day of your fast you do your own lusts, and gather up all your debts. And howsoever you fast, you never the later strive and fight and smite with fist cruelly. I have chosen no such fast and humbling of soul, etc. But that you loose wicked bonds, and let the oppressed go free, and to break bread unto the hungry, and to clothe the naked," and so forth.[41]

And concerning the temple,[42] Isaiah says in his last chapter, "What house will you build for me, or in what place shall I rest? Heaven is my seat, and the earth my footstool." As who should say, "I am too great for any place that you can make," and (as Stephen says, Acts 7, and Paul, Acts 17) "I dwell not in a temple made with hands."[43]

---

41. Margin Note: "Isaiah 58." Isa 58:3.
42. Margin Note: "Temple."
43. Margin Note: "Acts 7. Acts 17."

DOCUMENT 3

Martin Bucer,
A Treatise Declaring and Showing That Images Are Not To Be Suffered in Churches
(London, 1535)

INTRODUCTION

Born in the German free city of Selestat into a family of coopers, Martin Bucer (c.1491–1551) studied at the Dominican monastery in Heidelberg and at the University of Meinz. In 1518, he met Martin Luther at the Heidelberg Disputation and was deeply affected by the professor's arguments. Luther's influence was so great that by 1521 Bucer had his Dominican vows annulled and joined the Protestant movement.[1]

Arriving in Strasbourg in 1523, Bucer became associated with the city's leading reformer Matthew Zell. When the city erupted in religious violence the following year, Bucer was the person to whom the reformers turned to draft a basic statement of faith for adoption by the city council. Until the Schmalkaldic War in the 1540s, Strasbourg, under Bucer's leadership, became one of the leading cities of the Reformation, along with Worms, Geneva, and Zurich.

While Bucer admired Luther's reforms, his theology on images is marked by specific moves away from Luther and Tyndale. Bucer gradually came to oppose the notion that images could still be used in religious/

---

1. Eells, *Martin Bucer*; Wright, ed., *Martin Bucer*; Selderhuis, *Marriage and Divorce*.

devotional settings, exclaiming here that there is no "other more perilous mischief" than allowing images in churches. As William Dyrness explains, for Bucer and for an increasing number of reformed voices in France and the Low Countries, "the power of images . . . rests on their ability to distract the believer's attention from works that are truly acceptable to God."[2] The original German text *Das Einigerlei Bild* was published in 1530, and the English version that is below was translated from a Latin version. It is almost certainly the first large-scale reformed statement on images in English. In the text, Bucer shifted the emphasis away from the potential usefulness of images to their overwhelmingly more probable threat to healthy forms of worship. Bucer's own thinking on the matter shifted over several years, between the time that he ordered the images to be removed from Strasbourg's churches in the mid–1520s and when he universally condemned any religious use of images in the early 1530s.[3] No longer does the matter hinge upon the nature of images. Instead, as Bucer argues throughout this text, the crucial question is: what is the nature of holy worship?

Two key points arise from Bucer's text that become canons of the more reformed Protestant statements on religious imagery. First, that true worship cannot be performed with assistance of material things. As Bucer explains, "It is the spirit . . . that quickens," going so far as to say, "Christ did plainly witness that his bodily presence was nothing profitable." Here, Bucer sets down one of the simplest truisms of the Reformation image debate: to use images in religious devotion is necessarily corrosive to holy worship. Even those, like Luther, who would allow for images as aids of the unlearned or for the weaker brethren have "fallen in the flaming fire" of idolatry. Secondly, Bucer outlines the essential reformed response to the demand for images: that God has given all the images one should ever need or desire in his creation. He asks, "And why is not God known rather by the very lively creatures whose shapes or images for doubtless the glory of God should be more clearly and evidently known." In fact, for Bucer and those to follow him, to suggest that artists and artisans can somehow change stone, wood, or other substances into images that serve better as devotional aids is equally atrocious: "For trees or stones do more surely and lively put us in remembrance of God . . . having their own natural shape and fashion."

---

2. Dyrness, *Reformed Theology*, 92. While Michalski provides an excellent summary of most of the Protestant theologies, when it comes to Bucer he gives short shrift to Bucer's contributions, marginalizing him to the shadows of the theological mountains, Ulrich Zwingli and John Calvin.

3. Koerner, *Reformation of the Image*, 93.

TEXT[4]

That Images Wont To Be Worshipped Are Not To Be Suffered in the Churches of Christian Men

Albeit there are here many causes which might sufficiently satisfy the minds of Christian men and persuade them to take away images out of their churches, yet no man will deny this cause to be without a doubt the chief and principal, because it is forbidden in the first of God's commandments, that any manner of images should be had among his people. For this we read in the scriptures:

> I am that everlasting God. I am your God that has delivered you from Egypt, the house of thralldom and bondage. You shall have no strange gods besides me. You shall make unto yourself no graven or carved image, nor the similitude of any manner of thing which is above in heaven or beneath in the earth nor of those things which are in the waters under the earth. You shall not bow yourself before them, neither worship them. For I am your Lord and God everlasting, strong and mighty, punishing the faults of the fathers in the children, even unto the third generation of them which hate me. And pouring forth my goodness even unto the thousandth generation of them which love me and observe and keep my commandments.[5]

Lo, here are two laws of the Lord set forth unto the which, not without good cause among other, do challenge unto themselves the first place. The first of them requires of us that we do take this eternal and ever-being god (so as he is in very deed) for our God. The later does not only forbid strange gods, but also it forbids both the images of them and also of all other things to be had among the people of God unto which people doubtless that is to wit unto all true believers all such manner precepts do appertain. For these are the true Israelites, as it appeared in the scriptures. For Christ came not to break the law but to fulfill it, first of any man.[6] Now in very deed there are annexed to the law of God and also enclosed and contained in it whatsoever things bring any cause or occasion unto the love of God or of the neighbor to show or put forth itself more and more.[7]

---

4. Bucer, *A treatise declarying*, A5r–E3v.
5. Exod 20.
6. Rom 2.
7. Gal 3.

Indeed God commands very many things to his old people which were greatly available helping to the principal point and end of his law. But after that Christ was exalted to the right hand of the Father, and the Holy Ghost was sent all abroad into the world; we are delivered and freed from a great part of such manner legal ceremonies.

...

Besides all this I say (which is a thing more to be followed) this vain honoring of images has engendered such a confidence and trust in a great sort of men that those works which are in very deed good and godly laid clean aside, they have taken occasion to live a great deal the more at large and more licentiously because they are persuaded and in steadfast belief that with these works they have so gotten the favor of God that at all other sins and vicious living, he winks and will not see them and as though having liberty granted to sin unpunished they might give themselves at large to all manner of vices. . . . If this thing were not well enough known unto all men by experience, we could prove it with such manner of examples and proofs that even he that were blind should perceive plainly that there has not lightly any other more perilous mischief creeping into the church than this of honoring images.

Who is he then that does not somewhat smell and perceive the false, wily crafts of our old enemy, which has never ceased to drive the world into such madness that putting away the true honor of God, men should receive and embrace this honor, which makes them to go the clean contrary way from God, discerning all manner of men with the vain appearance and outward sight of images, as though men by them were put in remembrance of godly things, when in very deed by them nothing has been brought in but an innumerable heap of all evils. Moreover that man whom heaven, earth, and whatsoever is contained in them and most especially man which is created to the image of God, finally whom God himself the worker of all these things does not waken and stir up to love him and praise him, no man unless he be madder than a man of Bedlam will believe that this man will be moved greatly with deed and insensible images. If so many works of God, if so many creatures no less profitable than marvelous which set the goodness of God before your eyes cannot enflame you, then you are doubtless too insensible for to be admonished and stirred ever by insensible images. The goodness of God shines and appears in all his creatures. There is nothing but it expresses God himself. All the world is full of things, which do not cease to put us in remembrance of our duty that is, to wit, that we should continue to be unto other men as God is unto us, and that we should resemble him by a certain endless goodness....

And as for that which some men do feign that images are the books of laymen ... it is not only a weak reason but also foolish: as who should say that God of all most wisest and which is very wisdom itself either did not know these books or else through malice did withhold from his own people such manner of books and monuments whereby they might be put in remembrance of godly things. Forsooth, it is a wicked thing even once to think that God which according to his goodness towards us lest none of those things unshowed and as they say pointed with his finger which might help to further and increase the knowledge of himself and to stir us up also to the love of himself. I cannot tell of what evil will and hatred kept his worshipping of images from his own people. For not only did he not teach the worshipping of images but also he with express and plain words utterly forbade it, as it appears evidently by the first law of all. Now what is more unreasonable and unlikely than if the use of images be so profitable as these men do feign it to be that God did nothing esteem them, seeing that in the mean season he had begun to teach his people being yet but young beginners and having but small knowledge with so many outward things, even as one should induce a child seeing also that he would his works and benefits to be openly known by so many wonderful miracles and by so manifold ceremonies.... Since then it is so, that it was not lawful for the people which was yet rude and ignorant to have any manner images although the Lord did by many other diverse ceremonies by little and little teach and fashion the same people. Now much less shall it be lawful for us whom the truth succeeded into the place of shadows has now made free from outward ceremonies, requiring none other honor or service of us than that which stands in spirit and truth.

Let us therefore not have images of stone, not of wood, not graven, nor cast in any mold (all which God has once for all forbidden as well to us as to the Jews). But let us rather consider the very Word of God, let us occupy and busy ourselves in it both night and day. Besides this, let all the whole frame of this world be unto us a monument and token to put us in the remembrance of God, that whatsoever true godliness is remaining in us, it may not by the works of men but by the works of God well and after a godly fashion consider, enflame, and kindle us to the praising and loving of Him.

Now as touching this reason that some men make for the use of images, because (as they say) after that God taking the nature of man upon him had vouchsafed to live among men and to be nailed fast to the cross and willed the knowledge of himself to be equally published and declared unto all men, there is no cause why it should not be lawful to use images, but yet most specially of Christ crucified to the intent that we might oftentimes be put in remembrance how by his death we have gotten redemption and salvation. Verily we do not deny whatsoever wholesome and profitable thing has come to us by the death of Christ, which he suffering what he was conversant among men reconciled mankind to his Father, yet that notwithstanding the same Christ did plainly witness that his bodily presence was nothing profitable. It is the spirit (says he) that quickens.[8] It was therefore for our profit that he should bodily depart from us.[9] And for that cause after his resurrection he ascended up in to heaven to the right hand of his Father to the end that he might carry us also up to the same place, if it be so that we have risen with him in faith.[10]

. . .

It is undoubtedly stark madness to desire to be put in remembrance of the benefits of Christ by images when Christ himself ought to work the same in our minds, which in us and all creatures works all things. Let us (I say) have this Jesus nailed fast upon the cross, set up before the eyes of our mind, as oftentimes as he tries us and lays his cross upon us by patience of tribulations and adversity. Let Christ so possess and fill the breast of Christian man, of whom he has his name, that there be nothing but it puts him in remembrance of his Lord, the Creator and Maker, the Governor, and the Savior and Preserver of all things. Wherefore so oftentimes as he looks up towards the sky, he cannot choose but remember forthwith his Savior Christ, which reigns above all heavens on the right hand of his Father. As soon as he beholds the Son by and by he thinks upon Christ the Son of righteousness and the light of the world, which with his beams lights the heart.

. . .

Now, if any man will object that for the abuse (which peradventure no man will deny) images are not altogether to be taken away (for else the Supper of the Lord and Baptism with many other things which are encumbered with diverse abuses ought also in like manner to be abrogated) this answer we make unto him. That Christian men should not wink at any abuse and therefore whatsoever is brought into the church contrary to scripture it is to be amended and to be tried by the square and rule of God's word, if anything does not agree with it, it is to be cut away with all speed that may be. And

8. John 6.
9. John 16.
10. Col 3.

only that thing which is right, which is wholesome is to be restored to his own place, specially in the Lord's Supper, in Baptism, and other things, also which have been instituted by the Lord. But images are all manner ways to be taken away not only for the abuses but much more for the Word of God to which they are plain contrary and repugnance. For we cannot imagine any manner utility which may be said to have come by the reason of images. On the other side that the superstition of images draws with it a heap of all evils, we have heretofore declared.

To make short, God never forbade any of those things whereof any commodity or profit might rise, but rather whatsoever thing is profitable and may make us better he taught full largely as Paul very evidently witnesses, 2 Timothy 3.

But if any foolish wise man thinks that images are therefore not to be take away because he fears that those weak persons which now superstitiously worship images would be offended with the putting down of images, this man doubtless whiles he got about to avoid from the smoke (as it is said in the Proverbs) is fallen in the flaming fire. For while he fears to offed desperate persons with hurtful offenses of images, he backs and hinders better men which have begun to run the way of the Lord without any turning again.

. . .

But let us hear also Athanasius writing in this way against the Gentiles.[11] Let them say (I beseech you) how or after what manner God is known by images, whether is it by the matter and stuff put round about them or else is it by the shape and fashion brought to the stuff? If it be for the stuff of the images that he is known, then what need any shape or fashion to be brought in by the workman and why did not God appear as well by all manner of stuff before that any images were made, since all things witness his glory. But if the shape and fashion brought into the stuff is the cause of the knowledge of God, what needs than any painting or any other stuff at all? And why is not God known rather by the very lively creatures whose shapes or images for doubtless the glory of God should be more clearly and evidently known if it were shown by the live creatures both reasonable and unreasonable than by deed and unmovable creatures. Therefore when you grace or paint images for the intent to have understanding and knowledge of God, forsooth you do an unworthy and an unmet thing. Now Athanasius would never have purposed in his mind to write any such manner of thing against the Gentiles if he had seen the Christ of his time, entangled and wrapped in

---

11. Athanasius, *Against the Heathen*, in NPNF, vol. IV, I.22.

such superstition of images as we see a great part of the world to be virtuously shackled now in our time, but he would rather have exercised his pen against Christian men if they had been like our Christian men nowadays.

...

For whomsoever trees, stones, silver, gold, and other stuff whereof images are made finally whom the sight of man to whom God has given life and reason cannot stir nor put in remembrance of God, surely images shall not stir up that man with any fruit or profit for they (as Origen writes against Celsus) pluck away the memory of God and turn the eyes of the mind backwards to behold and consider earthly things.[12] For every man knows that the more near that one thing resembles another in nature and propriety, so much the more strongly it renews the remembrance in us of that thing which it is like. For trees or stones do more surely and lively put us in remembrance of God, when they are considered of us, having their own natural shape and fashion, so as they were first created of God, than when by the work and craft of men being bereaved of their own natural shape, they express and resemble unto us the image and likeness of man, or of any other thing. For sooner will the remembrance come to your mind of the carver or painter, whose workmanship you marvel at, than the remembrance of God the Creator and Maker of all things. It is therefore nothing else but a pure deceit of the devil, which calls us from the praising and charitable loving of the lively images of God unto dead images of wood or stone, which some man has carven or painted a foolish counterfeit of God.

---

12. Origen, *Contra Celsus*, in ANF vol. IV, I.5.

DOCUMENT 4

Woodcut title-page,
The Great Bible
(London, 1539)

INTRODUCTION

The title-page image (or frontispiece) of the English Bible known as the Great Bible was intended to illustrate the monarchy's authority over the religious reforms in the 1530s. While George Bernard has demonstrated that Henry was at least willing to "contemplate an official translation of the Bible in English" as early as 1530, the final product did not appear until April 1539.[1] Other translations, such as Tyndale's New Testament, the Coverdale Bible, and the Matthew Bible, appeared in the decade or so before the Great Bible was printed; however, the Great Bible represents the printing of the first complete, authorized version of scripture in a language other than Latin. Its importance to the Protestant cause was apparent even before it ever appeared, as the Inquisitor-General in Paris attempted to halt its production while it was still being printed in Francis Regnault's Parisian printing house.[2]

The text was unusual for the day, having no commentary notes or annotations; however, it did contain eighty-two woodcuts distributed throughout the text.[3] The magnificent frontispiece was similar to those appearing on Lutheran Bibles, and it seems that the Great Bible's producers

---

1. Bernard, *The King's Reformation*, 523.
2. Kastan, "'The noyse of the new Bible,'" 46–68; Bruce, *History*, 67–70
3. Luborsky and Ingram, *A Guide to English Illustrated Books*, I.96–103.

made the most of this opportunity to visually depict the unique character of English reforms. It was, in John King's words, "a revolutionary victory for Protestant ideology."[4] In the picture, King Henry VIII is enthroned, with the figure of Christ in the clouds above, and a smaller figure of the king kneeling before God in the right upper corner. The scroll on Christ's right reads, *Verbum meum quod egredietur de ore meo non revertetur ad me vacuum, sed faciet quaecunque volui.*[5] The scroll to his left reads, *Inveni virum juxta cor meum, qui faciet omnes voluntates meas.*[6] The scroll issuing from the king that folds down his left side reads, *Quod justum est, judicate. Ita parvum audietis et magnum.*[7] Flanking the king (enthroned) are his two closest advisers at the time, Archbishop Thomas Cranmer (on his right), with the clergy standing behind him, and chief minister Thomas Cromwell (left), with the nobility behind him. The king hands each of them a copy of the scripture (*Verbum Dei*). The scroll on the king's right, directed at Cranmer, reads, *Haec praecipe et doce.*[8] The scroll on his left, directed at Cromwell, reads, *A me constitutum est decretum, ut in universe imperio et regno meo homines tremiscant et paveant Deum viventem.*[9] Below these upper images, another figure of Cromwell (directly below the first) is shown presenting the Bible to the nobility, with a scroll reading, *Diverte a malo et fac bonum, inquire pacem et persequere eam.*[10] Likewise, on the opposite side, Cranmer, dressed in his episcopal vestments, gives the Bible to other clergy, with a scroll reading, *Pascite, qui in vobis est, gregem Christi, prima Pe. v.*[11] At the bottom of the page, a preacher ministers to the masses below, with a scroll above him saying, *Obsecro igitur primum omnium fieri obsecrationes, orations, postulations, gratiarum actiones, pro omnibus hominibus, pro regibus, etc.*[12] The crowds respond with either *Vivat Rex* or "God save the king."

Several things become apparent from a quick study of this image. First, the Bible represented an instrumental aspect of Henry's reforms. In

---

4. King, *Tudor Royal Iconography*, 70.

5. Isa 55:11, "So shall my word be that goeth forth out of my mouth: it shall not return unto me void, but it shall accomplish that which I please."

6. Acts 13:22, "I have found a man after mine own heart, which shall fulfill all my will." This is a reference to King David.

7. Deut 1:16, "Judge righteously." Ps 119:105, "Thy word is a lamp unto my feet."

8. 1 Tim. 4:11, "These things command and teach."

9. Dan 6:26, "I make a decree, that in every dominion of my kingdom men tremble and fear before the living God."

10. Ps 34:14, "Depart from evil and do good; seek peace and pursue it."

11. 1 Pet 5:2, "Feed the flock of God which is among you."

12. 1 Tim 2:1–2, "I exhort therefore that first of all supplications, prayers, intercessions, and giving of thanks be made for all men, for kings," etc.

the words of Jacobus Naudé: "The image projected is that of a unified nation, united under the monarch and the Bible, in which church and state work harmoniously together. The church upholds the monarchy and the monarchy defends true religion. It is an icon of a godly state and church under their supreme head, who in turn acknowledges his obligations to God, expressed in the Bible."[13]

Second, the image is an excellent example of sixteenth-century propaganda. The publication of the Bible was an ideal moment to reaffirm the Act of Supremacy and Henry's authority over the church. Employing religious themes to political ends was not a foreign concept to any early modern monarch. Deborah Shuger explained that one way of reading this image is that, "The divine word circulates out from the royal head through the hierarchical body-ecclesiastic and returns to the throne as a language of political obedience."[14] Third, it is evident even from the frontispiece that the Great Bible was intended for limited use, not to be distributed (in printed form) at the popular level, but to be guarded by the clergy and the nobility.

---

13. Naudé, "The Role of the Metatexts," 165.
14. Shuger, *The Renaissance Bible*, 190.

DOCUMENT 5

John Calvin,
The Sermons of M. John Calvin upon the Fifth Book of Moses called Deuteronomy
(London, 1583)

INTRODUCTION

In a much-quoted line, the theologian Karl Barth wrote of John Calvin, "I could gladly and profitably set myself down and spend all the rest of my life just with Calvin."[1] Calvin (c.1509–64) and his *Institutes of the Christian Religion*, along with dozens of sermons and smaller tracts, warrant more than a single lifetime can afford. His role as the leading reformer in Geneva, as well as his immediate influence upon the Protestant movements in France, the Netherlands, Scotland, and England have set him above his contemporaries in terms of his importance.

Over the past fifty years, Calvin's theology continues to engender vigorous study and continuous rereading and rethinking.[2] Recently, the work of Randall Zachman has challenged many preconceived notions about hard-and-fast Calvinist restrictions on divine images. Zachman argues for a key distinction in Calvin's thought between dead and living images, and that

---

1. Barth and Thurneysen, *Revolutionary Theology*, 101.
2. A full bibliographic account of Calvin studies cannot be given here. However, key works on his life and thought include Parker, *Calvin: An Introduction*; Bouwsma, *John Calvin*; McGrath, *A Life of John Calvin*; Selderhuis, *John Calvin*.

living images, for Calvin, were bound to words and the Word.[3] This distinction is vital when reading Calvin's sermon in this document, because when Calvin speaks of images/idols, it is almost entirely a reference to dead images (those created by human hands). However, living images, those created and ordained by God, are equally important, both as preventatives against idolatry and representations of God's love.

Initially, Calvin's vitriolic refutation of Catholic imagery seems iconophobic, promoting the banishment of all image-making ("meant to bar all images"). However, as the sermon progresses, Calvin clarifies that he is not among those reformers who are "too simple" in their understanding of the commandments, desiring to ban all images ("to paint any story or to make any portraiture"). Instead, his argument on the commandment against idolatry hinges upon making "any resemblance upon God," and what he believes such images reveal about our understanding of the divine nature. Zachman explains that "For Calvin there is no likeness between anything in creation and the invisible and infinite God."[4] As such, to fashion any representation of God is to suggest a likeness between God and his creation, since no visual representation can be made without reference to created things. While God himself may certainly condescend to give certain visual representations of his being (e.g., visions to Old Testament prophets, the smoke that filled the Old Testament Temple, the incarnation of Christ, etc.), it is arrogant for human beings to presume to represent him in such ways. It is a theological deception, an undermining of God's majesty to suggest an association and likeness of base material things with God's nature where none exists.

Finally, Calvin believes that crafting images of God also reveals our own human frailty and sinfulness, which is manifested in our desire "to have some representation of God." It is this lust that Calvin most adamantly condemns and seeks to root out of himself and his audience. Furthermore, since "our Lord has given us" as many images as he deemed fit for us, Calvin believes that to suggest we need more divine images scorns God's condescending love and grace.

TEXT[5]

But now let us come to the chief matter of this sentence. "You saw not (says he) any image or portraiture in the day that the Lord spoke to you on Horeb.

---

3. Zachman, *Image and Word*. See also the earlier work of Parker, *Doctrine of the Knowledge of God*.

4. Zachman, *Image and Word*, 52.

5. The only modern translation of Calvin's sermons on Deuteronomy, though it is

Take heed therefore that you mar not yourselves by making you any carved image, or the likeness of anything, whether it be of man or woman, bird or beast, worm or fish."[6] Beware of all such things. For your God has shown himself to you in such ways as was expedient, and not in any shape. So then let us bare this lesson in mind, namely to worship him in spirit, because he has not a body, nor any thing in him that can be represented by the things that are seen with our eyes. Now this doctrine is clear enough of itself, if men would follow it, and that the world would not willfully resist so certain a thing. But this pride has been in all ages and reigns yet still at this day, that men will needs have a presence of God after their own fashion and device. But surely their wits are fleshly, by reason whereof they conceive and imagine of God after their own nature, and thereupon make images unto him. Nevertheless it is not for us to counterfeit God, or to attribute anything unto him, but it belongs to him to utter himself: and therefore we must but only receive that which he showed us, and hold us wholly thereto.

Now let us mark the ground that Moses takes here, that is to wit, "At such time as God spoke unto you in mount Horeb, he showed not himself in any visible shape." In speaking after that manner, Moses showed that we must not be hasty beforehand to conceive what we ourselves think good, but must tarry until God shows himself. Take that for one point. For if men will needs give way to their own fleshly reason in that behalf, they shall overthrow themselves and brake their necks with their overmuch haste. But on the other side Moses showed that God did manifest himself in such ways to his people, as there is no cause why men should any more say, how shall we know God? How shall we be sure that he is near us? How shall we worship him? How can we call upon him? God therefore has cut off all occasion of fond curiosities, by showing himself to his people. . . . Then let us understand that God in manifesting himself by voice, meant to bar all images, not only in respect of the Jews, but also in respect of us too. And therefore we see that their beastliness is so much the greater, which nowadays maintain this corruption concerning images in the Popedom,[7] for they allege that this was spoken for the Jews and not for us. Truly, who would say that God's manifesting of himself by voice and not in shape of a man or of any other living creature served not for all ages, but only for the people of the old time.

Again, what is to be said of the reasons that are alleged through the whole Holy Scripture? Served they but only for a time? Or rather ought they

---

not comprehensive, is Farley, *John Calvin's Sermons*. This excerpt comes from Calvin, *Sermons*, 134–8.

6. Deut 4:15.

7. A derogatory term for the Roman Catholic Church.

not to stand fast forever? Behold, Isaiah upbraided the Jews that they had disfigured the majesty of God.[8] And why? To whom have you likened me, he said? The complaint that God made is this: does wood and stone resemble me? As for them, they were dead and corruptible things. Does it not well appear then, that dishonor and wrong is offered to my being, when men go about after that sort to represent me under such shapes?

Now is God changed since that time? Is he not the same that he was? Then if he had no likenesses to wood and stone in old time, neither is he like them now. And therefore it follows that this neither ought to be nor can be restrained to any one time, but must continue forever.

. . .

Furthermore, let us also take heed to ourselves. For as soon as we begin to entangle ourselves in our own imaginations, by and by there follows a sea of foolish thoughts, which make us to run gadding here and there, so as they carry us quite and clean from God. If men knew their own nature, surely they would never adventure to make any image. I told you at the first, that we ought to know God and that the same knowledge would be a good bridle to hold us in simplicity, and to make us to prevent all superstitions. And when we enter into ourselves that also ought to teach us well that it is a turning of all things upside down, when we make any image of God. For what is the cause that men are so eager to have some representation of God, but for that they cannot mount up into heaven, for as much as their wits go groveling downward and are always wedded to the earth? And therefore would they have God to come down unto them. Now it is true that God comes down unto us. However that is after his own manner and not at our appointment. And he must be feign to stoop unto us, because we cannot mount up unto him, but yet he keeps such a fashion and measure that therewithal he lifts us up to him. We for our part could find in our hearts that God were (as you would say) under our feet, so as we might tread upon him, and this is the cause why we have idols. For the beginning of idolatry springs from this, that men feeling their own infirmity would need to have God in such a way as their own wit was able to brook. . . . So then, if there be any idols or images to portray or represent God, it cannot be but that men shall be double seduced. Seeing they be too much naturally inclined, it is a great enforcement when they be further driven forward by the thing that they behold. Therefore if we wish it were such a vice, surely we would abhor idolatry, knowing that it turns us quite away from God. And for the same cause does the prophet Jeremiah say, that there is nothing but doctrine

---

8. Isa 44:9–20.

of falsehood in idols. And the prophet Habakkuk verifying the same and comparing idols with the living God, says that they are a school of lies.[9]

But yet for all this, the papists will affirm that images are laymen's books and that because all men cannot read nor are clerks, there must be some help for the ignorant. Very well, if a representation of God be made that is a book that is as good as the Bible, say the papists, and it is their chief anchor-hold that they flee to in this case.[10] True it is that this shift is not of their own devising. It was devised by a man not wicked of himself, notwithstanding that he was somewhat tainted with the corruption of the papistry. For he was a Pope himself, however not when the Popedome was in such plight as it is nowadays, but yet when it had already been greatly corrupted and the world was very degenerated. Now then, this good man Gregory thought it good to have images, and that they would be as books for the unlearned, and this have the papists received as if it were the oracle of some Angel from heaven.[11] Contrarily, the prophet Jeremiah avowed that all the doctrine of idols is mere falsehood, and likewise Habakkuk in the second chapter says that they teach nothing but lies.[12] Were it lawful for a man to coin false money on his own head, because he can get none of the right stamp? No, but you have God given his word to all men, so that he has vouchsafed not only to speak to great clerks but also to stoop to the rudeness of the little ones. And for all this, men stop their ears and say they cannot know God but by a puppet, and under that pretense they will need have it lawful for them to belie the things that God has reported of his own being. Forasmuch then as we have warrant that there is nothing but falsehood in images, let us send home such books to the devil, for it is certain that he is the author of them, and that they came all out of his shop.

. . .

But if they will needs that there must be visible images, our Lord has given us as many of them as he knew to be for our benefit. When we have baptism is it not a visible image of a thing that is spiritual? That is to wit of the washing which we have by the blood of our Lord Jesus Christ, when we

---

9. Hab 2:18.

10. Aston, *England's Iconoclasts*, 130-32; Wandel, *Voracious Idols*, 49-51.

11. This is likely a reference to the well-known and well-cited letter from Pope Gregory I to Bishop Serenus of Marseilles: Gregory, "Epistle XIII," in NPNF, 2nd Series, vol. XIII, II.297-98. Because of this letter, Gregory the Great's papacy became one of the more popular dividing lines for Protestants to mark when idolatry began to creep into Christian worship: Eire, *War Against the Idols*, 19-20; Aston, *England's Iconoclasts*, 58-59.

12. Jer 10:8.

are renewed by his Holy Spirit? And have we not a representation of the heavenly mystery set forth to us in the Lord's Supper? Yes, but yet for all that we must not make any image at all of God's being. And why? For it were not for our profit as I have declared before, but it would rather turn us away to lies and beset us in all manner of superstition. God therefore knowing that the having of images is an untoward thing and as a deadly plague has not listed to give us any, but rather holds us back to this, that having such signs as may convey us upward, we should travel toward him, howbeit without having any representation of his being. Thus you see that the thing which we have to remember in effect is that although the scripture did not expressly forbid us to have any image or bodily representation of God, yet the reasons are such as we ought to worship God in spirit, and to fly up into heaven and not to stick fast here below. Why so? For in knowing God, we must consider his majesty, how there is no proportion or likeness between him and the creatures. Therefore it is but a misshaping of him when we make any bodily image unto him; he that is the wellspring of life cannot be represented by a dead thing. . . . For although men be naturally contented to have some religion, yet they seek by all means not to come at God in truth. They will well enough say always, God is to be worshipped, and our intent is to do so, we must resort unto him. But how? Whereas they should seek God in heaven by faith, they will beat around the bush. Very well say they, we will have some image of God. And that is all one as if they should say, "Behold, here is a God that shall not trouble us for we will deal well enough with him at all times, he shall not speak a word, he shall but only make a move." See how the world making countenance to seek God drags back from him as much as possible, shrouding themselves under this pretense, that it is enough to have a representation of God, and that his power shall nevertheless be infinite still. But now we have to mark that God is not contented with such reasons, forasmuch as he has told us that it is not lawful for us to have any image of him to represent him. And shall we reply against him when we have the word of his mouth? What shall we win by it? When we have pleaded our fill, suppose we that we have any devices in our brain that can make God believe that he considered not all things well? No, and therefore (to be short) as many as covet to have any image of God betray themselves to be rank rebels against him; they betray a devilish malapertness,[13] in that they presume to forge and set up gods after their own fancy.[14] They betray their own beastliness also, in that they act against nature. For they would

---

13. Impudence

14. There is a similar comment to this in his *Institutes*. Calvin writes that the human imagination is a "forge of idols" (Calvin, *Institutes of the Christian Religion*, I.xi.8).

allow God such a representation, as agrees as fitly to him, as if they should liken him to a stick, or I wrote not what else. Men therefore do in all respects sufficiently show themselves to be inexcusable, when they turn so away after their images.

But, by the way, we have to mark further that all manner of images and representations are not meant here. For our Lord says expressly that he showed not himself to his people any otherwise than by his only voice, and therefore that it is a corruption to make images. If this should be drawn to conclude that it is not lawful to make any picture at all, it were a misapplying of Moses' testimony, as some do who being too simple in this behalf do say it is not lawful to make any image. That is to say, it is not lawful (to their seeming) to paint any story or to make any portraiture.[15] But when the Holy Scripture says, it is not lawful to shape any resemblance of God, because he has no body, it extends not so far. For it is otherwise as concerning men. Now then look what we see, that may we represent by picture. And therefore let us see that we apply the texts against the papists as we ought to do, that we may be armed to prove our case just. But yet must we be fully resolved of this, that if any man go about to express God's majesty by any shape, he does him wrong, and it is high treason to him, because he is incomprehensible in his glory. Mark that for one point. Now we see that the papists have gone about to express God by shapes, therefore it follows that they have marred all religion. When they allege that there were cherubim painted upon the veil of the temple and that two likewise did cover the Ark, it serves to condemn them the more. When the papists pretend that men may make any manner of image: what say they? Has not God permitted it? No, but the imagery that was set there served to put the Jews in mind that they ought to abstain from all counterfeiting of God, insomuch that it was a mean to confirm them the better, that it was not lawful for them to represent God's majesty, or to make any resemblance thereof. For there was a veil that served to cover the great sanctuary, and again there were two cherubim that covered the Ark of the Covenant.[16] Whereto comes all this, and what is meant by it, but that when the case concerning our going unto God, we must shut our eyes and not press any nearer to him than he guides us by his word? Then let us hearken to that which he teaches, and therewithal let us be sober, so as our wits be not ticklish, nor our eyes open

---

15. It is likely that Calvin has in mind the more radical reformers like Andreas Karlstadt: Sider, *Karlstadt's Battle with Luther*, 66–67.

16. The idea of images serving as preventatives to idolatry, to halt the human imagination from crossing the line to inappropriate adoration, has been studied most recently in Koerner, *Reformation of the Image*, 40–41, 209–11.

to imagine or conceive any shape.[17] That is the thing which God means to betoken in his Law. And so are we the more confirmed in the doctrine that I spoke of. But as for the images which the papists make of their saints as they term them, there are other reasons to condemn them. For God has forbidden two things. First the making of any picture of him, because it is a disguising and falsifying of his glory, and a turning of his truth into a lie. That is one point. The other is that no image may be worshipped. But now, do not the papists worship images? If they say, it is requisite so to do, for it is a continual stirring up of the people's devotion. That is too fond a reason. For first of all, when we come to the church, it cannot be but that we shall be caught in some error, if we have never so little occasion offered us. For (as I said) although there be no image at all to draw our eyes, yet are we inclined to earthly imaginations even of ourselves, and we nourish superstition in us of our own nature. Now then if we be furthered and thrust forward into evil, so as we find as it were spurs to prick us forward, I pray you, shall we not be as good as mad? Therefore the setting up of images in churches is a defiling of them, and can serve to no purpose but to draw folk from the pure and true knowledge of God. Again, to what end do the papists set up images in churches? Is it to have knowledge of their histories? No, but there stand a sort of puppets with demure countenances, as it were to summon folk to come to do them homage, insomuch that an image is not so soon set up in a church, but by and by folk go and kneel down to it, and do a kind of worship to it. And can a man devise to tear the majesty of our Lord Jesus Christ, and to deface his glory more than by the things that the papists do? Behold, they paint and portray Jesus Christ, who (as we know) is not only man, but also God manifested in the flesh, and what a representation is that? He is God's eternal son, in whom dwells the fullness of the Godhead, even substantially. Seeing it is said, substantially, should we have portraitures and images whereby the only flesh may be represented? Is it not a wiping away of that which is chief in our Lord Jesus Christ, that is, to wit, of his divine majesty? Yes, and therefore whenever a crucifix stands mopping and mowing in the church, it is all one as if the Devil had defaced the son of God.[18] You see then that the papists are destitute of all excuse. Again we see how they behave themselves. The images are worshipped among them, as if God

---

17. Stuart Clark has convincingly argued that the veracity of sight and seeing became increasingly scrutinized over the sixteenth and seventeenth centuries: *Vanities of the Eye*.

18. This was a contentious point among the reformers. Lutherans continued to depict Christ, while ardent Calvinists despised any such representation. Even reformers like Peter Vermigli, as we will see later on, remained ambiguous on the moral legality of such representations: Davis, *Seeing Faith*, 105–8.

were present there in his own person. Where say they their paternosters, but before some puppet? And yet are they not contented with that, for they will needs make idols of all things, even to the very sacraments, insomuch that they have falsified them, to draw the world from the right religion. Is there a more abominable idol, than that which they have invented under the pretense of the Supper of Jesus Christ? No, for they say, that God is there, and there he must be worshipped. So then, no marvel though they abuse their puppets and pictures after that fashion, seeing they have been so bold as to pervert the things that God has appointed to the furtherance of our faith.

. . .

Therefore let us learn to worship our God in spirit and truth, and to do him homage and to acknowledge the good that he does us, specially for that it has pleased him to adopt us to be his children, through freebestowed adoption in our Lord Jesus Christ.

Now let us kneel down in the presence of our good God with acknowledgement of our faults, praying him so to open our eyes, as we may no more adventure to devise anything after our own fleshly understanding, but resort altogether to his holy word whereby he hath revealed himself to us, and also receive his sacraments whereby we be yet better confirmed in his knowledge, so as our whole seeking may be to follow the pureness that is set forth in his doctrine, yet no error may lead us away form him nor from the pure religion that has been taught to us. And in the meantime, yet as we do him homage in spirit, so likewise we may serve him with all our heart, assuring ourselves that we cannot serve nor worship him by any ceremonies or outward things, without yielding him the honor and praise that he requires. And finally that it may please him to correct all the idolatry and superstition in the world, and to rid it in such ways from the earth which he has appointed to the use of men, as his name may be purely called upon there. For the performance whereof, it may please him to raise up true and faithful ministers of his word.

DOCUMENT 6

Roger Edgeworth, *Sermons, Very Fruitful, Godly, and Learned*

(London, 1557)

INTRODUCTION

Theologian and minister Roger Edgeworth (d. 1560) was an "alarmingly talented conservative preacher," delivering regular sermons in Bristol and Wells, and his writings are some of the most important expressions of Catholic piety to survive from the 1550s.[1] Often described as a moderate in his theology, Edgeworth weathered the tempestuous final years of Henry VIII's reign as well as the more adamant reforms of Edward VI. Most of his sermons which compose the collection *Sermons, Very Fruitful, Godly, and Learned* were likely preached during this tempestuous period and finally were printed in 1557 under the reign of the Catholic Queen Mary.

One of Edgeworth's appealing traits was, as Alec Ryrie explains, his "knack for using evangelical arguments against them." Edgeworth often conceded small points of Protestant criticism, such as certain corruptions in the church, only to level a greater condemnation upon the reformers.[2] In the fourth of his *Sermons*, Edgeworth employs his rhetorical style seemingly praising reformers for their "zeal and love to learning," only to argue that

---

1. MacCulloch, *The Boy King*, 84; Wizeman, *Theology and Spirituality*, 200-202.
2. Ryrie, *The Gospel*, 132.

this zeal had turned them arrogant and made them "renegades." As to the image debate, the sermon offers a response to Protestant attacks on Catholic image devotion, providing one of the earliest surviving, popular-level rebuttals of the Protestant conflation of terms like *imago* and *idolum*.[3]

While a more detailed, semantic argument is provided by the Catholic theologian Gregory Martin later in the century (document 16), Edgeworth strikes at the heart of the issue. He argues that this is a matter of definition, regardless of whether one is using a Greek or Latin term. An image "is a similitude of a natural thing," whereas an idol represents "a thing that never was nor may be." Thus, for him, the images of the pagan gods are all idols, but those based upon scripture cannot be, and the Protestant argument about *imago* and *idolum* is little more than a hall of linguistic mirrors.

Furthermore, Edgeworth plays on the theme of learning and arrogance throughout the text to get his point across. He pulls from Aristotle, Homer, Ovid, as well as more obscure sources like Pomponius Mela, subtly demonstrating his own education. He praises the Protestant ideal of having scripture in "the mother tongue," but questions "who be meet and able to take it in hand." Following his example of Aristotle, he believes that the people must first be educated in order to fully understand and appropriately engage with scripture. Of course, beneath this discussion of scripture and images, there is a larger underlying accusation that Protestantism was full of guile and deceit. While Protestants seem to promote learning in their insistence upon an English Bible, their actions, as Edgeworth sees it, were hypocritical and abusive. Far from "profound learning," he reports that Protestant preachers were "leaning" upon "vulgar noise" and "babble" when they preach.

TEXT[4]

The gift of science, or cunning, as we now speak of it, extends also to handcrafts and occupations as I shall declare hereafter. And it presupposes the gift of council (that I spoke of lately) by which we may with study, deliberation, and advisement attain to the knowledge of men's acts and to the knowledge of creatures. But because many times men's wits in their study and in their singular or private councils be ready to invent or imagine of

---

3. Aston, *England's Iconoclasts*, 395; Shagan, *Popular Politics*, 216.

4. Edgeworth, *Sermons*, 30v–32v, 40v–43r. The printer of Edgeworth's sermons loosely inserted many of Edgeworth's citations into the body of the text, making for cumbersome reading. This transcription has silently put these into footnotes for easier reading.

men's acts and of other creatures laying apart the gift of council and good judgment, so comes many times to man's mind deception, error, Lollardy, and heresy, contrary to true science and cunning, jealousy, suspicion, slander, and infamy, contrary to quietness of living. An example we have of the people of Israel, which had imbibed so much of Moses' law and wedded their wits so obstinately to that learning, and leaned so carnally to the same, that notwithstanding all Christ's doctrine and all the preaching of the Apostles, thought no way to salvation but by observing and fulfilling the works of the law of Moses, as except men were circumcised, they thought men could not be saved. And after a man had touched any dead thing or any unclean thing, except he should sequester himself seven days from the company of clean people, and except he were washed the third day and the seventh day with a certain water made for the same purpose, he should die, with many such ceremonies and usages which were then commanded to be used, and were no more but shadows and figures of our Savior Christ, and of the time of grace that now is, and they should now cease when the verity signifies by them is exhibited and performed, like as night ceases when the day comes, and darkness vanishes away by the presence of light. This they would not understand nor learn for any man's exhortation, but rather persecuted to death all them that instructed them in this verity. In this case was St. Paul, first before his conversion, and many of his countrymen and kinfolk the Jews, of which he says, *Testimonium enim perhibeo illis, quod et emulationem Dei habent, sed non secundum scientiam*.[5] I bare witness that they have a zeal and love to follow the learning that God has given them by Moses, but they lack science and cunning, they follow not good understanding, in that in which they think themselves cunning, for the said ceremonies were no more but *Justitiae carnis usque ad tempus correctionis imposite*.[6] Certain observances laid on their necks, carnally to be observed and kept, to occupy them and hold them under obedience, and to keep them from the rites and uses that the Gentiles used in their idolatry, until the time of correction, the time of reformation (which is the time of Christ's coming) at which time they should cease and be used not more. Such a zeal and love to learning has many nowadays. And of their learning and knowledge (which they think they have) they will make as great glory and boast as did the Jews of their learning. In this case be they that so arrogantly glory in their learning had by study in the English Bible, and in these seditious English books that have been sent over from our English renegades now abiding with Luther in Saxony. Of their study you may judge by the effect. When men

---

5. Rom 10.

6. No citation follows this Latin verse. It is found in Heb 9.

and women have all studied, and count themselves best learned, of their learning men perceive little else but envy and disdaining at others, mocking and despising all goodness, railing at fasting and at abstinence from certain meats one day afore another, by custom or commandment of the church, at Mass and Matins, and at all blessed ceremonies of Christ's Church ordained and used for the advancement and setting forth of God's glory not without profound and great mysteries and causes reasonable. By this effect you may judge of the cause, the effect is naught, therefore there must needs be some fault in the cause. But what say you? Is not the study of scripture good? Is not the knowledge of the Gospels and of the New Testament godly, good, and profitable for a Christian man or woman? I shall tell you what I think in this matter, I have been of this mind, that I have thought it no harm, but rather good and profitable that Holy Scripture should be had in the mother tongue, and withheld from no man that were apt and meet to take it in hand, especially if we could get it well and truly translated, which will be very hard to be had. But who be meet and able to take it in hand, there is the doubt. I shall declare this doubt by another like. The Philosopher declares who be meet and convenient hearers of the science of moral philosophy. And there he excludes from the study of that learning all young men and women, whether they be young in age or young in manners and conditions, they that be young in years, be no convenient hearers of moral philosophy, because they lack experience of things that be taught in that faculty, which be acts of virtue and virtuous living, principally intended in moral philosophy, of such manner of living, youth has no experience, or very little, and therefore they cannot discern them from their contraries when they hear them spoken of, neither discern the means which be virtues from the extremities that be vices, no more than a blind man can judge colors from their contraries, or can perceive yet how much the nigher[7] that any mean color draws to white, so much that more it scatters and disperses the sight, and hurts it, or on the contrary part, how much the nigh in degrees it approaches to the black color, so much the more it gathers the sight close together and helps the sight, and comforts it.[8] To tell this tale to a blind man is all labor lost, for he cannot tell what you mean (after Aristotle) because a child knows not the acts of virtue, of which moral philosophy treats for the end of that philosophy is well doing and good living. Therefore to teach a child the rules of that faculty is a vain labor.

. . .

7. Closer

8. "The Philosopher" referred to earlier in the paragraph is certainly Aristotle. Aristotle, *Nichomachean Ethics*, I.3.

And because I spoke even now of images and idols, I would you should not ignorantly confound and abuse those terms, taking an image for an idol, and an idol for an image, as I have heard many do in this city, as well of the fathers and mothers (that should be wise) as of their babies and children that have learned foolishness of their parents. Now at the Dissolution of the Monasteries and of free houses many images have been carried abroad and given to children to play withal. And when the children have them in their hands, dancing them after their childish manner, comes the father or the mother and says, "What nasse,[9] what have you there?" The child answers (as she is taught), "I have here mine idol." The father laughs and makes a gay game at it. . . . But if this folly were only in the insolent youth, and in the fond unlearned fathers and mothers, it might soon be redressed. But your preachers that you so obstinately follow, more leaning to the vulgar noise and common error of the people, than to profound learning they babble in the pulpits that they hear the people rejoice in.[10]

And so of the people they learn their sermons, and by their sermons they indurate their audience and make the people stubborn and hard to be persuaded to science, contrary to their blind ignorance, as well in this point of images and idols, as in many other like. They would have that this Latin word *imago* signify an idol, and so these new translations of the English Bibles have it in all places, where the translators would bring men to believe that to set up images, or to have images is idolatry. And therefore where the scriptures abhor idols, they make it images, as though to have imagery were idolatry that God so greatly abhors. But you must understand and know that an image is a thing carved, or painted, or cast in a mold, that represents and signifies a thing that is indeed, or that has been or shall be indeed. And so speaks our Savior Christ of an image, when the Pharisees send their disciples with Herod's servants, to ask him this question: whether it were lawful for the Jews to pay tribute to the Emperor or not? He called them hypocrites, and bade them show him the coin or money that was usually paid for the tribute. They brought him a *denarius*, we call it a penny. He asked them, *Cuius est imago hec et superscriptio*.[11] Whose is this Image and the scripture about? They answered: the emperor's. Note here (good friends) that Christ asked not *cuius est idolum hoc*? Whose is this idol? For he knew it was none, but that it was an image, as is the image of our sovereign Lord the king upon

---

9. There is likely a play on words here. "Nasse" in Old and Middle English meant "nose," however in French it means a "net" or fish trap.

10. Wooding, "From Tudor Humanism," 329–427; Wabuda, *Preaching*.

11. Matt 22:20.

his money coined in London, in Bristow,[12] or in other places, which no man that has wit would call an idol. For St. Paul says, *Scimus quia nihil est idolum in mundo et quod nullus est dues nisi unus.*[13] We know that an idol is nothing in the world, and that there is no God but one. Where the blessed Apostle refers much unto science in this matter of idols, and of meat offered unto them, and spoke to them that were learned, and should have cunning to discern in this matter, saying in the beginning of that eighth chapter, *Scimus quoniam omnes scientiam habemus.*[14] We know, for all we have science and cunning to judge of these meats that be offered to idols, what know we? *Scimus quia nihil est idolum in mundo et quod nullus est dues nisi unus.* We have this science, and this we know, that an idol is nothing in the world, and that there is no God but one. An image is a similitude of a natural thing that has been, is, or may be. An idol is a similitude representing a thing that never was nor may be. Therefore the image of the crucifix is no idol, for it represents and signifies Christ crucified, as he was indeed. And the image of St. Paul with the sword in his hand, as the sign of his martyrdom is no idol, for the thing signified by it was a thing indeed, for he was beheaded with a sword indeed, but an idol is an image that signifies a monster that is not possible to be, as to signify a false god which is no God indeed. For as St. Paul said, "There is no God but one."[15] As the image of Jupiter set up to signify the god Jupiter is a false signifier and signifies a thing of nothing, for there is no God Jupiter. And the image of Venus to signify the goddess Venus is nothing, for that is signified by it, is nothing, for there is no she goddess Venus. As in a like speaking, we say Chimera is nothing, because the voice is sometime put to signify a monster, having a head like a lion, with fire flaming out of his mouth, and the body of a goat, and the hind part like a serpent or a dragon, there is not such a thing, although the poets feign such a monster, therefore the voice Chimera is a false signifier, and that which is false is nothing, therefore we say Chimera is nothing but Chimera signifying a certain mountain in the country of Lycia, flaming fire out of the top of it, breeding and having lions closer about the higher part or top of the same hill, and downward about the middle part, having pastures where breeds goats or such other beasts, and at the foot of the it marshes or moist ground breading serpents: such a hill there is in the said country, and of the diverse disposition of the parts of the said hill, the fiction of the foresaid monster is imagined, which is nothing, and therefore so we say that Chimera is noth-

12. Bristol
13. 1 Cor 8.
14. 1 Cor 8:1.
15. 1 Cor 8:6.

ing, but the same word put to signify the hill in Lycia aforesaid is somewhat, and a true signifier, for it signifies a thing that is indeed.[16]

As appeared by Pomponius Mela and Solinus, with their expositors, and even so it is true that Paul says that an idol is nothing, for there is no such thing as is signified by it, there is no God Saturn, there is no god Jupiter, there is no goddess Venus, but I say more, that if a man could carve or paint an image of Jupiter's soul burning in the fire of Hell, or likewise an image of Venus's soul there burning.[17] If St. Paul had seen such a picture or image, he would never have called it an idol, or a thing of nothing, for it should signify a thing that is indeed, for Jupiter's soul is in Hell indeed, and so is Venus's soul, and other like taken for gods made of mortal men. After this manner, good friends, you must by science and cunning learnedly speak of images and idols, and not to confound the words, or the things signified by them, taking one for another. And by this you may perceive, that when you will arrogantly of a proud heart meddle of matters above your capacity, the Holy Ghost withdraws his gift of science from you, and that makes you to speak you cannot tell what, for the Holy Ghost will not inspire his gifts but upon them that be humble and lowly in heart. And because I said heretofore that this gift of science as it is here taken extends to mechanical science and handy-crafts. This appears by the text Exodus 31, when the holy tabernacle should be made in the desert, Almighty God provided an artificer and workman for the same, one called Beseleel, son of Uri, son of Hur, of the tribe of Judah.[18] "I have filled him (says God) with the spirit of God." *Sapientia, intelligentia, et scientia in omni opera.* I have given him *sapience*, by which he might well discern and judge of the things that God would have made, in so much that he was able to teach others the things that he knew by God's revelation and instruction. And this properly pertains to the gift of *sapience*, as I have said before. I have filled him with the spirit of intelligence or wittiness, and fine and clear perceiving and understanding, by which he may more perfectly pierce and enter with his wit into the things that be taught him, than he should have done if he lacked the said gift of intelligence. I have also (says God) fulfilled Beseleel with the gift of science. Of which speaks John Chrysostom in a sermon of the Holy Ghost after this manner.[19] When Moses made the tabernacle in the wilderness, he had need then not only of doctrine and learning, but also of the gift of a master craftsman, to know how we should sow together fine clothes

---

16. Pliny, *Natural History*, II.105.
17. Mela, *De situ orbis*, book I; Solinus, *De mirabilibus*, ch. 52.
18. Exod 31:1–3.
19. Chrysostom, "Homily XX on Ephesians," in NPNF, vol. XII, 374.

and silks of precious colors, and how to weave them, plate them, and shape them together. And how he should cast gold and other metals necessary for the ceremonies there to be used, and how to polish precious stones, and also to frame the timber for the same tabernacle. For these and such other purposes Almighty God gave him and to his workman Beseleel the spirit of science, that they might frame all such things accordingly. And even so in your occupations and handy-crafts, when you exercise yourselves diligently and truly without sloth, without deceit, guile, or subtlety in all your exercise, ordering yourselves to your neighbor, as you would be ordered yourself, so long your occupation, exercise, and labor is annexed and joined with charity and seems plainly to come of the Holy Ghost. For without charity this gift of science coming of the Holy Ghost will not be, no more than other virtues infused. And contrary, like as every good thing has an enemy, or at leastwise an ape or a counterfeiter, as fortitude or manliness has foolhardiness or rash boldness, which seems manliness and is not so, so has science or cunning, guile or subtlety, which counterfeits cunning, and is not true cunning, in as much as it is without charity, and also without justice.

DOCUMENT 7

John Hooper, *A Declaration of the Holy Ten Commandments*

(London, 1549)

INTRODUCTION

John Hooper, bishop of Gloucester, was certainly among the firebrands of the first generation of English Protestants. Martyred in 1555 in the reign of Queen Mary, Hooper is one of England's earliest nonconformists and perhaps most zealous of the English Protestant zealots.[1]

As a Catholic cleric in the 1530s, Hooper underwent an evangelical conversion, and by 1544 he had fled to the Protestant havens of Strasbourg and Zurich. Heavily influenced by the writings of Calvin, Bucer, and Ulrich Zwingli, Hooper's own theology honed the Calvinistic dogma to a radically sharp, and often simplistic, point. For example, during the vestment controversy in the reign of King Edward VI, Hooper stood alone, even against the advice of fellow Protestants like Thomas Cranmer and Bucer, in refusing to conform to the use of clerical vestments during his consecration as a bishop. He relented only after a few weeks in prison.

A Declaration of the Holy Ten Commandments was going to print while Hooper was returning to England from Zurich in 1549.[2] Although in

---

1. Newcombe, *John Hooper*.
2. Aston, *England's Iconoclasts*, 436.

certain respects, Hooper parrots his great mentors (i.e., Calvin and Bucer), his text is not unimportant in the history of the image debate. Despite the Edwardian official iconoclasm that had already swept across the English countryside, cleansing much of what Henry VIII's officers had missed, it is apparent that Hooper—and likely others with him—believed that more still needed to be done. As Margaret Aston commented, Hooper was one of those reformers who had "run ahead of official policy," heralding what would come to be known in the 1570s and 1580s as the puritan movement.[3] He insisted upon reforms that were a challenge to, and at times in violation of, the official religious policies of the English monarchy.

Moreover, Hooper's text is important in the evolution of the English debate on images precisely because he parrots the continental reformers so closely. In his argument, Hooper stresses the origins and growth of idolatry in the Christian churches, with particular reference to the church father Lactantius's *Divine Institutes*. This archaeology of idolatry became a staple of the image debate in the second half of the sixteenth century. As Michalski explains, Lactantius's teachings had "a big impact on the image dispute," because he was the first to say that Christian cults derived from pagan practices. By extension, the Christian use of images could be understood as having pagan roots. In fact, Lactantius's influence was so profound that he was specifically mentioned in the Second Helvetic Creed in 1566, as an authority that sanctioned iconoclasm.[4] By tracing the development of idolatry, Protestants could provide a historical trajectory and roadmap, explaining that images were first used with little corruption but were slowly perverted into idolatrous beliefs and practices.

TEXT[5]

Ch. 5 The Second Commandment

Epigraph: You shall make no image, or any similitude, of things in heaven above, in earth beneath, or in the water under the earth. You shall not worship, nor honor them: for I am the Lord, thy God, a Jealous God, punishing the iniquity of the fathers in the children that hate me in the third and fourth generation.

---

3. Aston, *England's Iconoclasts*, 438.
4. Michalski, *Reformation and the Visual Arts*, 184.
5. Earlier edition: Hooper, *Early Writings* , 316–22. The following excerpt is taken from Hooper, *A declaration*, 69–78.

In the first commandment we learned that God is the only and sole God, and that we should not think nor feign any other besides him. Further, that commandment expresses what this our one God is, and how affectionate or minded towards us, fully of mercy, and ready always to succor and aid both soul and body in all affliction, shows us further how we should honor and reverence this our almighty and merciful God, so that the end and whole sum of the first commandment is, that only God would be known of his people to be God and honored as God. So does God first instruct the mind and soul of man before he requires any outward work or external reverence, or else altogether were hypocrisy, whatsoever show or perfection it seems to have in the eye of the world. He lays therefore the first commandment as a foundation of all true religion, as the original and spring of all virtue, and opens the well and foundation of all mischief and abomination in these words, "You shall have no strange gods before my face."[6] This second precept and the two others that follow in the first table teaches us how to honor God in external religion or outward works and to show the fear, faith, and love that we bear unto God in our hearts unto the world. Two of these last commandments show what we should do; and the third, which I now expound, what we should not do. The purpose, end, and will of this second commandment is: that God's pleasure is unto us, that we should not profane, or dishonor, the true religion, or honor of God, with superstitious ceremonies, or rites, not commanded by him. Wherefore, by this second commandment he calls man from all gross and carnal opinions or judgments of God, which the foolish and ignorant prudence and wit of man conceives, where as it judges without the scripture and forbids external idolatry, as in the first internal.

This commandment has three parts. The first takes from us all liberty and license that we in no case represent or manifest the God invisible and incomprehensible with any figure, or image, or represent him, unto our senses that cannot be comprehended by the wit of man nor angel.

The second part forbids to honor any image.

The third part shows us that it is no need to represent God unto us by any image.

Moses gives a reason of the first part, why no image should be made: "Remember," says he to the people, "that the Lord spoke to you in the vale of Oreb. You heard a voice, but saw no manner similitude, but only a voice (heard you)."[7] Isaiah chapters 40, 41, 45, 46 diligently shows what an absurdity and indecent thing it is to prophane the majesty of God, incomprehen-

6. Exod 20:3.
7. Deut 4:15.

sible with a little block or stone, a spirit with an image. The same does Paul, Acts 17. The text therefore forbids all manner of images that are made to express, or represent, Almighty God.

The second part forbids to honor any image made.

The first word honor signifies: to bow head, leg, knee, or any part of the body unto them as all those do that say they may with good conscience be suffered in the church of Christ. To serve them is to do somewhat for their sakes, as to sense them with incense, to gild, to run on pilgrimage to them, to kneel, or pray before them, to be more affectionate to one than to the other, to set lights before them with such like superstition and idolatry.[8] God be praised, I may be short or write nothing at all in this matter, because such as I write unto my countrymen be persuaded already aright in this commandment.

The second part shows us how idolatry proceeds and takes place in men's conscience. The mind of man, when it is not illuminated with the Spirit of God, nor governed by the scripture, it imagines and feigns God to be like unto the imagination and conceit of his mind, and not as the scripture teaches. When this vanity or fond imagination is conceived in the mind, there follows a further success of the ill. He purposes to express by some figure or image God in the same form and similitude that his imagination has first printed in his mind; so that the mind conceives the idol and afterward the hand works and represents the same unto the senses.

Therefore God first forbids this inward and spiritual idolatry of the mind, when he says, "You shall have no strange gods before my face." If the mind be corrupted and not persuaded aright: then follows the making of images and, after, the honoring of them. The cause therefore of external idolatry is internal, and inward ignorance of God, and his word, as Lactantius writes in his book of the original error.[9] As it cannot be otherwise, but whereas the air is corrupted, there must follow pestilence and infection of the blood.[10] So where the mind is not purely persuaded of God in an idol. The original cause why they are made is that man thinks God would not be present to help him, except he be presented some ways unto their carnal eyes, as the example of the Israelites declares, that required Aaron to make them gods that might lead them in their journey.[11] They knew right well that there was but one God whom they knew by the miracles that he wrought

8. This is essentially, though perhaps not intentionally, a condemnation of Tyndale's teachings in document 2.

9. Lactantius, *Divine Institutes*, II.13, 122–23.

10. This was a common misconception, stemming from Greco-Roman medicine, that foul smells were indicative of disease: Galen, *De differentiis frebrium*, I.3–5.

11. Exod 32:1.

among them. But they thought he would not be present and at hand with them except they might see him in some corporal figure and image and that the image might be a testimony of his presence. So see we that no man falls into this gross idolatry, but such as be first infected with a false opinion of God and his Word. Then say they, they worship not the image, but the thing represented by the image. Against whom writes St. Augustine, in Psalm 118 and 113, in the fourth book of the *City of God*, that "images take away fear from men, and bring them into error. The ancient Romans more religiously," says he, "honored their gods without images."[12] Seeing there is no commandment in either of the testaments to have images but as you see the contrary, and likewise, the universal catholic, and holy church, never used images as the writings of the apostles and prophets testify: it is but an ethnic verity and Gentiles' idolatry to say God and his saints be honored in them, when that all histories testify that in manner for the space of five hundred years after Christ's ascension, when the doctrine of the gospel was most sincerely preached was no image used. Would to God the Church were now as purely and well instructed as it was before these avaricious ministers and dumb doctors of the lay people were made preachers in the church of God.... Therefore St. John bids us not only beware of honoring of images, but of the images' selves.[13] You shall find the original images in no part of God's word, but in the writings of the Gentiles and infidels or in such that more followed their own opinions and superstitious imaginations than the authority of God's word. Herodotus, in book two, says that, "the Egyptians were the first that made images to represent their gods." And as the Gentiles fashioned their gods with what figures they listed, so do the Christians.[14] To declare God to be strong, they made him the form of a lion, to be vigilant and diligent, the form of a dog; and, as Herodotus says, in book two, Mendes formed their god Pan with a goat's face and goat's legs, and thought they did their god great honor, because among them the herdsmen of goats were had in most estimation.[15] So do those that would be accounted Christians paint God and his saints with such pictures as they imagine in their fantasies. God like an old man, with a forehead, as though his youth were past, which has neither beginning nor ending. St. George, with a long spear, upon a jolly hackney, that gave the dragon his death wound, as the painters say, in the throat. St. Whit, with as many round cheeses as may be painted about

---

12. Augustine, *City of God*, IV.9, 30.
13. 1 John 5:21.
14. Herodotus, *Histories*, II.4.
15. Ibid., II.46.

his tabernacle.[16] No difference at all between a Christian man and Gentile in this idolatry, saving only the name. For they thought not their images to be god, but supposed that their gods would be honored that ways, as the Christians do. I write these things rather in a contempt and hatred of this abominable idolatry, than to teach any Englishman the truth. For my belief and hope is, that every man in England knows praying to saints and kneeling before images is idolatry, and instruments of the devil to lead men from the commandments of God. And that they are appointed in many places to be as doctors to teach the people: these doctors and doctrine the bishops and pastors shall bewail before the judgment seat of God at the hour of death, and likewise the princes of the world. Whose office is daily to read and learn the scripture that they themselves might be able to judge the bishops' doctrine, and also see them apply the vocation they are called unto. It is not only a shame and an indecent thing for a prince to be ignorant, what curates his subjects has through all his realm, but also a thing so contrary unto the Word of God that nothing provokes more the ire of God against him and his realm than such a contempt of God's commandment.

The third part declares that there is no need to show God unto us by images, and proves the same with three reasons. First, "I am the Lord your God," that loves you, helps you, defends you, and is present with you. Believe and love me, so shall you have no need to seek me and my favorable presence in any image.

The second reason, "I am a Jealous God" and cannot suffer you to love anything but in me and for me. When we two were married and knit together for the love that I bore unto you I gave you certain rules and precepts, how in all things you may keep my love and goodwill towards you; and you promised me obedience unto my commandments.[17] So honor me and love me, as it stands written in the writings and indentures written between us both. I cannot suffer to be otherwise honored than I have taught in my tables and testament.

The third reason is that God revenges the prophanation of his divine majesty if it be transcribed to any creature or image. And that not only in him that commits the idolatry but also in his posterity in the third and fourth generation, if they follow their father's idolatry, as I "give mercy into the thousandth generation," when the children follow their father's virtue. Then to avoid the ire of God, and to obtain his favor, we must use no images

16. In Carr's edition, this is transcribed "Saint White . . .," believing that the text "Sainct whit" was a typographical error, typical of sixteenth-century English printing houses. However, it is more likely a reference to the rural custom on Whitsunday of distributing bread and cheese during the Mass.

17. Exod 19.

to honor him withal. This you may read, Numbers 12, Jeremiah 32, and Isaiah 39, how King Hezekiah's sons lost their father's kingdom, and were carried into captivity for their father's sin. Read the thirteenth, fourteenth, and fifteenth chapters of Deuteronomy, and see how Moses interprets this second commandment more at large.

God's laws expel and put images out of the church, Exodus 20, Deuteronomy 5: then no man's laws should bring them in. As for their doctrine they teach the unlearned, it is a weak reason to establish them in. A man may learn more from a live ape than a dead image, if both should be brought into the school to teach.

PART 2

THE ELIZABETHAN REFORMATION

HISTORICAL OVERVIEW

The English church under Queen Elizabeth I has been characterized in many ways, from a successful compromise immortalized in the Thirty-Nine Articles, to a disastrous tension of rivalling religious and political factions. Neither of these two extremes is fully accurate nor wholly misleading, however, in regards to the question of religious images it is important to pay attention to the divisions within Protestantism, more than the compromise.

While scholars like Julie Spraggon have described a "broad consensus of suspicion towards, if not active dislike of, images with Elizabethan Protestantism," the reality is much more complicated. Certainly, there was a general distrust among many mainstream clergy, as the following documents attest, particularly as Catholic apologists like John Martiall, Nicholas Sander, and Gregory Martin continued to defend them (documents 13, 14, 16).[18] But over this period, the general distrust was qualified and nuanced by several factors, including the continued Protestant use of certain images (e.g., woodcuts) and the increasing diversity of what images were permitted.

While the beginning of Queen Elizabeth's reign was met with a fresh wave of image destruction, there was tension between the monarch and her Protestant clergy about the extent of religious reform that was needed

---

18. Spraggon, *Puritan Iconoclasm*, 16.

in England.[19] It quickly became apparent that the queen's policies on images would not be as straightforward as her younger brother Edward's had been. On the one hand, Elizabeth's first articles "administered by the royal visitors" were based off Thomas Cranmer's visitation of Canterbury in 1548, adamantly condemning images in churches. Elizabeth's royal injunctions, on the other hand, "played down" the dangers of idolatry.[20] In practice, she proved equally enigmatic. Elizabeth preferred to err on the side of ordered removal, where it was necessary, rather than celebratory destruction wherever it could be accomplished. At Bow Church in London, when a crowd of iconoclasts gathered to destroy images inside the church, Elizabeth ordered the Lord Mayor to "use the best means to bolt out the Doers . . . and to cause them to be apprehended and committed to Ward."[21] In other cases, the Queen arrested unauthorized iconoclasts like John Ramsden and John West in Dover and Theodore Pike in Shobury for "plucking down the images before a Law did authorize him so to do."[22] While the queen permitted her officials to condemn image worship across the country (removing countless crosses and crucifixes), she herself kept an altar cross in her private chapel in Whitehall Palace (document 12).

Divisions within the consensus grew even more apparent as the 1560s wore on, with fissures appearing first at a convocation of clergy in 1563, and then a controversy over the wearing of clerical vestments (mandated by the monarch) threatened to undermine clerical unity. Respected leaders in the church, like John Jewel (document 12) expressed their concerns over the seeming hypocrisy. Reformers like William Fulke found themselves cornered by Catholic polemicists who pointed out the differences between various Protestant groups, like Calvinists and Lutherans.[23] The emergence of a puritan faction led by figures like Thomas Cartwright, John Field, and Thomas Wilcox crystalized in the early 1570s. At the same time, a rearguard movement led by Richard Hooker and Lancelot Andrewes toward "greater ceremonialism" and sacrament-centered worship was gaining ground in Protestant England, slowly restoring certain elements of traditional worship. As Kenneth Fincham and Nicholas Tyacke have demonstrated, this group of small but well-placed clerics began to outline a new kind of Protestant

---

19. Aston, *England's Iconoclasts*, 302; Phillips, *Reformation of Images*, 114–16.

20. Aston, *England's Iconoclasts*, 297–304. Fincham and Tyacke, *Altars Restored*, 37–8.

21. Strype, *Annals of the Reformation*, I.49.

22. Ibid., I.48.

23. Fulke, *A Defence*, 204–5.

conformity, which emphasized more sensual forms of worship, including a greater emphasis on the altar.[24]

Nevertheless, destruction continued in varying degrees of intensity depending upon the time and place, and at times it seemed more virulent than ever. In one example in 1567, nine parishioners from Yorkshire, probably former churchwardens and officials, were commanded to do penance for withholding images from the royal visitors, and then they were forced to publicly burn the images.[25] Such examples of antagonism toward Catholic practice only increased in number after Pope Pius V excommunicated Queen Elizabeth in 1570.[26] The increasing tension is evident in the late 1570s and 1580s as Catholics suffered mounting suspicion from both the local and royal authorities who believed that conspiracies to overthrow the government were fomenting across the kingdom.[27] The searching and ransacking of Catholic homes was amplified, and images, particularly crucifixes that had been blessed by the Pope, were targeted by royal officials.[28]

---

24. Fincham and Tyacke, *Altars Restored*, 74–97 (quote p. 74).

25. Purvis, ed., *Tudor Parish Documents*, 145–46.

26. For more on this period of English Catholic history see Walsham, *Church Papists*; Questier, *Catholicism and Community*.

27. These suspicions were not mere paranoia, as three major plots, the Ridolfi Plot, the Throkmorton Plot and the Babington Plot, were uncovered by royal officials.

28. Phillips, *Reformation of Images*, 132; Davis, *Seeing Faith*, 109–12.

DOCUMENT 8

Woodcut of Ezekiel's Vision of Heaven, *Geneva Bible*
(Geneva, 1560)[1]

INTRODUCTION

In her study of the *Bishops Bible*, Margaret Aston argued that images depicting visions and dreams of God were in a "different category" for Protestant reformers.[2] Visions of God recounted in scripture, particularly those in the Book of Revelation and those visions had by Isaiah and Ezekiel, were popular subjects for illustration in Protestant Bibles. Between 1534 and 1603, five different series of woodcuts representing scenes from Revelation were printed in at least forty-five editions of English Bibles and New Testaments. The more popular of these were created by continental artists like Albrecht Durer and Lucas Cranach and imported or copied for English use.[3] Representations of Ezekiel's vision of heaven appeared in at least thirty-one editions of scripture, and other images of divine visions—those experienced by Adam and Eve, Jacob, Moses, Peter, Paul, and Stephen—were included in early English Bibles as well. Despite the general Reformation fear of idolatry, printed images of God were intended to illustrate and exposit the divine

---

1. Luborsky and Ingram, *A Guide to English Illustrated Books*, I.115–18.
2. Aston, "The Bishops' Bible Illustrations," 280.
3. Interestingly, the Cranach series that first appeared in Luther's German Bible (c.1522) was used in English Bibles in the 1530s. While the German woodcuts were altered to remove the anti-Catholic symbolism of the antichrist wearing a papal tiara, the English copies retain the original imagery (Bauckham, *Tudor Apocalypse*, 239–40).

revelations in scripture. Thus, when Isaiah exclaimed, "I saw the Lord seated on a throne," or when Ezekiel described God as "a figure like that of a man," the images followed suit by depicting God as a man.[4]

The woodcut below was included in the Geneva Bible (c.1560), which became the most popular English translation until the mid-seventeenth century. Taken mostly from John Calvin's French translation, the Geneva Bible was created by the more Calvinist English reformers, before returning from exile after the ascension of Elizabeth I. The woodcut of Ezekiel's vision was one of twenty-six woodcuts (a relatively low number for an illustrated Bible) and was part of a larger apparatus of notes, commentaries, maps, and other readers' aids. The vision of Ezekiel along with other passages specifically was identified in the letter to the reader of the Geneva Bible as one of the many passages in scripture that was "so dark that by no description . . . could be made easy to the simple reader."[5]

This particular woodcut remained in the subsequent editions of the Geneva Bible, seemingly never coming under iconoclastic scrutiny for its content. The reason for this permissiveness may be found in the intended purpose of the image. While it is technically a similitude of God, one could make the argument that it is a visual representation of how Ezekiel describes what he sees, rather than an attempt to capture the divine essence in pictures. Ezekiel says that what he saw was "like the appearance of a man." Moreover, there are clear indicators of the image's purpose as something other than visual stimulation and devotion. Small letters are scattered around the image, indicating a description key, which has usually been lost in surviving copies, that would explain to the reader each portion of the image. Also, the artist has gone to great lengths to capture exactly what Ezekiel describes, without any visual embellishments, even including a personification of the North Wind (Aquilon) blowing the vision into view. Finally, when compared to similar images of prophetic visions that were appearing in European art, the depiction of God here is rather banal and slight.

Nevertheless, its presence and popularity should not be overlooked because of its poor artistic quality. In fact, there is an argument to be made that this inferior aesthetic is intentional. Elsewhere, I have made the argument that this image is a good example of the kind of anti-image that other scholars, like Joseph Koerner, have identified in Lutheran art.[6] It is intended to halt the reader's imagination, providing a visual diagram more

---

4. Luborsky and Ingram, *A Guide to English Illustrated Books*, I.84–85. I have explored the reasons for this imagery and how Protestant theology maneuvered around the question of idolatry in Davis, "Godly Visions."

5. Geneva Bible, sig. 4v.

6. Davis, *Seeing Faith*, 163–65.

than visual stimulation. The unusual and awkward placement of the image, between verses 4 and 5 of chapter 1, bears out this idea, that the image was intended to subvert any wild imaginings and fix in the readers' minds a particular presentation of the divine revelation.[7]

7. Efforts to control reading habits and interpretation have been explored in Slights, *Managing Readers*.

DOCUMENT 9

Woodcut of Isaiah's Vision of Heaven, *Bishops Bible*
(London, 1568)[1]

INTRODUCTION

Although similar in certain respects to the image of Ezekiel found in the Geneva Bible, the image of Isaiah's vision of heaven printed in the 1572 edition of the *Bishops Bible* represents a slightly less iconoclastic Protestant theology.[2] The image itself was a copy from a woodcut used in the 1537 Coverdale Bible, printed in Antwerp, and the continental (and Renaissance) elements of this woodcut are fairly obvious. Unlike the Ezekiel image, the artist has taken liberties to include a framing set of pillars and an arch. Also, the entire scene is divided along two axes. Horizontally, saints kneel in prayer on God's right, and sinners flee on his left. It is divided vertically as well, with the spiritual world in the top half of the page and the material world in the bottom, as the holy altar serves as a bridge between the two. Not only was this a reflection of Renaissance ideals of proportion and symmetry, it also echoed a popular reformed theme: the division between the sheep and the goats, between the true and false church. Moreover, the figure of God is more evident and three-dimensional, and he sits atop some sort of castle or turret, which is quite different from the image in the Geneva Bible.

1. Luborsky and Ingram, *A Guide to English Illustrated Books*, 1.133–37. For commentary on some of the woodcuts in the Bishops Bible, see King, *Tudor Royal Iconography*, 105–9; 233–36.
2. Davis, *Seeing Faith*, 166.

In the history of the image debate, this woodcut stands as a visual example of the growing rift between the nascent puritan movement and the more conforming Protestants. In 1572, puritan leaders published *An Admonition to Parliament* and *A Second Admonition to Parliament*, demanding that the Queen continue to purify the English Church by ridding it of what remained of Roman Catholic practices. In the *Second Admonition*, Thomas Cartwright condemned the "blasphemous pictures of God the father" that appeared in the original Bishops Bible (1568).[3] Despite the apparent hypocrisy of the Puritans in promoting the Geneva Bible (with its image of Ezekiel's vision) while condemning the Bishops Bible, it was the Bishops Bible that became the appointed scripture to be read in Elizabethan churches. While the woodcuts used for the first edition of the Bishops Bible, created by the German artist Virgil Solis, could not be utilized subsequently, more woodcuts (like this image of Isaiah's vision) were created or copied for later editions, insisting upon the importance of visual images in religious contexts.

3. Frere and Douglas, eds, *Puritan Manifestoes*, 118.

DOCUMENT 10

Marcus Gheeraerts the Elder, *The Allegory of Iconoclasm*
(London, 1566–1568)

INTRODUCTION

A native of Flanders, the artist Marcus Gheeraerts (c.1520–90) was among the many Protestant artisans and other skilled laborers who made their way over to England during the 1560s, as religious warfare ripped through France and the Netherlands.[1] As a highly skilled printmaker with a strong reputation in Europe, Gheeraerts arrived in England in 1568 and was immediately sought after by the leading members of the printing trade. Most notably, one of the leading stationers John Day (who was responsible for the printing of John Foxe's *Actes and Monuments*) made great use of Gheeraerts's abilities.[2]

The Allegory of Iconoclasm, completed in 1566 or shortly thereafter, is one of Gheeraerts's works that has garnered a great deal of scholarly attention, with its eerie Golgatha-like face swarmed by a legion of people, serpents, and religious accoutrements.[3] The print is almost certainly a commentary on the iconoclastic riots that rocked the Low Countries in late summer and autumn of 1566. Carlos Eire estimates that in Flanders over 400 churches were attacked, with iconoclasts destroying not only statuary

   1. Hodnett, *Marcus Gheeraerts*; Evenden, "The Fleeing Dutchmen?"
   2. Evenden, *Patents, Pictures, and Patronage*, 96–99.
   3. Prints and other artworks that illustrated the violence of iconoclasm in both scripture and early modern accounts has been studied in Aston, *King's Bedpost*, 57–59, 62–65, 78–80, 114–27.

and paintings but curtains, books, altars, windows, seats and benches, and gravestones.[4] It was nothing short of a holocaust of material religion, and Gheeraerts makes his own feelings abundantly clear about Catholic rituals, images, and liturgical practices, by visually depicting "an image war" against the material corruption.[5]

Upon the hill, Catholics participate in the sacraments, along with other practices like kneeling before the bishop (right eye), praying to a wayside cross (bridge of the nose), selling indulgences (crown of the head), saying the Mass (in the mouth), giving confession (in the ear), and processing with the crucifix and an image of the Virgin (beneath the chin). Catholic ritual, as Margaret Aston explains, has "stopped up" the head's ability to hear, speak, and see, creating a visual representation of the description of idols in Psalm 115:4–6.[6] At the bottom of the print, Protestants with pickaxes, wheelbarrows, hammers, and shovels hack a part what they saw as a mountain of corruption and idolatry.[7] The image was a visual display of the culture war that had been waged in the Low Countries and other places in Europe for the past few decades.

---

4. Eire, *War Against the Idols*, 280.
5. Koerner, *Reformation of the Image*, 112.
6. Aston, *King's Bedpost*, 170.
7. Similar to the anti-Catholic imagery typical of the early Lutheran movement: Scribner, *For the Sake of the Simple Folk*, chs. 4, 5.

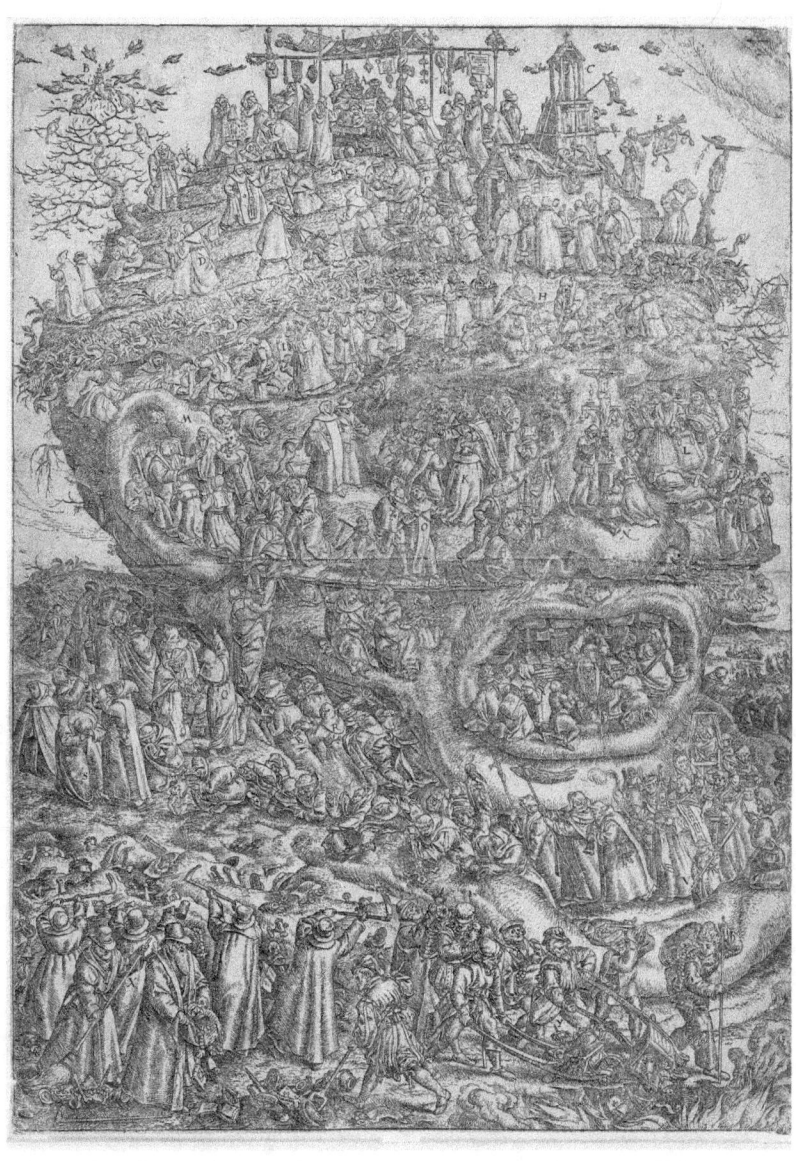

DOCUMENT 11

Heinrich Bullinger, *Fifty Godly Sermons*
(London, 1577)

INTRODUCTION

Too little attention has been paid to the influence Heinrich, or Henry, Bullinger (c.1504–75) had upon the English Reformation.[1] Torrance Kirby goes so far as to suggest that Bullinger should be considered "the theologian *par excellence* of the reformed Church of England."[2] He was the spiritual and intellectual "mentor to almost half the bench of bishops" under Queen Elizabeth I, including John Cheke, professor of Greek at Cambridge University.[3] Unfortunately, scholars tend to focus on some of Bullinger's more unusual theological positions, such as his views of the Virgin Mary, distracting attention from his more formidable and influential works of theology.

As the son of a concubinage relationship, his father being the dean of the church in Bremgarten (Switzerland), Bullinger knew full well the need for reforming clerical practices. Bullinger rose to prominence in the international Protestant world as a thundering preacher in Zurich, who eventually

---

1. The most important works include Kirby, *Zurich Connection*; Gordon and Campi, eds, *Architect of Reformation*; Biel, *Doorkeepers*. Unfortunately, Bullinger's theology on images has often been overlooked, when compared to that of Calvin's or Zwingli's. Michalski does him the great disservice of saying that "he added little of theological substance" to the image debate (Michalski, *Reformation and the Visual Arts*, 59).

2. Kirby, *Zurich Connection*, 26.

3. Ibid., 25n.2.

replaced Ulrich Zwingli, after Zwingli's death in 1531. While Bullinger's written and oral discourse often carried scathing and brusque remarks like "God very often and earnestly beat into our heads," he was known across Europe as a conciliatory reformer, who strove to fashion Zurich into a nexus of Protestant unity and consensus. His writings were a part of a theological canon for reformed preachers in the sixteenth century. Among these works were his widely published *Decades* (or *Fifty Godly Sermons*), sermons of pastoral theology, which proved to be more popular in Elizabethan England than John Calvin's *Institutes* and became required reading for all English clergy during the tenure of Archbishop John Whitgift.[4]

In this document, the second of Bullinger's sermons in *The Decades* under the title "Of God's Law and the First Two Commandments of the First Table," Bullinger makes several key points about the Protestant reading of the second commandment against idolatry. First, that the prohibition against idolatry was not a new law when God handed it to Moses, but instead was part of the natural law "writ" into men's "hearts," which is exemplified Bullinger says, in the actions of people like Jacob and Abraham. As we have already seen in previous texts, there was a powerful emphasis on the Decalogue as the groundwork for Protestant iconoclasm, and Bullinger is a good example of how Protestants deployed the commandments against image veneration. Second, that the figure of Christ should be included in this prohibition. The question of depicting the Son of God—something on which Protestants are not entirely unified—will be taken up by both Protestants and Catholics (documents 11, 12, 13, 18). Finally, Bullinger is adamant that the making of images, in general, is not wrong; instead, the error can be found in both the fashioning of images with the intent of worship and in the actual act of worshipping. This is a distinction that Protestants (with few exceptions) resolutely expressed in various ways throughout the Reformation, in order to avoid the untenable radicalism of iconophobia.[5]

TEXT[6]

The law of God openly published and proclaimed by the Lord our God himself sets down ordinary rules for us to know what we have to do, and what to

---

4. McNeill, *The History and Character of Calvinism*, 310

5. This radicalism had been well documented and publicized in the debates between Martin Luther and the radical reformer Andreas von Karlstadt, who advocated the destruction of all images: Sider, ed., *Karlstadt's Battle with Luther*.

6. Bullinger, *Fifty Godlie Sermons*, 109–25. An earlier edition of the entire text of Bullinger's sermons can be found in Harding, ed., *The Decades of Henry Bullinger*.

leave undone, requiring obedience and threatening utter destruction to disobedient rebels. This law is divided into the moral, ceremonial, and judicial laws. All parts and every point whereof Moses has very exquisitely written and diligently expounded. The moral law is that which teaches men manners and lays down before us the shape of virtue, declaring therewithal how great righteousness, godliness, obedience, and perfectness God looks for at the hands of us mortal men. The ceremonial laws are given concerning the order of holy and ecclesiastical rites and ceremonies, and also touching the ministers and things assigned to the ministry and other holy uses. Last of all, the judicial laws give rules concerning matters to be judged of between man and man, for the preservation of public peace, equity, and civil honesty.

. . .

First of all therefore, let no man think that before Moses' time there was no law, and that the law was by Moses first of all published. For the selfsame special points of the moral law, which Moses set down in the Ten Commandments, were very well known to the Patriarchs even from the beginning of the world. For they worshipped the one true God alone for their God, whom they reverenced and called upon him. Jacob took away with him the Syrian idols of Laban out of his house, and hid them in Bethel under an oak or terebinth tree, which was near to Shechem. Abraham in taking an oath used always a reverenced fear and a spiced conscience, whereby it followed that to him the name of the Lord was holy and not lightly taken.[7] All the holy fathers did both diligently and devoutly solemnize and observe holy rites and sacrifices. . . . For the Lord with his finger writ them in their hearts, which the lively tradition of the fathers did exquisitely garnish and reverently teach. The law is everywhere the same, and the will of God is always one, because God is but one and is never changed. Nevertheless, the commandments were first of all set down in tables by God, who was the beginner and writer of them, and after that again were written into books by Moses.

. . .

All [of these laws] . . . Moses gathered together into a certain number of decreed laws, setting down many things more plainly than they were before and ordaining many things which the Patriarchs were either altogether without, or else had used in another order. Of which sort were the tabernacle, the holy vessels, the Ark of the Covenant, the table, the candlesticks,

---

7. Gen 35:2–4.

the altar for burnt offerings and for incense, the Levitical priesthood, and the holy vestments.... But because manners cannot consist if the Ten Commandments be broken, the moral law—although it has properly the name of a law—is notwithstanding not abrogated or broken. For the Ten Commandments are the very absolute and everlasting rule of true righteousness, and all virtues set down for all places, men, and ages to frame themselves by. For the sum of the Ten Commandments is this: to show our love to God and one another, and the Lord requires this at all times and everywhere of all kinds of men.

...

The second precept of the Ten Commandments is, "Thou shalt not make to thyself a graven Image, nor any likeness of those things, which are in heaven above, or in the earth beneath, or in the water under the earth: thou shalt not bow down to them, nor worship them: I am the Lord thy God, strong and jealous, visiting the fathers sins in the children, unto the third and fourth generation of them that hate me, and showing mercy unto thousands to them that love me, and keep my Commandments."[8] In the first commandment, the Lord did teach and draw out before our eyes, the pattern of his inward worship and religion: now, here in the second he amended that which might be amiss in the outward rites and ceremonies. If we could have rightly judged of God and have kept (as devout as we should) the first commandment, then should there have been no need of the second, but because God knew our disposition and nature, he therefore expressly forbid the things that otherwise we would have done. For many there are which think that God ought to be portrayed in some similitude or likeness and to be worshipped with some bodily or visible reverence, in offering gold, silver, pearls, ivory, and precious things of price. Wherefore, the general end of this commandment is to draw them from those gross imaginations and carnal worshipping of God, who is an incomprehensible power and an eternal spirit.... Under the name of the idol, or imagined likeness, is contained all the outward reverence done thereunto; when therefore the idols are forbidden, together with them is also forbidden all outward honor irreligiously exhibited to the true and very God. For wherever an idol is, there must the idolaters set him up a pillar, place him in a seat, erect him an altar, and build him a temple. And all these again require keepers and overseers, ministers or priests, sacrifices and offerings, ceremonies, furniture, holy days, cost and labor that will never be ended. In this sense did the prophets say that idolatrous images were endless labors and infinite miseries. For after images

8. Exod 20:4.

are once received, there is no end or measure of expenses and toil. This does experience teach to be true.

Now to proceed, this commandment consists of three separate parts. First of all, God flatly forbids us to make a graven image or other kind of idol. That is, God utterly forbids [us] to set up or hallow to him any image of any shape or substance. For as God will not, so indeed he cannot, be represented in any manner of likeness. Now, in this commandment are reckoned up, in a manner, all the similitudes of those things, whereunto we are wont to portray, to liken our pictures. "Thou shalt not," says he, "fashion like unto God any shape or figure of those things which are in heaven, which are I say above us." Above us are the celestial bodies, the sun, the moon, the planets, the stars, and diverse birds of sundry fashions. In all which figures and shapes, almost, no small number of the Gentiles did solemnly honor, and reverently worship the name of God. "Thou shalt not liken unto God," says he, "any shape or fashion of those things that are in ye earth." In the earth are men, beasts, herbs, shrubs, trees, and such like. Now it is manifest that the Gentiles worshipped God under the likeness of men and beasts. Cornelius Tacitus writing of the Germans, says: "But the greatness of the visible celestial bodies, they do conjecture and verily think, that the Gods are neither enclosed in walls, nor yet in favor resembling men's visages, and therefore do they hallow woods and groves, calling that hidden mystery by the name of the gods, which with outward eyes they see not, but with inward reverence alone."[9] Here our ancestors worshipped God in the likeness of trees and woods, which nevertheless men are forbidden here to do, even as also we are prohibited to worship our God in the likeness of anything that is in or under the water. The Philistines worshipped God in the image of a fish. Dagon their god bore the shape of a fish. Egypt honored God in the similitude of serpents. All which, and many other, Paul knitted up together in the first [chapter] to the Romans, where he argued against the Gentiles, and said: "Their foolish heart was blinded: when they counted themselves wise they became fools and turned the glory of the incorruptible God unto the likeness, not only of a mortal man but also of birds and of four-footed beasts and of creeping beasts."[10] Against this madness is the first part of the law directly given.

But now the cause why God will not be represented in any visible or sensible image is this. God is a spirit, God is unmeasurable, incomprehensible, unspeakable, all over and everywhere, filling heaven and earth, eternally, living, giving life unto and preserving all things, and lastly of a

9. Tacitus, *Germania*, IX.
10. Rom 1:22.

glorious majesty exalted above the heavens. But what is he that can portray a spirit in any image or substance? God is an incomprehensible power, quickening and preserving all and everything. . . . To go about therefore to express God in any visible likeness, is the next way to dishonor God, and to bring him into contempt. God's eye beholds all things, idols see nothing. God's ears hear all things, idols hear nothing. By God all things live, move, and are preserved. The idols themselves neither live nor move, and unless they be upheld by the men that make them, they fall and are dashed in pieces. An idol breaths not, God gives to other a breathing spirit. How then, and wherein, are these two alike? In substance, or in shape? If you say in substance, I answer, is God then of gold, of silver, or of wood? If in shape, mine answer is, has the invisible power of God then, put on visible and mortal members? How greatly therefore did the Anthropomorphites offend herein? If then there be no similitude of God, how comes it to pass (I beseech you) that images and idols be called the likeness and pictures of God? Among us, he that calls another an idol or an image does seem to have spoken it too despitefully in reproach of the other. For we know that idols are counterfeits of men and not men indeed, and therefore do we call him an image, that is a sot, a fool, a dolt, an idiot, and one that has not wit, nor knows any more than he hears of others.

. . .

Furthermore, for Christ our Lord and very God, though he took on him the nature of us men, yet that notwithstanding, there ought no image to be erected. For he did not become man to that intent. But he drew up his humanity into heaven, and there gave us a charge, that so often as we pray, we should lift up the eyes of our minds and bodies into heaven above. Moreover, being once ascended, he sent his spirit instead of himself, unto the Church wherein he has a spiritual kingdom and needed not any bodily or corruptible things. For he commanded that if we would bestow anything on him or for his sake, we should bestow it on the poor and not on his picture or image. And now, since without all controversy, our Christ is the very true God, and that the very true God forbids to hallow to him any likeness of man, that is to say to represent God in the shape of a man, it follows consequently that to Christ no images are to be dedicated, because he is the true and very God and life everlasting. In the second part of this commandment, we are taught how much more it is unlawful for us to make any image of God or else of feigned gods. . . . Images ought not in any case to be made for men to worship, or otherwise, to use as means or instruments to worship God in. But if so it happens, that any man make them to the intent to have them worshipped, then must the zealous and godly dispose, despise, neglect, not worship nor honor them, nor yet by any means be brought to do them service.

For in this precept are two things set down especially to be noted. The first is, "Thou shalt not bow down to them." To bow down, is to cap and to kneel, to duck with the head, and bend the body, fall down, to honor, to worship, and to reverence. The saints of old did bow down (that is to bend the knee, to uncover the head, and to fall down) to the magistrates, the prophets, the princes, and teachers of the people, and unto all sorts of revered men. And that they did partly, because God had so commanded, who used their ministry to common men's commodity, and partly again, because men are the lively image of God himself. But deaf, dumb, and blind idols are wood and stone, whereunto we are forbidden to bend or bow down, how so ever we are made to believe, that they do bear the likeness of God. The latter is, "Thou shalt not worship them, or else. Thou shalt not do any service unto them." In this clause is forbidden all outward and unlawful honor done to God, or to the gods in the way of religion, nay rather in the way of superstition, and devilish hallowing of churches, relics, holy days, and such like trash and trumpery.

For to serve is to worship, to reverence, to attribute some majesty and divine authority to that which we do worship, to have affiance[11] in, to burn incense, to offer gifts, and to show ourselves dutifully serviceable to that which we worship. There is no man that knows not what it is to serve and what is meant by service in matters of religion. We are forbidden therefore to run in pilgrimage to idols, yea, though they be the images of God himself. We are forbidden to do them any service, in offering gifts, or attributing unto them one iota of God's preeminence, thereby to blind ourselves to maintain and uphold their unlawful honor, in mingling such superstitions with better points of true religion. This therefore considered (since we may not attribute to Images any serviceable honor) I do not see how we can ascribe to them the office of teaching, admonishing, and exhorting, which are the offices and benefits of God's Holy Spirit and Word.

This does the most true God very often and earnestly beat into our heads throughout Ezekiel and the whole scripture beside.

---

11. Trust or faith

DOCUMENT 12

John Jewel, "Homily Against the Peril of Idolatry and Superfluous Decking of Churches"

(London, 1571)

INTRODUCTION

The Elizabethan book of homilies was written in the early 1560s, in order to provide parish ministers around England a collection of sermons to serve as a guide for preaching. As leading English Protestants returned from exile after the reign of Queen Mary, the homilies became one of several efforts that the newly elected Protestant bishops made to bring a certain amount of uniformity and continuity to the various liturgical practices in Elizabethan England. Eventually, the name of John Jewel (c.1522–71), the Bishop of Salisbury, became attached to the 1571 printing of the homilies; however, the first editions have no stated author, and the original authorship remains in dispute.[1]

For our purposes, the book of homilies, and more specifically the "Homily Against the Peril of Idolatry," has two major elements that highlight aspects of the image debate. First, the homilies were part of a growing tension between Elizabeth and her newly minted bishops, particularly those

---

1. The complete edition of the Elizabethan homilies was last edited in Griffiths, ed., *Two Books of Homilies*. Griffiths argued for Jewel as the author (Griffiths, xxxii). Although, Aston makes a strong case for Edmund Grindal, Elizabeth's future archbishop (Aston, *England's Iconoclasts*, 322n.96).

of a more reformed temperament. Elizabeth argued with her bishops over the extent to which reforms should be carried out. Patrick Collinson has demonstrated that the homilies became a lightning rod for this larger dispute, in which the Calvinist tendencies of many of the English clergy came into contention with the will of the monarch.[2] Comparisons of earlier and later manuscripts of the homilies have revealed a marked shift away from virulent iconoclastic language, limiting the destruction to abused images. It is likely that these changes were made at the Queen's behest.[3] Part of the Queen's reticence certainly had to do with her own demonstrated proclivity toward certain religious images, like her own chapel cross.[4]

A second key aspect in the homily against idolatry is the nature of the documents as a guide for preachers and other clergy. Unlike many of the theological treatises and polemical tomes found in *From Icons to Idols*, the homilies were intended to buttress the low level of education found among many parish preachers. They were directed at an audience that were not likely to have read much theology, and so the homily against idolatry was something of a commonplace of Protestant arguments, a compilation of what had already been said. It serves modern scholarship as a lowest common denominator, a statement on what English Protestants believed that every minister of the gospel should know.

The "Homily Against the Peril of Idolatry" is divided into three parts, which all together equal over twenty thousand words, the longest of all the homilies. The selections here, from all three parts, are intended to demonstrate the style of the author and what matters were seen to be of primary importance. The first homily deals with the church fathers and draws on a host of sources—including Tertullian, Clement, Origen, Athanasius, Lactantius, Epiphanius, Cyril of Alexandria, Jerome, Augustine, Ambrose, and Eusebius—in demonstrating the patristic condemnation of idols. The second part follows the historical argument, charting how idolatry crept into the churches. Here, the writer reaches a fever pitch of polemic asserting that Christian idolatry has brought about the division of the Church into East and West, "the utter overthrow of the Christian religion" in Greece to "Muhammad's false religion," and "the cruel dominion and tyranny of the Saracens and Turks." Perhaps most importantly for the history of the image debate, the homilies assert two key moments in church history as the

---

2. Patrick Collinson demonstrated that the first major split between Elizabeth and her bishops came during the 1563 Convocation, over the language of the homilies: Collinson, *Elizabethans*, 113–14. For a more detailed examination of them in the context of images, see Aston, *England's Iconoclasts*, 320–24.

3. Aston, *England's Iconoclast's*, 321–2; Haugaard, *Elizabeth*, 273–76.

4. Aston, *The King's Bedpost*, 101–7.

beginning of institutionalized idolatry (echoing earlier reformers like John Calvin, document 5): Pope Gregory the Great's letter to Serenus in which Gregory allows images to remain the churches and the Second Council of Nicea, which opposed the iconoclasm in the Byzantine Church.[5] Finally, the third part argues that the practices of the Catholic church concerning images are "all one which the Gentile idolaters used."

TEXT

First Homily[6]

In what points the true ornaments of the church or temple of God consist and stand have been declared in the two last homilies, entreating of the right use of the temple or house of God and of the due reverence that all true Christian people are bound to give unto the same. The sum whereof is that the church or house of God is a place appointed by the Holy Scriptures, where the lively Word of God ought to be read, taught, and heard; the Lord's holy name called upon by public prayer, hearty thanks given to his majesty for his infinite and unspeakable benefits bestowed upon us, his holy sacraments duly and reverently ministered, and that therefore all that be godly indeed, ought both with diligence at times appointed to repair together to the said Church and there with all reverence to use and behave themselves before the Lord. And that the said Church thus godly used by the servants of the Lord in the Lord's true service for the effectual presence of God's grace, wherewith he does by his Holy Word and promises endow his people there present and assembled to the attainment as well of worldly commodities necessary for us, as also of all heavenly gifts, and life everlasting. It is called by the Word of God (as it is indeed) the temple of the Lord, and the house of God, and that therefore the due reverence thereof, is stirred up in the hearts of the godly, by the consideration of these true ornaments of the said house of God, and not by any outward ceremonies, or costly and glorious decking of the said house or temple of the Lord, contrary to the most manifest doctrine of the scriptures, and contrary to the usage of the primitive church, which was most pure and uncorrupt. And contrary to the sentences and judgments of the most ancient learned and godly doctors of the church (as

---

5. The Seventh Synod, or the Second Council of Nicea (787), was a key "target" in the Protestant debates: Aston, *England's Iconoclasts*, 55. John Jewel, in his debates with Catholic apologists, wrote: "There was never any assembly of Christian bishops so vain, so peevish, so wicked, so blasphemous." (Jewel, *Works*, IV.792).

6. Jewel, "Homily Against the Peril of Idolatry," 25–26.

hereafter shall appear) the corruption of these latter days has brought into the church an infinite multitude of images ... decked with gold and silver, painted with colors, set them with stone and pearl, clothed them with silks and precious vestures, fantasizing untruly that to be the chief decking and adorning of the temple or house of God, and that all people should be the more moved to the due reverence of the same if all corners thereof were glorious and glittering with gold and precious stones.

Second Homily[7]

Hear you see what Christian princes of most ancient times decreed against images which then began to creep in among the Christians. For it is certain that by the space of three hundred years and more after the death of our Savior Christ and before these godly emperors' reign, there were no images publicly in churches or temples.[8] How would the idolaters glory if they had so much antiquity and authority for them, as is here against them? Now shortly after these days, the Goths, the Vandals, Huns, and other barbarians and wicked nations burst into Italy and all parts of west countries of Europe, with huge and mighty armies, spoiled all places, destroyed cities, and burned libraries, so that learning and true religion went to wrack and decayed incredibly. And so the bishops of those latter days, being of less learning and in the middle of wars, taking less heed also than did the bishops before, by ignorance of God's Word and negligence of bishops, and especially barbarous princes, not rightly instructed in true religion, bearing the rule, images came into the Church of Christ in the said west parts, where these barbarous people ruled not now in painted clothes only but also embossed in stone, timber, metal, and other like matter, and were not only set up, but began to be worshipped also.

...

But of Gregory's opinion, thinking that images might be suffered in churches, so it was taught that they should not be worshipped: what ruin of religion and what mischief ensued afterward to all Christendom.[9] ... First, by schism rising between the East and the West Church about the said images. Next, by the division of the empire into two parts by the same occasion

---

7. Jewel, "Homily Against the Peril of Idolatry," 61–70.

8. The emperors referenced here are those that followed after Constantine the Great. This is something of a dead argument, because until Constantine, Christianity was not celebrated publicly, so it had no public places of worship *per se*.

9. Gregory the Great, "Epistle XIII," in NPNF, 2nd Series, vol. XIII, II.297–98.

of images, to the great weakening of all Christendom, whereby last of all has followed the utter overthrow of the Christian religion and noble empire in Greece and all the east parts of the world and the increase of Muhammad's false religion, and the cruel dominion and tyranny of the Saracens and Turks, who now hang over our necks also that dwell in the west parts of the world, ready at all occasions to overrun us. And all this we owe unto our idols and images, and our idolatry in worshipping them.

But now give your ear a little to the process of the history, wherein I do much follow the histories of Paulus Diaconus, and others, joined with Eutropius, an old writer.[10] For though some of the authors were favorers of images, yet do they most plainly and at large prosecute the histories of those times, whom Baptist Platina also in his history of popes, and in the lives of Constantine, and Gregory II, bishops of Rome, and other places (where he entreats of this matter) chiefly follow.[11]

After Gregory's time, Constantine, bishop of Rome, assembled a council of bishops in the western church, and did condemn Philippicus, then emperor, and John bishop of Constantinople for the heresy of the Monothelites, not without a cause, indeed but very justly.[12] When he had done so by the consent of the learned about him, Constantine, bishop of Rome, caused the images of the ancient fathers which had been at those six councils which were allowed and received of all men to be painted in the entry of St. Peter's Church at Rome. When the Greeks had knowledge hereof, they began to dispute and reason the matter of images with the Latins, and held this opinion, that images could have no place in Christ's Church, and the Latins held the contrary and took part with the images. So the eastern and western churches which agreed evil before, upon this contention about images fell to utter enmity, which was never well reconciled yet. But in the mean season, Emperors Philippicus and Arthemius, or Anastasius, commanded images and pictures to be pulled down and raised out in every place of their dominion.[13] After them came Theodosius III. He commanded the defaced images to be painted again in their places, but this Theodosius reigned but one year. Leo III succeeded him, who was a Syrian born, a very wise, godly,

---

10. Paul the Deacon, *History*; Eutropius, *Abridgment*.

11. The first complete translation of Platina's history is underway. The first volume is Platina, *Lives of the Popes*.

12. Ekonomou, *Byzantine Rome*, 245–47.

13. This is a reference to the first iconoclastic period of the Orthodox Church. For further reading see Brubaker and Haldon, *Byzantium*. Aston explains that the Byzantine precedent was vital to the Protestant attack on images, but it was also problematic, particularly the dubious source text known as the *Libri Carolini* (Aston, *England's Iconoclasts*, 47–61).

merciful, and valiant prince. This Leo by proclamation commanded that all images set up in churches to be worshipped, should be plucked down and defaced, and required especially the bishop of Rome that he should do the same, and himself, in the mean season, caused all images that were in the imperial city Constantinople to be gathered on a heap in the midst of the city, and there publicly burned them to ashes and whited over and raised out all pictures painted upon the walls of the temples and punished sharply diverse maintainers of images.[14]

. . .

Now on the contrary, note you that the bishops of Rome were no ordinary magistrates appointed by God out of their diocese, but usurpers of princes' authority, contrary to God's Word, and stirrers up of sedition and rebellion and workers of continual treason against their sovereign lords, contrary to God's law and the ordinances of all human laws, being not only enemies to God, but also rebels and traitors against their princes.

Third Homily[15]

Now remains the third part, that their rites and ceremonies in honoring and worshipping of the images and saints are all one with the rites which the Gentile idolaters used in honoring their idols. First, what means it that Christians after the example of the Gentile idolaters go on pilgrimage to visit images, where they have the like at home but that they have a more opinion of holiness and virtue in some images than some others, like the Gentile idolaters had? Which is the readiest way to bring them to idolatry by worshipping of them and directly against God's word, who says, "Seek me and you shall live and do not seek Bethel, neither enter not into Gilgal, neither go to Beersheba."[16] And against such as had any superstition in the holiness of the place, as though they should be heard for the places' sake, saying, "Our fathers worshipped in this mountain," and you say that at Jerusalem is the place where men should worship. Our savior Christ pronounces, "Believe me, the hour comes when you shall worship the father neither in this mountain nor at Jerusalem, but true worshippers shall worship the father in spirit and truth."[17] But it is too well known that by such pilgrimage going,

14. The most recent research questions the existence of any such edict from Leo III: Brubaker and Haldon, *Byzantium*, 151.

15. Jewel, "Homily Against the Peril of Idolatry," 103–21.

16. Amos 5:5.

17. John 4:20–21.

Lady Venus and her son Cupid were rather worshipped wantonly in the flesh than God the Father and our Savior Christ his Son, truly worshipped in the spirit.[18]

And it was very agreeable (as St. Paul teaches) that they which fell into idolatry, which is spiritual fornication, should also fall into carnal fornication and all uncleanness by the just judgments of God, delivering them over to abominable concupiscence.

What does it mean that Christian men, after the use of the Gentile idolaters, cap and kneel before images? Which, if they had any sense and gratitude, would kneel before men: carpenters, masons, plasterers, founders, and goldsmiths, their makers and framers whose means they have attained this honor, which else should have been evil favored and rude lumps of clay or plaster, pieces of timber, stone, or metal, without shape or fashion, and so without all estimation and honor, as that idol in the pagan poet confesses saying, "I was once a vile block, but now I am become a god, etc."[19] What a fond thing is it for man, who has life and reason, to bow himself to a dead and insensible image, the work of his own hand? Is not this stooping and kneeling before them, adoration of them, which is forbidden so earnestly by God's word? Let such as so fall down before images of saints, know and confess that they exhibit that honor to dead stocks and stone, which the saints themselves—Peter, Paul, and Barnabas—would not to be given them being alive, which the angel of God forbid to be given to him.[20] And if they say they exhibit such honor not to the image but to the saint whom it represents, they are convicted of folly to believe that they please saints with that honor, which they abhor as a spoil of God's honor. For they be no changelings, but now both having greater understanding and more fervent love of God more abhor to deprive him of his due honor, and being now like unto the angels of God, with angels flee to take unto them by sacrilege the honor due to God.[21] And here withal is confuted their lewd distinction of *latria* and *dulia*, where it is evident that the saints of God cannot abide that as much as any outward worshipping be done or exhibited to them. But Satan, God's enemy, desiring to rob God of his honor desires exceedingly that such honor might be given to him. Wherefore, those which give the honor due to the Creator to any

---

18. This sort of interlacing of paganism and Christian worship was a popular criticism that reformers levelled at Catholic practices. In the sixteenth century, the accusation was popularized in Erasmus's colloquy "The Shipwreck" in *Collected Works of Erasmus*, 351–67.

19. Likely a poor translation of Horace, "Satire VIII" in Horace, *Satires, Epistles, Ars Poetica*.

20. Rev 19:10.

21. Rev 19:10.

creature does service acceptable to no saints (who be the friends of God) but unto Satan. ... And to attribute such desire of divine honor to saints is to blot them with a most odious and devilish ignominy and villainy and indeed of saints to make them satans and very devils, whose property is to challenge to themselves the honor which is due to God only.

...

Now images will continually, to the beholders, preach their doctrine, that is the worshipping of images and idolatry, to which ... mankind is exceedingly prone and inclined to give ear and credit, as experience of all nations and ages too much proves. But a true preacher to stay this mischief is in very many places scarcely heard once in a whole year and somewhere not once in seven years, as is evident to be proved. And that evil opinion which has been long rooted in men's hearts cannot suddenly by one sermon be rooted out. And as few are inclined to credit sound doctrine, as many and almost all be prone to superstition and idolatry. So that herein appears not only a difficulty but also an impossibility of the remedy.[22]

Further it appears not by any story of credit that true and sincere preaching has endured in any one place above one hundred years. But it is evident that images, superstition, and worshipping of images and idolatry have continued many hundreds of years. For all writings and experience testify that good things do by little and little ever decay, until they be clean banished and contrariwise, evil things do more and more increase, until they come to a full perfection of wickedness. ... For preaching of God's word (most sincere in the beginning) by the process of time waxed less and less pure ... and other inventions of men crept in place of it. And on the other part, images among Christian men were first painted and that in whole stories together, which had some signification in them. Afterwards, they were embossed and made of timber, stone, plaster, and metal. And first they were only kept privately in private men's houses. And then after, they crept into churches and temples, but first by painting and after by embossing. And yet were they nowhere at the first worshipped. But shortly after, they began to be worshipped of the ignorant sort of men, as appears by the epistle that Gregory I, Bishop of Rome, wrote to Serenus, Bishop of Marseilles. Of the which two bishops, Serenus for idolatry committed to images, braked them and burned them; Gregory although he thought it tolerable to let them stand, yet he judged it abominable that they should be

---

22. A similar argument was made by Martin Luther against Andreas Karlstadt, over the role and place of images in worship: "Against the Heavenly Prophets," in *Luther's Works*, LI.81–100

worshipped and thought (as is now alleged) that the worshipping of them might be stayed by teaching of God's Word, according as he exhorts Serenus to teach the people, as in the same epistle appears.[23] . . . For notwithstanding Gregory's writing, and the preaching of others, images being once publicly set up in temples and churches, simple men and women shortly after fell on heaps to worshipping of them. And at the last, the learned also were carried away with the public error, as with a violent stream or flood. And at the Second Council of Nicea, the bishops and clergy decreed, that images should be worshipped and so by occasion of these stumbling blocks, not only the unlearned and simple, but the learned and wise, not the people only, but the bishops, not the sheep, but also the shepherds themselves (who should have been guides in the right way, and light to shine in darkness) being blinded by the bewitching of images, as blind guides of the blind, fell both into the pit of damnable idolatry.[24]

---

23. Gregory the Great, "Epistle XIII," in NPNF, 2nd Series, vol. XIII, II.297–98.

24. Percival, ed., *The Seven Ecumenical Councils* , in NPNF, 2nd Series, vol. XIV, 549–51.

DOCUMENT 13

John Martiall,
A Treatise of the Cross
(Antwerp, 1564)

INTRODUCTION

John Martiall (c.1534–97) was one of many young Catholic men who, upon the ascension of Queen Elizabeth I in 1558, believed it was wise to leave England for exile in continental Europe. Martiall was part of the founding of the English Catholic College in Douai, which became a hub of English Catholicism abroad, and he later became a canon at St. Peter's Church in Lille.[1]

While he never returned to England, Martiall's name was well known at home. In the 1560s, Martiall was one of a few English Catholic exiles who locked horns in published theological disputes with leading Protestants like John Jewel, bishop of Salisbury, Alexander Nowell, dean of St. Paul's Cathedral, and James Calfhill, archdeacon of Colchester.

In perhaps his most important book, *A Treatise of the Cross*, Martiall offered a thorough defense of images, specifically images of the cross. Martiall's scholarship is both impressive and intriguing. He not only demonstrates a familiarity (whether directly or indirectly through authors like John of Damascus) with sources that had previously been employed in the debates (e.g., Tertullian, Augustine, church councils, etc.), but also he introduces into the debates a number of apocryphal stories and legends from the early Church that deal with the cross as a miraculous object.

---

1. Lucy Wooding, "John Martiall," ODNB.

The work was dedicated to Queen Elizabeth, who, being "well affectioned" to the cross, continued to use a large golden cross for her own private chapel, and it was part of an ongoing controversy with Jewel. In the book, Martiall lays out the significance of the word "cross" and the sign of the cross, demonstrates how the cross was prefigured in the Old Testament, provides scriptural and patristic examples of how the cross (and images of the cross) was used in Church history, and finally gives examples of the miraculous works the cross had performed in the early Church.[2] More than the other documents in this volume, Martiall seems particularly concerned with *praxis* and the tradition of the cross as part of Christian worship than with the theological and linguistic wrangling found in other documents. He outlines the basic Catholic defense for image reverence, arguing "he that adores and honors an image does adore and honor that which is resembled in the image." Image reverence became idolatry when what was represented was either not real or not worthy of reverence.

TEXT

Preface

To the Most Gracious and Clement Princess Elizabeth by the grace of God Queen of England, France and Ireland, your loving and faithful subject John Martial wishes all heavenly grace and peace from God, with long reign and much felicity to his honor and health of your majesty's subjects.

It has ever been (most gracious Sovereign) the want of most men that commit any matter to the view and fight of the world, to recommend the same to some noble personage, either studious in the art of which they write, either well affectioned to the matter upon which they discourse: whose usual practice I thought it expedient for me to follow in dedicating this little treatise of mine. And knowing your Majesty to be one of the noblest personages that lives this day in Europe, in all princely prowess and gifts of nature equal with the chief and inferior to none, and so well affectioned to the cross (which is the matter that I have taken in hand to treat) that your Majesty has always kept it reverently in your chapel, notwithstanding many means have been made to the contrary, by the privy suggestions and open sermons of such, as without order of law, or authority given by express commandment

---

2. It is interesting that this final point, concerning the miracles of the cross, diminishes in popularity among Catholic apologists at the end of the sixteenth century. Martiall is perhaps the last of the English Catholic apologists who spends any significant energy stressing the miracles of the cross to a Protestant audience.

from your Majesty (as it is thought) have in all churches, chapels, oratories, highways, and other places of your most noble realm thrown down the sign of the cross, and image of our savior Christ, and in most despiteful manner abused it, and in common assemblies have called it an idol, and keepers of the same idolaters, I have adventurously presumed to recommend and dedicate this little treatise of the cross to your Majesty.[3] Whereby sufficient authority out of the old ancient fathers it is declared, that ever since Christ suffered death upon the cross, and sanctified that holy wood with the water and blood that fell from his precious body rent upon the cross, Christian men have had the sign of the cross in churches, chapels, oratories, private houses, highways, and other places meet for the same. And that the holy fathers of the primitive church worshipped and reverenced the sign of the cross and counselled others to do the same. And that there can be no fear nor mistrust of idolatry in Christian men, having and worshipping the cross, with many other special matters which I omit to repeat here, upon hope that your grace at some vacant time, and opportune leisure will take a view of the whole. Which if it may happily stand with your Majesty's pleasure I hope the variety of the history and truth of the cause shall both ease that tedious pain, and also give your Majesty soon after occasion to see whether their meaning (who have blasphemously railed against it, and bereaved your faithful subjects of the sweet sight of it) be sincere and correspondent to the fathers of the primitive church (as they pretend).

. . .

That Every Church, Chapel, and Oratory Erected to the Honor and Service of God Should Have the Sign of the Cross

For declaration and proof of this article that every church, chapel, and oratory erected to the honor and service of God should have the sign of the cross, I will declare it unto you, first by a miraculous dedication of a church by an angel sent from God to that purpose, who made the sign of the cross in four corners of the church. Secondarily by the example of St. Philip, Christ's apostle, preaching to the Gentiles in Scythia and exhorting them to pluck down their idol and set up a cross.[4] Thirdly, by the authority

---

3. The reference to "open sermons" may well be directed at a well-known 1564 Lenten sermon of Alexander Nowell, Dean of St. Paul's Cathedral, wherein Nowell was shouted down by the Queen for making a derogatory remark about crucifixes (McCullough, *Sermons at Court*, 64).

4. The text referred to here is likely Pseudo-Abdias, *Apostolic History* (Elliott, ed.,

of counsels and doctors, fourthly by the laws of Justinian the Emperor and custom of the church. Touching the first, after that the apostles receiving the Holy Ghost, had authority to loose and bind and commission to go into all nations and preach the glad tidings of the gospel, St. Bartholomew went into India, where was a great temple and famous idol called Ashtoreth, in which the devil by vain illusions, false miracles, and pretended curses, had long time miserably afflicted the people. The apostle entering into that temple, and tarrying there for a time, did with his presence make the devil so dumb and impotent that he could neither dissolve the riddles which were propounded unto him, neither cure, nor help the lame Lazarus, whom he had tormented. And that he made the wicked spirit himself acknowledge and confess, and before the king and all the people to detect his impotency, how he did hurt and was not able to heal. And further he compelled him to break in pieces that and all other idols in the temple, so that there remained not one. At which sight the people cried: *Unus Deus omnipotent quem praedicat Bartholomeus.* That only god is omnipotent whom St. Bartholomew preaches. Whereupon he taking occasion to confirm that which God by grace began to work in them, and to deliver that temple from that idol, and people from idolatry, lifted up his hands to heaven, and desired god for his son Jesus Christ his sake, that the multitude of lame Lazarus and sick persons lying there hurt by the malice of the devil might be cured and healed. And when he had ended his prayer, and the people said Amen, *Apparuit angelus domini splendens sicut sol, habens alas, et per quattuor angulos templi, circumuolans digito suo in quadratis saxis sculpsit signum crucis et dixit: Haec dicit dominus qui misit me: Sicut uos omnes ab infirmitate vestra mundamini, ita mundavit templum hoc ab omni sorde. Et habitatore eius,* etc. The angel of God appeared bright as the son having wings, and fleeing by the four corners of the temple, engraved with his finger in the square stones, the sign of the cross, and said, "Thus says our lord God, even as all you are healed of your infirmities, so have I purged this temple from all filthiness, and the devil inhabits and dwells there."[5] Further God commanded me that I should say unto you, that look what sign I have engraved in the stones, such you should make in your foreheads, and all evil shall flee from you.

Here, good readers you may note three things, first how God moved with the prayer of his apostle delivered the people India from the thralldom of the devil and sent his angel from heaven to sanctify the temple polluted with idols, which sanctification was done by making the sign of the cross,

---

Apocryphal New Testament, 525-31).

5. This is from the *Passio Bartholomaei* (Bonnet, ed., *Acta apostolica apocrypha*, II.1.145-6). See also Rose, *Ritual Memory*, 113-15.

which sign God commanded to be engraved in the square stones at the four corners of the temple. The second is how he willed them to make the sign of the cross in their foreheads. The third how all evil shall flee from them that so do, whereby you may learn that even from the beginning it has not only been God's will, but also commandment, that the sign of the cross should be set up in churches, and made in men's foreheads, which heretics deride and accompt, superstition and folly, as peradventure they will this story, but whatsoever it pleases them to say, I trust every good Christian man stayed by the grace of God in the unity of his church, and grounded upon that sure rock against which Hell gates shall not prevail, will more esteem the authority of him that wrote it, than the levity of such as again say it, especially seeing it is, written by him that saw our Lord in flesh, and followed Simon and Jude into Persia and was at the death of St. Andrew, and made bishop of Babylon by the apostles, Abdias I say, who wrote a little discourse of the apostle's life.[6]

Concerning the example of St. Philip, the aforesaid author writes in this sort. After Christ's ascension St. Philip preached the gospel zealously to the Gentiles in Scythia, where when he had been kept in prison and should have been compelled to have done sacrifice before the idol of Mars, there came out of the pillar where the idol stood a great hideous dragon and struck the priest's son that ministered fire at the sacrifice, and the two tribunes whose officers had the apostle in prison. Besides diverse were infected with his venomous blasts, and began to be sick, which thing the apostle espying, said unto them, "Hear my advice and counsel, and you shall have your health again: they which are dead, shall be revived, the dragon which has hurt you, in the name of God shall be put to flight." Then said the sick men, "Sire what is best for us to do?" *Deiicite hunc Martem et confringite*: "Cast down this idol Mars and break him in pieces," said the apostle: *Et in loco in quo fixus starevidetur, crucem Domini mei Iesu Christi offigite, et hanc adorate*. "And in the place where he seems to stand fast set up the cross of my Lord Jesus Christ, and adore the same."[7] Here, mark good readers, how St. Philip, Christ's apostle, exhorts the Scythians both to set up the cross and also to adore it, which if it were idolatry or superstition as these gay gospellers, and new presented reformers of Christianity would make simple souls believe, St. Philip endued with the Holy Ghost, highly esteeming the honor of God, and zealously desiring the salvation of man's soul, would not have counselled the Scythians to have done it, and in the minds of those late converses for true honor and worshipping of God, have planted supersti-

---

6. Abdias of Babylon was one of the apocryphal apostles mentioned in Luke 10.
7. Elliott, ed., *Apocryphal New Testament*, 531.

tion and idolatry. Nor here can they use their slight shift and say that the apostle commanding the Scythians to set up a cross and adore it meant only that they should set the passion of Christ on high in their minds, and be thankful to the Lord for it. For the apostle not only commanded them to set up a cross, but also he appointed the place where it should be set, that was in a stone wall or pillar, where faith in the passion of Christ could not be fixed nor set, for that the wall receives no faith. Unless the melody of these meal-mouthed minstrels be so sweet, that they can (as the poets feigned of Orpheus) move hard stones, or make brazen pillars understand.

Touching the authority of councils, ... a Synod kept at Orleans in France this canon. *Nemo Ecclesiam adificet, antequam episcopus civitatis veniat et ibidem crucem figat.*[8] "Let no man build a church before the bishop of that diocese come, and set up a cross." And in the second Synod kept at Tours, we find this canon. *Ut corpus domini in altari non in armario, sed sub cruces titulo componatur.*[9] "That the body of our Lord consecrated upon the alter be not reposed and set in the vestry, but under the rood," by which decree we perceive that then there was a rood and cross in the church and the sacrament reserved and laid up reverently under the rood. For under that the sign of the cross was kept and had in churches it may well be gathered by the fixed general council kept at Constantinople in Trullo, and by the whole discourse of the seventh general council kept at Nicea.[10] Where three hundred and fifty bishops, men of great virtue, profound knowledge, and deep sight in divinity made this decree. *Hiis se sic habentibus*, etc. These things being so, we going on the king's highway and standing to the doctrine of our holy and most godly fathers and observing the tradition of the Catholic Church, in which the Holy Ghost dwells, determine and define with all diligence and care that honorable and holy images made handsomely in colors, stones, boards, or any other matter be dedicated and set up in holy churches, *ad modum et formam venerande trucis*, after the manner and form of the holy and reverend cross. And that they be had in hallowed vessels, and vestments, and in walls, tables, private houses, and high ways, and especially the image of our Lord and God Jesus Christ our Savior, and the image of the immaculate Virgin Mary, mother of God, and the images of holy men, that by this beholding of painted images all that look upon them may come to the remembrance and desire of the first samplers and patterns which they resemble. And with all exhibit unto them some courtesy, and reverent

---

8. This is a reference to the seventeenth canon of the First Council of Orleans in 511: Hefele, *A History of the Councils*, 87–93.

9. Council of Tours, 567, Canon 3: Hefele, *A History of the Councils*, 389.

10. "The Canons of the Council in Trullo," in NPNF, 2nd Series, vol. XIV, 765; Percival, ed., *The Seven Ecumenical Councils*, in NPNF, 2nd Series, vol. XIV, 549–51.

honor, for honor and reverence done to an image redounds to the glory of the first sampler and pattern, and he that adores and honors an image does adore and honor that which is resembled in the image.

The Sign of the Cross Used in All Sacraments

As Sozomenus, a Greek author and one of the compilers of the tripartite history, writes, Probianus a pagan newly converted to Christ, in some part behaved himself like a Christian man, but the cause of our salvation that is the most holy cross he would not worship and adore, whereupon while he was in this determination and mind, *Divina virtus apparens signum monstravit crucis, quod erat positum in altario eius ecclesiae, et aperte palam fecit quia ex quo crucifixus est Christus, omnia quae ad utilitatem humani generis facta sunt, quolibet modo praeter virtutem sanctae crucis gesta non essent, neque ab angelis sanctis, neque ab hominibus piis.*[11] That is to say, "The divine power appearing showed him the sign of the cross which was set upon the alter of that church and made it plainly appear that ever since Christ was crucified, all things which were done for the commodity and weal of man, were done by no manner of means without the virtue of the holy cross, neither of holy angels, neither of good men." St. Cyprian says, whatsoever the hands be which dip those that come to baptism, whatsoever the breast is out of which the holy words do proceed, *Operationis authoritas in figura crucis, omnibus sacramentis largitur effectum.*[12] "The authority of operation gives effect to all sacraments in the figure of the cross." St. Augustine confirms the same, saying, *Crucis mysterio rudes cathechizantur, eodem mysterio fons regenerationis consecratur, per manus impositionem baptizati dona gratiarum accipiunt. Cum eiusdem crucis caractere Basilicae dedicantur, altaria consecrantur, altaris Sacramenta cum interpositione Dominicorum verborum conficiuntur, Sacerdotes, et Levitae per hoc idem ad sacros ordines promoventur, et omnia Ecclesiastica Sacramenta in huius virtute conficiuntur.*[13] That is to say, "with the mystery of the cross the ignorant are instructed and taught, the font of regeneration is hallowed, by imposition of hands such as are christened received the gifts of grace, churches are dedicated, alters

---

11. The text here is Sozemenus, *Historiae Ecclesiasticae*, II.9. For an English translation see Sozemenus, *The Ecclesiastical History*, in NPNF, 2nd Series, vol. II, 1146.

12. Cyprian, "Epistle LXII," ANF, vol. V, 208–21. See also Mayes, "The Lord's Supper," 307–24. James Calfhill responded to this citation in *An Answer*, 203.

13. This sermon is not among the English translations of Augustine's sermons from the Augustinian Heritage Institute, and it only appears in an appendix in the Latin *Opera Omnia*, which suggests that its authorship is uncertain (Augustine, *Sanctii Aurelii*, V.2994).

hallowed, the sacraments of the alter with the putting in between of our Lord's words are made, priests and deacons promoted to holy orders, and all sacraments of the church perfected." And in another place he has these words, *Quid est, quod omnes noverunt, signum Christi, nisi crux Christi? Quod signum nisi adhibeatur sive frontibus credentium, sive ipsi aquae ex qua regenerantur, sive oleo quo chrismate unguntur, sive sacrificio quo aluntur, nihil eorum rite perficitur,*[14] that is to say, "What is the sign of Christ which every man knows, but the cross of Christ? Which sign unless it be put to the foreheads of faithful believers or to the water with which we are regenerate, or to the oil with which men are anointed in the holy Chrisme,[15] or to the sacrifice with which men are nourished, not one of all those is done rightly and in due order." To this, Chrysostom agrees, saying, "The passion of our Lord is the beginning and original of our felicity, with which we live and by the which we be." With as good a will let us carry about with us the cross, as we would a crown: *Omnia enim quae ad salute nostrum conducunt per ipsam consummator. Nam quum regeneramur, quum sacratissimo alimur cibo, quum in ordine consecrandi statuimur, ubique et semper id victoriae insigne nobis assistit.* That is to say, "For all things which avail to our salvation are consummated and made perfect by the same cross."[16] For when we are regenerated or christened, when we are nourished with the most holy meat, when we are placed and set to be consecrated in holy orders that flag, banner, and sign of victory always assists us.

In these authorities and first in the story of Probianus note good readers the goodness of God driving him by a vision from heaven to the worshipping of his cross in earth and that in those days there were alters and the sign of the cross upon them. And that things are done by angels and men for the wealth of man's soul here upon earth, but yet not without the sign of the cross. Next in St. Cyprian note that men have authority by commission from God to make and minister his sacraments and that in the figure and sign of the cross by that authority and operation, all sacraments have their effect. And note how in St. Augustine's time, churches, fonts, and alters were hallowed, children after baptism confirmed, and anointed with holy oil, and that all sacraments of the church are made with the sign of the holy cross and none rightly in due order without it. Further Chrysostom notes that all things available to our salvation are consummated and made perfect by the cross. And unless they who envy us the effects and fruits of Christ's blessed sacraments make you believe that all is to be meant and referred to Christ

---

14. Augustine, *Tractates on the Gospel of John*, in NPNF, vol. VII, 430–32.
15. Oil
16. John Chrysostom, "Homily 55 on Matthew," in NPNF, vol. X, 342.

his passion, only consider that Probianus being converted to Christ and believing also that all things necessary to our salvation have their operation and effect by the virtue and merits of Christ's passion had also the sign of the cross, she wed him upon the alter. And that St. Augustine says unless the sign of the cross be put to the sacrament of confirmation, holy orders, and the body and blood of our Lord, nothing is rightly done.[17] And besides mark how St. Chrysostom affirming all things to be consummated by the cross, says in the end: *Ubique, ac semper id victoriae insigne nobis assistit*, that banner or ensign of victory in all places and at all times assists us and in diverse places uses this word (cross) for the sign of the cross, as in his demonstration against the Gentiles, he says, *Reges positis diadematis crucem suscipiunt mortis symbolum. In purpuris crux, in diadematis crux, in precibus crux, in armis crux, in mensa sacra crux, et in toto orbe crux*, that is to say: "Kings laying down their crowns take up the cross a sign of death, in their purple robes there is a cross, in their crowns a cross, in their prayer books a cross, in their armor a cross, in the holy table a cross, and in all the world a cross."[18]

Here you see good readers by the authority of Sts. Cyprian, Chrysostom, and Augustine and by the vision showed to Probianus from heaven that nothing was ever done for the weal of man Christ suffered, without the cross and that all the sacraments of the church are duly perfected and made with the sign of the cross and never rightly and in due order without it.

And here to take away occasion from all malicious mummers of cavillation, I give you to understand that the cross in celebration of Christ's sacraments is used for two causes specially. The first is to put us in remembrance of our redemption by Christ's death upon the cross. The second to declare that all sacraments have their virtue and effect of the merits of his passion. And albeit the ancient teach and the Catholic Church command that the sign of the cross should be used in all sacraments. . . . But when of self-will and set purpose the order of the Church is contemptuously broken and the intention of the minister evil and faith worse (as theirs is who be Zwinglians, Calvinists, and such like) there is doubt but that they offend the goodness of God in omitting the sign of the cross in the celebration of Christ's sacraments, transgress the ordinance of the Holy Ghost, and the tradition of the apostles and ancient fathers, which they pretend to keep and restore unto Christendom.

. . .

---

17. Augustine, *Tractates on the Gospel of John*, in NPNF, vol. VII, 430–32.
18. Chrysostom, *Adversus Gentiles*.

The Apostles and Fathers of the Primitive Church Blessed Themselves with the Sign of the Cross

In this article three points remain to be proved. The first is that the apostles and fathers of the primitive church blessed themselves with the sign of the cross. The second that they counselled every good Christian man to do the same. The third that in their days a cross was set up in every convenient place. To discourse of the first and run over the lives of all the apostle and fathers of the primitive Church, it were a long labor, unpleasant for the reader and impertinent to my purpose. For that I am desirous in this treatise to be short, not long and tedious. Wherefore I will only lay before your eyes the examples of certain, by whom you may be easily induced to conjecture and think the like of others. St. Paul being brought to the place of execution, where he should suffer martyrdom under the cruel tyrant Nero for his constant faith in Jesus Christ, and truth of the gospel, which he had preached, turned himself to the east, and holding up his hands to heaven prayed a great while, and when he had ended his prayer and given peace to the brethren which followed him, and taken his leave of them all, *Flexis genibus, crucisque signo se muniens, cervicem praebuit percussori.*[19] "Falling down upon his knees, and blessing himself with the sign of the cross, held out his neck to the bureau or hangman."

When St. Andrew had done many miracles and converted diverse to the faith in Patras, a city of Achaia, it fortuned that Maximilla the lieutenant's wife instructed in the faith did so diligently attend upon the apostle, while her husband was in Macedonia, that at his return home he had almost taken her and a great company of other men and women hearing the Word of God in his palace with the Apostle, which thing St. Andrew foreseeing, fell down upon his knees and prayed in this sort. "Suffer not Lord the lieutenant to come into this place, before all be departed hence," which when he had done, the lieutenant before he could come in was by necessity driven to go into a secret place to the secrets of nature. And while he tarried there, St. Andrew laying his hands upon them that were with him, and signing them with the cross, suffered them to depart. . . .

When St. John had in Ephesus by his word only forced the temple and idol of Diana to fall down and fitter in pieces, as dust, which the wind blows from the face of the Earth, Aristodemus, chief minister and superintendent over the idols, possessed with a wicked spirit raised a great sedition among the people in so much that they were ready to fight. Then said St. John, "O

---

19. Pseudo-Abdias, *Apostolic History*, book II (Elliott, ed., *Apocryphal New Testament*, 525–31).

Aristodemus, what shall I do to take this rancor and malice out of your heart." "Marry," said he, "if you will that I believe in your God, I will give the poison to drink, which if you drink and do not die, then shall it appear that your God is the true God." St. John said, "if you give me poison to drink after that I have called upon the name of my God, it shall not be able to hurt me." To be short he took the pot of poison and blessing it with the sign of the cross, made his prayer to God, and his prayer being complete and ended. He blessed his mouth and all his body with the sign of the cross and drunk up all that was in the pot.[20]

. . .

Lo good readers, in the time of the apostles, the sign of the cross was used and has continued ever since. In Tertullian's time within two hundred years after Christ, men commonly blessed themselves with the sign of the cross. In holy Ephrem's time, they did the like, the year of our Lord 380. They did so in Chrysostom's time, the year of our lord 431. They did so in St. Jerome's time the year of our lord God 422. They did so in St. Augustine's time, the year of our lord, 430. They did so in Cyril's time in the year or our lord 436. . . . And shall we so far discredit, and dis-authorize these grave, virtuous, and learned men, as though they knew not the scriptures and true interpretation of the same? As though they knew not light from darkness, verity from heresy, true religion from vain superstition? Alas God forbid.

---

20. The story comes from the apocryphal text known as *The Acts of John* (Elliott, ed., *Apocryphal New Testament*, 343–45).

DOCUMENT 14

Nicholas Sander,
A Treatise of the Images of Christ
(Louvain, 1567)

INTRODUCTION

Nicholas Sander (or Sanders) was born in 1530 and became a fellow of New College, Oxford, where he distinguished himself until he was forced to flee into exile, rather than recognize Queen Elizabeth's oath of supremacy. By 1560, Sander was residing in Rome where he was ordained and worked in the final session of the Council of Trent. After the council's conclusion, Sander moved to Louvain where he became a leading figure in the English Catholic community, writing several polemical works against the Elizabethan reforms.[1]

The last of these polemical works *A Treatise of the Images of Christ and of his Saints* (1567) is different in both tone and style than John Martiall's work on *Treatise of the Cross*, written a few years earlier. Sander cites very little scholarship, making his work a much easier read, and his prose is poignant and biting at times. His stated intention is to "to answer an objection moved by certain Protestants" as justification for the widespread iconoclasm in the Low Countries in 1567.[2] As a member of the English Catholic community in exile, Sander possibly witnessed some of this destruction firsthand. Also, the text reflects the Tridentine (Council of Trent)

1. T. F. Mayer, "Nicholas Sander," *ODNB*; Veech, *Dr. Nicholas Sanders*.
2. Sander, *Treatise on Images*, 5.

view of images. Sander keeps very close to the council's wording when he writes that his purpose is to defend the fact that, "it is not only lawful but commendable and most agreeable to reason and to the law of nature and to the universal custom of the church to make images, which may put a man in remembrance of good, holy, and honorable verities." In the first section that is transcribed here, Sander reminds his readers that Catholics do not believe that all images should be reverenced, nor should those that are due reverence receive the same degree or kind of reverence ("honor to God himself, another due to His saints, another to our prince, another to his lieutenant").

For Sander, and for most Catholics in the latter half of the century, the image debate rested on questions of degrees and distinctions between abuse and appropriate use. Much of his treatise deals with the kinds of appropriate uses that Catholics put to religious images. For example, unlike Martiall and Thomas More, he concedes that images may be given "false worship," but argues that instead of destroying the image "charitably" correct the "abuse." Also, Sander stresses the uncharitable actions of Protestants who destroy images rather than communicating "right knowledge" of images and criticizes those who oversimplify the matter by leaning on the Greek word "Idolarum." Finally, Sander believes that images should be permitted, because they are good reminders, they inform "our understanding most lively and speedily," and they are "more rightly joined to the original verity" than any other manufactured representation.

TEXT[3]

Before that images can be worshipped, they must be made. And when they are made, seeing we do not defend that all images, but only that certain may be worshipped, it must be known, which are the images that may be worshipped, and which may not. Then because it is not always expedient that everything which may be done, should be done, it is another question, whether though some images may be worshipped, it were well done to let them be worshipped, especially when a further danger might be feared thereby.

Further, for as much as there are diverse degrees of worship, one which is due to God alone, another which is due to good men, it is doubted whether the same worship which is due to the principal pattern (as to the saints themselves) be also due to their signs and images, or else whether

---

3. Note on the text: this transcription is based upon the 1624 edition (Sander, *Treatise on Images*, 16–28). Each paragraph for each section of the text begins with a number. These have been removed in this transcription for ease of reading

it be some inferior degree of worship, which becomes their images and representations.

Concerning the first question, the Catholics defend that images may be made and that no general or immutable commandment of God is against the making of them.

Secondly, we defend that only those images may be worshiped (in respect of Christian religion) which represent and bring us in mind, either that there is a God or that there are three persons of the Blessed Trinity, or which represent Christ, or his holy angels and saints.

Thirdly, we think it expedient that these holy images should be permitted to be worshipped for their sakes whom they represent.

Fourthly, we defend it for the more probable that the same degree of honor is not due to the image of Christ, of our Lady, or of other saints, which is due to Christ, our Lady, and to other saints themselves. But that there is a certain proper honor due to holy images, which may be called a worship or honor due to a good remembrance, or monument.

Now in the first questions, whether it be lawful to make images or no, there is no great difficulty, albeit some Calvinists do speak up and down in that behalf. But for the most part, it is granted of all men that images may lawfully be made, so that they be not abused.

In the second, as well the Lutherans as the Calvinists defend against us, that no image at all may be worshipped in one sort or other. And much more they must judge it unprofitable to have images worshipped, which was the third question.

In the fourth and last question, there has been thought to be some controversy between the Catholics, because some have thought that the honor due to the thing itself (by reason that the image is all one with the thing when it exercises the act of an image) might be given to the image thereof. Others be of another mind, because they consider an image otherwise.

Of every of these questions somewhat (God willing) shall be said, but most of all, concerning the second question, wherein the greatest controversy consists.

To make it then plain what shall be defended in this treatise, I say, it is not only lawful but commendable and most agreeable to reason and to the law of nature and to the universal custom of the church to make images, which may put a man in remembrance of good, holy, and honorable verities.

It is likewise lawful and commendable when the images are made to use them as we ought to use the remembrance of good, holy, and honorable verities. And then we do use well the remembrance of an honorable verity, when we show so much honor to the verity itself, that we suffer not the very sign and token or as it were the messenger and step of it, to be without some honor for that verity's sake, which it shows and puts us in mind of.

How much did St. John esteem Christ, when he thought himself unworthy to unbuckle the latchet of his shoe? And who does not naturally embrace never so mean a servant or messenger mourning for his dear friend? Who kisses not the ring, which he receives from him? Who loves not the honorable naming of him? Who esteems not his pictures and image?

But when we say, images may and ought to be honored, no man may by and by think that we make them gods, as though there were not one honor due to God himself, another due to His saints, another to our prince, another to his lieutenant, another to our father and mother, another to our master, another to our friends and fellows, yea another also to the holy monuments and remembrances of just persons, whose monuments are in blessedness. Among so many degrees of honor, we give one degree to holy images and by God's grace I will prove it to be due to them.

...

Because the whole mischief done in the Low Countries had its beginning upon this pretense, that the Catholics abused the images of Christ and of his saints, worshipping them, like as the Gentiles heretofore did worship the idols of their false gods, I will first show that our images, although they had been falsely worshipped, yet they ought not to have been so broken and destroyed, as they were.[4] And afterward I will show that they are no idols but may and must be conveniently worshipped by us according to the Word of God, and the example of the first six hundred years.

Concerning the first point, if we had given false honor to the images of Christ or of his apostles and martyrs, it was their part who thought so, to have exhorted us to leave that false honor and not to have committed any injurious fact, whereby we might be justly offended with their whole doctrine. For if charity did persuade them to break our images, lest we should worship God in a false manner, the same charity, if it had been ruled by right knowledge, would have told them that the way for them to make us worship God better had been to have gotten credit with us by their good deeds. And when we had thought them to have been good and honest men, afterward to have proposed their great reasons whereby we might have been moved to leave that our false worship (as they imagine it) and so to have both kept our images for the instruction of them who cannot read, and to have left

---

4. While iconoclasm became something of a staple practice of Dutch reforms, the previous year 1566 was particularly violent: Arnade, *Beggars*, 103–4. See also Pettegree, *Emden and the Dutch Revolt*; Vanhaelen, *Wake of Iconoclasm*.

idolatry, as they call it. For seeing the image neither is evil of itself nor the resemblance of any false god or of evil men (as the Gentiles' idols were) I see not but the false worship might have been taken away from the true representation which the images make and so both the images quietly let alone and the abuse charitably amended.

. . .

But these men being not so much as inferior magistrates, much less kings, did without order, by stealth, by force, and by night (and therefore with an evil conscience) destroy not obscure figures but known images of Christ and of his friends, and those also no worshipping concerning their metal, but only concerning that they represented a truth.

. . .

Last of all, if an image might be broken and stolen by any means, yet what fault has silver crosses and gilded chalices committed? Why they must need be broken and carried away? What offense did white linen cloth? What deserved the Holy Bibles and the works of the ancient fathers, why they should be torn, burnt, or spoiled? Did Hezekiah spoil the whole Temple of Solomon because the brazen serpent was abused?

To return to images, although they had been abused and falsely worshipped (as they were not) yet according to the authority of Holy Scripture, they ought not to have been thrown down by private men against their wills whose goods they were. For thus it is written touching the idols of the very false gods: "When the Lord thy God hath brought thee into the land which thou goes to possess" (and afterward) "when he hath delivered them to thee" (again afterward). "Destroy their altars and brake their images."[5] . . . Whereby we are taught on the other side that if we be not lords of the land, we may not destroy other men's altars or images albeit they be false.

. . .

Whereas[6] there are two kinds of images, one which represents a truth, as that Christ redeemed us, another which represents a stark falsehood, as that Jupiter is God. Again, whereas there are diverse kinds of honor, one, which is due to God alone, another which is in diverse degrees due to good

---

5. Deut 7:1–5.

6. The subsequent portion of this document can be found in Sander, *Treatise on Images*, 131–71.

men, the heathens invented such images to represent a falsehood, and such honoring of them as is not due to them.[7]

But images which represent a truth and the true honoring of them came indeed from God and that first of all by the law of nature and of nations, which permits the art and knowledge of graving and painting, if they be well used. Secondly, God in the law showed the images might be made, by willing the two cherubim and the images of lions and of oxen to be set in the tabernacle and in Solomon's temple. Thirdly, God in the time of the New Testament inspired his apostles and servants to allow the making of good and true representations, the which were laudably made in the first three hundred years after Christ, as Eusebius does witness, about whose words our chief disputation shall be.[8]

Now comes Mr. Jewel and taking upon him to write against Dr. Harding (who defended only such images as God has allowed, and such as Christ's church has used) brings in that which was spoken either of wicked idols or of the false worshipping of bawdy and wanton images, so that his long discourse is answered in one word.[9] They are idols (Mr. Jewel) or wanton pictures, and not the images of holy men, whereof the Book of Wisdom, St. Cyprian, St. Ambrose, St. Augustine, Lactantius, and St. Athanasius did speak of.[10] . . . Is every image an idol? If you think so, then since "the Son of God is the image of God and the figure of his Father's substance," the Son of God is with you an idol. Or is every idol an image? Then the pictures of those who are made with dogs' faces are images and consequently there are such men indeed. For every image, if it be properly an image, is the likeness of some truth. Otherwise it is an idol and no image, as I showed before . . . But know you not the difference between idol and an image? Then you are very simple, in good faith, and too meanly learned or if you do know the difference (because doubtless you are no foal) why then turn you the Greek word *Idolarum* by this English word images? But only because you must maintain your cause by falsehood?

. . .

---

7. Aston, *England's Iconoclasts*, 48; Eire, *War Against the Idols*, 20.

8. Eusebius, *Ecclesiastical History*, VII.18.

9. For more on the debate between John Jewel and Thomas Harding see Jenkins, *John Jewel*, 42–49.

10. Cyprian, "Epistle LXII," ANF, vol. V, 208–21; Ambrose, "Epistle XVII," in NPNF, 2nd Series, vol. X; Augustine, *The City of God*, XX.10; Lactantius, *Divine Institutes*, II.xiii, 122–23; Athanasius, *Against the Heathen*, in NPNF, vol. IV, I.22.

Whereby we learn that an image is not a thing made for itself, but for another end, which end is not only more principal than the image but also it is naturally more acceptable unto him, who takes joyful information thereof. Insomuch that, when a man hears tidings which he most desired to hear, although he learned it by the mean and service of his own inward imagination, yet he so much thinks of the thing that he forgets all other matters in the world.

But when the mind is loosed from that great and sudden affection which it bare to the thing itself, and will again solace itself with repeating and calling to remembrance the same thing, then the image thereof (whereunto the mind returns) being viewed at leisure, pleases more and more, and according as it is good, virtuous, and delectable, so does the man love, honor, and embrace the same. And while the mind reads backward (as it were in its inward book) the whole order of the history, it comes to his remembrance at length who told that matter to him, that consequently he loves, honors, or embraces him also. Of this natural instinct it comes that all princes and great men give rewards to those who bring them good tidings.

Thus, whereas three things do concur, the thing which is told, the inward image whereby I learned it, and the reporter, the chief and first honor naturally belongs to the thing itself, the second to the inward image, which was the next mean of apprehending the tidings, the third to the reporter.

Now seeing the outward image made artificially bears the office of a reporter (so often as I see an image, the signification whereof is known to me) it cannot be denied but the said image necessarily and naturally deserves so much honor of me, as he that should have told me that self thing, if no image had been there to have done it.[11]

...

If then also the painter as the orator provokes many to fortitude and yet the painter does it by leaving an image behind him which may work that feat, it is clear that a good image deserves that place of honor (be it little or great) which is due to him who tells us good news.

Moreover, the image is by so much in the better case to be honored (than that orator) by how much it has more affinity with my inward image, then the orators' word had. For it serves to be both in the whole steed of the orator and also in part of the steed of forming the inward image, because it gives me the very express form and figure already made, which my understanding must conceive, whereas if I learned the matter by words, I must

---

11. Gombrich, *Symbolic Images*, 125; Aston, *England's Iconoclasts*, 32.

have taken the pain to have changed the shape of the words into another form and thereof to have formed a visible image.

For the eye being the highest and most spiritual outward sense is most ready to instruct the mind after that sort, as it apprehends everything.[12]

By which means we are come to the case that the painted image is an easier and a more lively way to instruct us than any orator, and thereby it deserves also more honor than any orator, insomuch that we say of him who can tell his tale most lively that he seems to paint forth and to do it rather than to speak and report it.

...

But for as much as I write to instruct, let it be no grief to the reader if I say once again that the image of an honorable truth represented, and as it were lively reported is by good and right reason worthy of some honor, not as deserving honor by grace and free will, but as having it belonging to its condition and propriety, and that for three causes.

First, for it makes us to know or remember a good thing. Secondly, because it informs our understanding most lively and speedily. Thirdly, because it is a thing more rightly joined to the original verity (in that it bears the natural shape thereof) than any other thing is (such I mean as yet is no natural part or relic of the verity itself) excepting only a natural image, which represents the very substance of his original. If common sense and sound judgment show this matter to be true, if when I may honor the truth represented to me, I may, and must necessarily honor the inward image wherein it is represented (because I cannot at that instant divide the one from the other) and if thence I may come to honor the occasion of the said image, and of that my good remembrance (least I acknowledge not those means whereby God has informed me) if an artificial image communicates most entirely with all three causes, which are all worthy of honor: if it be the shape of the thing itself, the pattern of my inward image, and the occasion thereof, let either man's nature be made a new (which is abominable to think of) or let nature have its course, in honoring the inward and outward image, of a trustworthy to be honored. This much for the finding out of honor naturally due to images, according to the way of right and sound reason.

But if when Christ crucified is represented to me, I give honor to the inward image, and must do so by force of nature (if at the least Christ crucified do please me) doubtless the necessity of honoring good and honorable internal images (for of them now I speak) is grounded in us, and born with us, according to the first and highest order of nature.

12. Woolgar, *The Senses*, 147–50.

But yet the use of making external and artificial images, rather came in (according to the imitation of nature) long afterward (as all other handcrafts) then was born together with us. And for that cause, also the law of Moses in the old time, as now the law of the church, might for just causes moderate or, in some part, inhibit the making of artificial images. For that which was begun by man's own invention may be restrained by the law of wise governors.

DOCUMENT 15

Peter Vermigli, *The Common Places of the Most Famous and Renowned Divine Doctor Peter Martyr*

(London, 1583)

INTRODUCTION

A Florentine by birth, Peter Vermigli (c.1499–1562) was trained at the University of Padua and eventually abandoned his position as prior at the Basilica of San Frediano in Lucca, after reading the writings of Martin Bucer and Ulrich Zwingli. Fleeing into exile, he was invited in 1547 by Archbishop Thomas Cranmer to take up the Regius Professor of Divinity position at Oxford University, which he occupied until Queen Mary's reign in 1553.[1] Even after he left England, Vermigli continued to have a powerful influence over the young theologians and ministers whom he taught.[2] Many of them, like the future Bishop John Jewel, followed Vermigli into exile, to the reformed cities of Strasbourg and Zurich.

His most influential work *Loci Communes* (or Common Places) (Latin, 1576; English, 1583) was a posthumous compendium of his writings. Compiled by the exiled Huguenot Robert Masson, living in London, the *Loci* was intended as a systematic theology to be read in the same spirit as Philip Melanchthon's *Loci Communes* and John Calvin's *Institutes*. While

---

1. McNair, *Peter Martyr in Italy*; Campi, ed., *Peter Martyr Vermigli*.

2. Jenkins, "Peter Martyr and the Church of England after 1558," 47–69; Overell, "Peter Martyr in England."

it is impossible to know what Vermigli would have thought about the organization of the *Loci*, its systematic purpose presents his writings in an accessible way to the learned pastor or theologian.[3]

Moreover, the *Loci* offers an intriguing, and at times unique, theology of images. Since Vermigli did not struggle, like so many other reformers, under the toil of being a pastor, he seems more at freedom to explore the ambiguities and possibilities surrounding visual images, that someone who is battling idolatry in the parish would not be at liberty to consider.[4]

In many ways, his chapter on images is straightforward in its reformed theology, condemning the religious uses of images as corrupt and charting the historical progression of idolatry in the Catholic churches. In other respects, however, Vermigli strikes a more moderate chord. While he does not disagree with Calvin that images of God undermine human understanding of the divine essence, he stresses other issues, like the cost of images and the concern for social disorder in a riot of iconoclasm. Also, Vermigli believed it was "lawful sometimes to picture" angels, according to the ways "they have shown themselves unto men." He even went so far as to suggest that "the law stands in ambiguity" about images of Christ, arguing that "there are no firm reasons brought" why Christ's humanity cannot be portrayed. Finally, while earlier reformers dismissed the distinction between *dulia* and *latria*, Vermigli is willing to acknowledge a "difference of honors," even though he believes Catholics "invented the word latria." This, as we will see in later documents, seems to have had a lasting influence on the Protestant position, as theologians as diverse as William Perkins and Richard Montagu will follow Vermigli in this acknowledgement.

TEXT[5]

Ch. 5 The Second Precept, which concerns Images

In treating upon this place, it seems good to use this method, that first we consider as touching the original and beginning of images; afterward of the use of them, whether it be lawful; last of all, if they have any use, whether they ought to be suffered in temples and holy assemblies.

. . .

---

3. McLelland, "A Literary History," 479–94.
4. Davis, *Seeing Faith*, 54–60.
5. The chapter in the original text runs to over 12,000 words. What follows is a sizeable representation of the text: Vermigli, *The Common Places*, 333–55.

But as touching the thing, we must understand that the thing signified by the image, is no absolute thing; but must be placed in those things, which have relation to another. For every image is the image of something, even as the likeness is called the likeness of another thing. And those things, which be compared either in quantity or quality, have relation one to another. And the things, which be compared together in quantity, be either equal, or greater, or lesser; and in quality they are reckoned like, unlike, and diverse. Seeing therefore that an image is counted (as I have said) among those things, which have relation one to another, it is among the number of those, which appertain unto quality. For it expresses the lineaments, figures, and colors, and such other like of a living creature. And therefore we may thus define the same. An image is a certain similitude, whereby something is represented unto us, which may be discerned with the eyes. And this I therefore say, because we may as well read, as hear many things alike, which properly be not called images. The matter of images is not all one. For sometimes they be made of stone, of wood, metal, plaster, clay, and such other like. And sundry artificers do make them of that matter, which they have in hand: the potter, of clay; the carpenter, of timber; the mason, of stone; the founders, of metal, brass, silver, and gold; the painters also, of their colors.

And we must not pass it over, that idols also are images, whereof Tertullian wrote an elegant book, which he entitled *De idolatria*; and he examining the word derived it from *eidos*, and *eidos* is a likeness, image, or form: whereupon comes *eidolon*, which may be called, a little form.[6] The form of images is the view of a similitude, wherein something is expressed, so as it may be perceived of the beholders. The end where to images are, seems to be delight. For Aristotle in his *Rhetoric*, among other things which breed pleasure, reckons imitation, where an image seems to be a certain emulation of God.[7] For God created all things, wherefore men being unable to create the things themselves, do imitate the production of God, when they make images of those things, which he himself has brought forth in nature. Images also are made for adorning sake, for they beautify the places where they be put. Furthermore, they have invented them, to the intent they might not suffer the remembrance of them which be absent, or dead, or things done, to be extinguished. Also, they have been devised for honor sake, for if a man had well deserved of the commonwealth, images were erected to him. So did Cicero counsel that there should be an image set up unto Servius Sulpitius, who died in his embassage.[8] And there have been some among

---

6. Tertullian, *On Idolatry*, in ANF, vol. III, I.3.
7. Aristotle, *Art of Rhetoric*, I.11.1371b2–10.
8. Cicero, "The Ninth Oration," *The Orations*, IV.147–54.

them in old time, which would not only have others, but also themselves to be worshipped with images. For Nebuchadnezzar, king of the Chaldeans, commanded that within his own kingdom he should be honored by an image of gold.[9] And among the princes of the Romans, Gaius Caligula Caesar, a god. And such an image he endeavored to bring into the temple of Jerusalem; whereupon, there arose very great troubles, seditions, and tumults in Judea.[10] The which thing Nero afterward would have to be done, and for that cause the Hebrews revolted from the people of Rome, whereof appears that images were also translated to the service of God. Neither did there want some, which erected images to the affects or appetites wherewith they were corrupted

...

Seeing we have said enough touching the end, it remains that we examine the efficient cause of images. Artificers indeed were authors of them, and surely cunning workmen. Wherefore, from them they received their estimation. For the honor of images consists not of the matter, seeing they may be made unhandsomely even of gold. Certainly, all their honor is of the form, that in very deed they may in perfect similitude finely represent that thing, which they betoken. Jupiter Olympius obtained honor and estimation of Phydias, and the picture of Alexander the Great by Apelles, even as the well graven pots of Alcimedontes, and the instruments of Solomon's house by Iramus that notable artificer. To these things let us add that our forefathers, to bring more estimation unto their images, feigned them to have fallen from heaven. Wherefore, the image of Pallas of old time was called Diomedes, that is to say, "Fallen from Jupiter." Wherefore we read in the nineteenth chapter of Acts that the town clerk of Ephesus said to the people, "Who knows not that you are worshippers of the great goddess Diana, whose image came down from heaven?"[11] And it must not be omitted that seeing the ages in times past were very rude, the images at first were not orderly and perfectly wrought, as afterward they were. For of a long time men had unwrought stones, stocks, and pillars, instead of images. Yea, and in Rome, at the first, a spear was the ensign of Mars; afterward, by little and little, there succeeded more cunning artificers, who so greatly prevailed in the perfecting of art that as the poet wrote, "they drew lively countenances out of the marble stone." ... Images were made so fair and beautiful, that

---

9. Dan 3.

10. Though Vermigli does not cite his source, the events are described in Philo, *On the Embassy*, XXX.203.

11. Acts 19:35.

there were found, which doted in love towards them, and as it were coupled with them most filthily.

Moreover, there might be somewhat spoken of the antiquity of images, but that thing is very obscure and all be not of one mind touching the same. Some call back the beginning of them unto Prometheus, who first shaped a man of clay, and afterward gave life thereunto. The Hebrews ascribe the original of images unto the nephew of Adam, who was called Enoch. For it is said that then began the name of God to be called upon. Tertullian in his book against idolatry brings the testimony of Enoch, which is reckoned among the Apocryphal books of scripture, which was yet extant when Tertullian lived.[12]

And among the Gnostics, one Marcellina is much celebrated by Epiphanius, who had such manner of images. The very same thing Augustine touches in his book *De haeresibus*. Eusebius in the seventh book and eighteenth chapter writes, that there was kept among some the images of the apostles and martyrs, which they had private at home with them, and he adds that he himself saw them, and it is not to be omitted that he confesses this custom to be derived from the Ethnics.[13] Damascene, where he purposely treats this matter, says that Christ sent unto Abgarus the picture of his physiology, printed in a cloth to the intent he might comfort himself therewith when he could not see him present.[14] They feign also that Christ going to suffer delivered the print of his face in a handkerchief to Veronica, the which they say is kept at Rome, and under that name they honor and reverence a certain picture at this day with great superstition.[15] Also Eusebius writes that in the city of Caesarea, which was afterward called Apamea, there was an image of Haemoroussa, together with the image of Christ, which afterward was removed and thrown down by Julian the Apostate.[16] And there want not some rash men, which affirm that Luke was a painter and that he drew very many pictures of the blessed Virgin, which

---

12. Tertullian, *On Idolatry*, in ANF, vol. III, I.4.

13. Eusebius, *The Church History*, in NPNF, 2nd Series, vol. I, VII.18. By "Ethnics," here, it seems that Vermigli is referring to Eusebius's mention of Gentile customs and traditions.

14. This is a reference to the Byzantine theologian John of Damascus. See Louth, *St. John of Damascus*. Damascus presented a robust defense for holy images in Louth, ed., *Three Treatises*.

15. Though the most well-known of these sorts of images of Christ, the Veronica legend is intimately connected to the previous legends that Vermigli mentions from Eusebius and Damascus. For more on the roots of the Veronica legend see *Butler's Lives*, VII.84–6; Belting, *Likeness and Presence*.

16. Eusebius, *The Church History*, in NPNF, 2nd Series, vol. I, VII.18. "Haemoroussa" refers to the woman with the issue of blood, in Mark 5:25.

were dispersed abroad among the cities and provinces. . . . Surely, if we shall believe Jerome, Luke did exercise the science of physic. And indeed Paul in his epistle to the Colossians makes plain mention of Luke the physician.[17] But whether the same was he that wrote the history of the Gospel and of the Acts of the Apostles, I know not; but that he was a painter or a drawer of pictures, none of the ancient writers tell. And thus much touching the beginning of images.

. . .

The partition of them must be taken from those things that are represented by them, for such things as are referred to another thing are wont to be distinguished by their correlatives. Wherefore, images either represent God the Creator of all things or else things created, which be the sundry workmanship of God. And among those things which were created, we place even Christ himself as touching his humanity. This being set down, it seems necessary to determine whether all creatures may be represented by images, even the very angels themselves. I mean not in respect of their spiritual nature, but in such sort as they have exhibited themselves to be seen by men. Wherefore the godly men, which either be dead or yet living, kings, stars, plants, stones, earth, sea, and such like may be represented by pictures. Also we make a distinction of images, that some of them be true and some of them false. Among the true, those be reckoned which represent those things, which either be, or have been, or hereafter shall be. But those are called false, which represent those things that neither be, have been, nor yet ever will be, like the chimeras and centaurs. There are also some filthy images and some honest, according as those things be, which are expressed by them. Also they may be distinguished according to the circumstance of the place, because some are set in a holy place, and some in profane places. Again, other distinctions there be, which are appointed in respect of worship and religion, but others are erected as ornaments and only for the remembrance of a thing.

. . .

Now . . . it seems good to dispute whether it is lawful to represent God by them. And it must be determined, and that freely without exception, that the same is not lawful. For God commanded the children of Israel that they should remember they saw no image upon Mount Horeb, and therefore forbade that they should make any such. . . . For there he commanded that

---

17. According to legend, mainly originating in the eastern churches, the gospel writer Luke was also a painter: Schaefer, "Saint Luke as Painter," 413–27.

they should not make any images at all to do worship unto them. And in the fortieth chapter of Isaiah he says, "To whom will you resemble God, or by what similitude will you express him?" And in the forty-fourth chapter he confirms the same, saying, "Who will be so hardy to fashion out God or to make a molten or graven image that is profitable for nothing?"[18] I marvel that among the papists, Dominicus Azotus, upon the epistle of Romans, the first chapter, writes that by that commandment it is not forbidden unto the Christians to make images resembling the shape of man, seeing the law has only made mention there of creeping things, of birds and fishes, whereas nevertheless it is there by express words forbidden that no images should be made either of the male or of the female.[19] Moreover it is thus written in the Psalms, "Mouths they have and speak not, feet they have and walk not, ears they have and hear not, noses they have and smell not."[20] And although the rest of the members may be understood touching brute beasts, yet that saying that "They have mouths and cannot speak" belongs peculiarly unto men, for speech was not given unto brute beasts.[21] Wherefore Lucretius called them beasts without mouths. Which interpretation, Augustine brought in the same place.[22] Furthermore, Isaiah in the forty-fourth chapter laughs the carpenter to scorn, who of the one part of a tree being cut down makes an image, of the other part kindles fire, and therewith dresses bread and meat. He carves it and marvelously works it, that he may express the similitude of man.[23] By all these things it appears that even the images of men (which are ordained for divine service) are forbidden. It proves therefore that images, which represent God himself, be forbidden by testimonies of the Holy Scriptures. Whereunto we must add that by the testimony of them we are taught that God is spirit. Whereof it follows that by lineaments and colors he cannot be expressed.

. . .

But at this day in Christendom, there are such kinds of images suffered, whereby God himself may be represented. For to express the blessed Trinity, you may see everywhere in the churches, a man painted with three heads.[24] In another place they put a tall old man for God the Father, who

---

18. Isa 40:18; 44:10.
19. Vermigli leaves no citation concerning Azotus.
20. Ps 115:5.
21. Ps 135:16.
22. Lucretius, *On the Nature*, IV.
23. Isa 44:13.
24. Such images of the Trinity were not without their concerns for the early modern

has standing before him a young man, that is to say the Son, and between both they place the picture of a dove, that is instead of the Holy Ghost.... The Seventh Synod which was held at Nicea in the reign of Constantinus and Irene concluded that it is God which the image teaches, but it is not God. Look upon this but worship with your mind that which you behold in the same image.[25] But what is to be judged of this Synod, we shall see in due place. In the meantime, let us hear the objections of the adversaries.

First of all they say that the Holy Scriptures have given occasion to form images, for seeing they have attributed unto God the parts of a man, namely: eyes, ears, head, nostrils, feet, etc. There seems no cause why, but that the painters and gravers may form the very same unto him. Also it is written in Hosea, "I am likened by hands of the prophets."[26] And in the seventh chapter of Daniel, "The ancient of days was showed unto the prophets, which had the ears of his head white like wool."[27] Also there was shown unto Ezekiel the similitude of a man. Isaiah says that he saw, "the Lord sitting upon a throne, etc."[28] And Moses also with the elders say God sitting upon a throne and upon the mountain he beheld his hind parts like unto a man going away. Wherefore they say that seeing those things have been shown and have been seen by the prophets, why shall it be thought a wicked part to plant out the self-same things in colors and engravings?

. . .

Indeed he expressed himself sometimes by certain apparitions, but in them there was no danger of idolatry, for who is there that worships words either spoken or written or offers sacrifices unto them? For words pass away, knowledge also and conceits of the mind are put out of remembrance, but these things themselves are painted or graven outwardly, men will readily adore them, burn incense to them, and pay unto them. Further, let us

---

Catholic hierarchy. In fact, the Inquisition officially condemned the three-headed or three-faced image of God in 1625: Davis, *Seeing Faith*, 145; Hallebeek, "Papal Prohibitions," in van Asselt, et al., eds, *Iconoclasm and Iconoclash*, 353–86.

25. The passage which Vermigli is rephrasing from the Synod is most likely the statement: "For the honor which is paid to the image passes on to that which the image represents, and he who reveres the image reveres in it the subject represented." Percival, ed., *The Seven Ecumenical Councils* in NPNF, 2nd Series, vol. XIV, 549–51 (quote on p. 550).

26. Hosea 12:10. Vermigli, or his translator, is using the Wyclif translation in this instance. Most of the English translations of the time, such as the Geneva translation, translate this passage: "used similitudes by the ministry of the prophets."

27. Dan 7:9.

28. Isa 6:1.

consider that the prophets, which had such kind of forms in their mind, never picture them nor yet made images of them. For they knew that God forbade such things to be done. Neither did they dispute with themselves in this manner. God has declared himself unto us, therefore it is lawful so to express him out in images. Besides this, God commands that there should be a propitiatory upon the Ark, as though his seat should be there, but the same was an empty seat, neither was there any image of God therein. . . . What shall we do then? Will not God be in some manner counterfeited, that our minds thereby may be carried or lifted up to the consideration of heavenly things?

We answer that of his images they are now already extant. For Christ is the lively image of him; let us therefore behold him and his acts and in him we shall know God abundantly. Furthermore, we have in the Holy Scripture, which most perfectly painted out God to us, so much as is requisite to the painting out of him. What need have we either of wood, brass, gold, silver, or other sensible matter? Again, if it delight us to behold the lively images of him, let us look upon godly men, which now are and sometime have been in the church for the they undoubtedly were from the beginning created and afterward were restored to the image in the church, for they undoubtedly were from the beginning created and afterward were restored to the image of God. We have moreover as it is above declared all the works of nature, wherein the printed steps of God's power appear. Further, we have the visible sacraments, wherewith the Word of God is joined. Surely these things may suffice and ought to be enough to lift up men's minds to the beholding of God and his properties. But curious and importunate men, besides these things which I have recited, bring yet into the church, marble, brass, and wood. But they which do these things be reprehended in the Holy Scriptures and are most weightily reproved of whoredom, because they be not content with God to whom all the faithful are married. But call unto themselves other husbands, that is images and idols and with them commit most abominable idolatry.

. . .

Now as touching those images which resemble things created, let us see how they may be suffered or not suffered. And first of all, Christ comes very well to remembrance, in that he is man. For in that respect he may be resembled and painted out. For that is not against the nature of the thing, seeing he was very man. Neither is it against the art of painting, which may imitate bodies. True indeed it is that in the Seventh Synod, which the papists allow not (being held by Constantine and his son), it was decreed that

Christ should not be painted or fashioned out. ... And the reason is set down, because nothing but his humanity can be expressed by art. Wherefore they, which make such things, seem to embrace the Nestorian heresy, which separated the human nature from the divine. But to say truly, I do not much allow of this reason, which if it were true, it should not be lawful to picture any man, because the soul which is a spirit cannot be expressed. And they which describe the human nature of the Lord do not exclude the divine nature from the understanding, neither do they show or allow that the humanity of Christ, either was or is destitute of his Godhead. Although Theodosius and Valentinian seem to have commanded that Christ's picture should not be set forth in metal nor in flint stones nor yet in tables of wood.[29] As we have in the first book and eighth title of the Code. The law stands in ambiguity which seems to signify that he should not be expressed in the pavement, least it should be trodden under foot or spat upon. But Petrus Crinitus says that he saw that law written absolutely, whereby is commanded that the image of Christ should not be made of any matter.[30] But that he cannot be counterfeited as touching his human nature, there are no firm reasons brought.

The angels as touching their substance and nature, seeing they are spirits, cannot be expressed, yet is it lawful sometimes to picture them in such ways as they have shown themselves unto men.[31] For they are not, as God is, infinite but are bounded and limited. Neither does the commandment of God forbid this, unless their pictures were made to the intent they should be religiously and devoutly worshipped. Also men may be pictured and counterfeited, seeing the same is not repugnant either to the thing, either to art, or else to the commandment of God. So is it lawful also to form and picture forth the cross of the Lord, tree, fruits, and other sensible or visible bodies, for the arts of painting and counterfeiting[32] are very gifts of God, wherefore they must serve to some use.

...

Neither does he take away the use of those gifts, because many abuse them, and this is easily confirmed by many similitudes. The power of

---

29. See Kolrud and Prusac, eds, *Iconoclasm from Antiquity*; MacMullen, *Christianizing the Roman Empire*.

30. Crinitus, *De honesta disciplina*, IX.9.

31. Interestingly, while saints were almost entirely abandoned by English Protestants, angels continued to hold a particularly powerful place in their religious belief and devotion: Walsham, "Angels and Idols," 134–67; Walsham, "Invisible Helpers," 77–130.

32. Manufacturing

procreation is given unto men, although some shamefully abuse the same unto lusts. So the sight is granted, which they perversely use, who for the sake of lust behold women, which are not their own. And so it might be said of the rest. Again, we know that Solomon would have images to be made for his royal throne, which should have the forms of young lions; neither was he for that matter reprehended by any prophet. Wherefore in a profane thing it is lawful to have pictures and graven images. I am not ignorant that the ancient fathers, especially Clement and Tertullian, detested the acts of painters and image-makers. But I understand this in respect that these workmen professed Christ, and yet they made images and pictures, which might easily be worshipped and peradventure they divided them among the idolaters, thinking it sufficient to their own salvation if they themselves did not worship them.

. . .

The use of images may be good for the keeping of things in memory, for the garnishing of houses, especially of kings and noble personages, and also to serve for some honest pleasure, wherewith men sometimes may both delight and recreate themselves. Howbeit, in such light commodities, there are oftentimes many faults; for false images are sundry times thrust in, instead of true images. . . . We must therefore take heed, unless men are perniciously seduced by false images. I have added perniciously because the centaurs and other things of this sort may for garnishing sake be expressed without any harm unto them, which are the beholders. Others attempt to paint out virtues, which have no bodies, but do belong unto the mind, which is a spirit. Also they painted or fashioned them like virgins or matrons, and therein I think is no deceit, whereby the beholders can be deceived. Howbeit, this seems the safest way of all other, that if things should be painted, the profitable and holy histories should chiefly be painted, whereby the beholders may receive some edifying.

Further we must beware of lavishing out of money, for there are some, which in procuring pictures and images, are stark mad. These costs must not be preferred before the necessities of the poor. How greatly herein it has been offended, the temples of our forefathers which be yet extant do evidently declare. Besides this, we must take very diligent heed that there be no filthy things painted, for we are otherwise, or our own vileness and corruption of nature, sufficiently kindled unto lust. If it be truly said that evil speaking corrupts good manner, no less do filthy images corrupt the beholders.

...

It cannot be denied but that the honor which we attribute unto God is not that which we give unto men, for that is the highest honor, which is given to only one God, and it chiefly consists in these things. First, that we repose in him all the hope of our salvation, that we account him for our chief happiness by submitting ourselves unto him, without adding of any condition, but even simply and absolutely. But unto princes we must submit ourselves, and all that is ours yet so, as they command us not to do things repugnant unto the Word of God. But unto God we are subject, without any manner of condition or exception.[33] Furthermore, it is necessary that we believe in him simply and absolutely, and that we declare him to be as the fountain of all good things, in giving him thanks for all the benefits which daily happen to us, and we must declare his honor by outward calling upon him. Also, some honor is due unto the excellent creatures, such as princes, prophets, and godly men. Wherefore Augustine in *De civitate* book 22 and chapter 10 writes that, "Those are to be honored in the right of charity and society."[34] For we hold them for our fellows and brethren, and therefore we love them, we wish well unto them, and we rejoice with them in their good fortune.... And of this kind of honor, Paul wrote saying, "In giving honor, go one before another."[35] Again, as brethren, they are to be held with mutual good turns.

Further, in the churches the saints are only commended, and the noble gifts which God bestowed upon them are celebrated after such a manner, as Christ allowed of the faithful and diligent servant, which rightly and prudently behaved himself in ordering the money which he had received. But and if so be they will use the word *dulia* in this kind of worshipping. We will that they may retain it so that they know the same distinction to be contained in the Holy Scriptures. They also have invented the word *latria*, which they would have to be attributed unto the most excellent creatures, namely unto Mary, and to the human nature of Christ. A difference of honors we disallow not, but those things which appertain only to the high God we cannot suffer to be attributed unto creatures. Which ... they prostrate themselves before images, they light wax candles to them, and at them they invoke those dead men which are represented by them. Augustine in many places takes away from all creatures, churches, priesthoods, sacrifices, and

---

33. The phrasing here is subtle but important in the wider debate over church-state relations that would create rifts within the Protestant communities in Europe, particularly over the role of the civil authority in the ordering of the Protestant congregations.

34. Augustine, *The City of God*, XX.10.

35. Rom 12:10.

altars.... Yet the papists have communicated all these things, not only unto men departed this life but also unto images and pictures, and for the defense of this, they use many sophistications, when as God notwithstanding plainly speaks and forbids that images should in any way be made unto religious worshipping. And that, which he has absolutely spoken and commanded must not be cunningly shifted off by man's craftiness.

...

Seeing therefore it is plentifully enough confirmed that images must not be worshiped nor adored, now it rests that we examine this, whether it be lawful to set them in holy places, where the congregations of the faithful resort. Some affirm that it is lawful, so the worshipping of them be forbidden. But (in my judgment) it must not be allowed that they should be in churches. First, because it is a dangerous thing, and experience has taught that whether men at length, through beholding of them, fell, when they saw them in places in the temples, for they worshipped them. The way therefore that leads unto idolatry must be cut off from the faithful. Augustine writes very well and religiously of this matter upon Psalm 113. When images, he says, are set in a high place, or else in some tabernacle, a naughty affection is bred in men's minds, whereby the devil is invited to intermeddle himself.[36]

...

Besides, it may be proved by the example of Epiphanius that they ought not to be had in churches. He being on his journey and happening into a certain town that was called Anablatha,[37] saw a certain candle burning, and demanding what place it was, he understood that it was a church or a place of prayer for the faithful. Whereunto he entered in that he might pray unto God, and he saw a curtain hanging, wherein was painted the image of a man as if it had been of Christ or of a holy man. Insomuch that when he saw the picture of a man hanged in the church, contrary to the authority of scriptures, he both plucked down and rent the curtain and counselled the sextons of the church that they should carry it forth and wrap a poor dead man in it. Moreover he wrote unto John, Bishop of Jerusalem (unto whom the cure of that place belonged), that from then forward he should take heed that such hangings, otherwise than religion would permit, should not be suffered in the Church of Christ.[38] And that epistle seemed unto Jerome to

---

36. Augustine, *Expositions on the Psalms*, NPNF, vol. VIII, 548–49.
37. Anabantha
38. This is among Jerome's letters: "Letter LI," NPNF, 2nd Series, vol. VI, 83–89. For more on Epiphanius's theology on images see his *The Panarion*, 28–31, 63, 323.

be of such weight that he vouchsafed to turn it into Latin, which he would not have done if he had not been of the same mind. Also the latter synod of Ephesus condemned images, howbeit the same synod is not allowed and that upon just cause, insomuch as it favored the heretics Nestor and Eutychus.[39] Such is the fortune not only of human affairs but also many times of ecclesiastical, that evil things are mingled with good. Whereupon it comes to pass afterward that not only evil things but also good things together are therewithal rejected.

. . .

Paul undoubtedly, in the first letter to the Corinthians, exhorts the faithful, and that with many words, that they should beware of offending the weak. Wherefore, although there are many which say that they know that images must not be worshipped, yet let them think this that everyone does not sufficiently know it. And surely the consideration of images and of things dedicated unto idols seems to be all one, which the wise men of Corinth said they knew what they were. And yet nevertheless, Paul commanded that they should not eat them, and he said, "Buy meat in the market, eat at home and not in places appointed for idols."[40] Even so may we say, if you will have images, have them at home and not in the temples. Neither do images placed in the temples do less unto the Church than did the dissembling of Peter. For he, in suffering the ceremonies of the Jews, nourished an evil opinion of them. In like manner is the fall of the weak, and perverse adoration confirmed when images are suffered to be in churches. . . . And when as they be at any time removed out of the temples, I think it good to beware that they not be kept sound and whole, for if the state changes they may easily be restored again into their places. When Constantine the Great was converted unto Christ, he shut up the temples of the idols, but he destroyed them not. Afterward came Julian the Apostate and opened them again. . . . Which thing afterward Theodosius and other Christian princes noting, they either destroyed them utterly or else granted them to the use of Christians.[41]

But we must understand that it is not the part of private men to cast down images, therefore it must be done by the public authority of a magistrate. . . . Of this matter Augustine, in his sixth homily *De sermone domini in*

---

39. In reality, the second synod at Ephesus only spoke of images tangentially, as they were related to the personhood and deity of Christ and his representation: Perry, ed., *The Second Synod of Ephesus*, 225, 235.

40. 1 Cor 8.

41. For more see Brown, *The Rise of Western Christendom*, 74–76.

monte, wrote very well, where he brings the place out of the seventh chapter of Deuteronomy: "When the land shall be yours, you shall subvert the altars and images of them."[42] First, says he, it behooves them to possess the land and to have it in their power before they could subvert the images thereof. And it is evident that temples be public places and not the possessions of private men. Wherefore it is not every man's part there, either to cast out or to destroy anything. They then, which bear rule, as well in civil as ecclesiastical causes ought not to suffer those images in churches. Otherwise, the simple sort, when they perceive them to be suffered, even for that cause they attribute the more unto them, for that they see the princes, bishops, and pastors do not cast them away. And it is very frivolous that they have always in their mouth that images are certain visible words of God, which help the faith of them that are ignorant. For Paul testifies that, "Faith comes by hearing and hearing by the Word of God," not by pictures or images. If any desire to have Christ pictured, let him read the Holy Scriptures, let him have in his hand the Gospels, the apostolic epistles, and the Acts of the Apostles, and let him be oftentimes present at godly sermons.[43]

. . .

At the last they come unto that which was the cause that we took in hand this treatise. And they say that in the time of Moses and Solomon, God would have cherubim and other images in the tabernacle or temple. Hereunto, some say that those images were placed in the innermost holy place, where none might see them. It is a weak answer, for there were such also in the court of the priests where they made the burnt offerings and sacrifices. Also in the engines that sustained the lavatories, there were cherubim, lions, and oxen. Moreover the sea of brass was set upon the oxen of brass. Whereupon others answer that those images were not there to the intent they should be worshipped, but to be as it were a certain training and that they might garnish the holy temple. But the papists would, after the same manner, excuse their images. Wherefore it is more fitly answered that God gave the law, not to himself but unto us; so then, we must follow the same, neither may we bring him into order if he otherwise would anything of a special prerogative. He must be suffered to do after his own will, but we

---

42. Augustine, *Sermon on the Mount*, in NPNF, vol. VI, 93–94.

43. Rom 10:17. This was a fundamental argument of most Protestant iconoclastic movements: that true faith cannot be communicated visually. In fact, hearing the Word was often set up in contradiction to seeing idols: Dyrness, *Reformed Theology*, 72–84. The exceptions to this are, of course, the imagery that was employed by Protestants to either condemn Catholicism or otherwise encourage true faith: Scribner, *For the Sake of the Simple Folk*, 190–228.

must obey the law that is made. Certainly those images had some figurative meaning, but they were not set forth as an example for us to follow. With them was joined the Word of God, which the images placed in our churches want. And seeing they were external things and had the word added to them, they were (after a sort) sacraments of those times, and it is only God, and not men, which can make sacraments.

And it is to be noted that Solomon and Moses, which made the Cherubim did not make any other. They only made that which was commanded unto them by God. They painted not upon the walls the acts of Abraham, neither the acts of Adam or Moses, nor the other fathers. They (papists) are also accustomed sometimes to say, "We have the images of Christ, to the intent we may convince the Marcionites and Valentinians, which denied that Christ had a true body." Surely a very plausible and sharp argument! But I would have them answer wherefore they have the images of other saints. Was there any man that admitted them to have no true bodies? Doubtless there be other reasons to be used for the convincing of heretics, who, if they are not moved by the testimonies of scriptures and by the acts which Christ did, surely they will not be confuted by images.

. . .

Wherefore, in vain do our adversaries clatter that images are the books of laymen, that while they notify the acts of holy men they teach the rude and unskillful sort. We indeed confess that something is signified by pictures or images, howbeit very slenderly. But the minds of the unskillful be so rude as that they have need of the ministry of the Word. And it comes oftentimes to pass that by images they are rather led into error than truly taught. Let the idiot or unlearned return as often as he will unto a picture, it will always tell one thing, and if any doubt comes upon him while he beholds the same, it will never answer anything for resolving thereof. But in the Holy Scriptures and in godly sermons, whatsoever shall appear somewhat dark in one place is plainly enough expounded in another. . . . Howbeit, we grant that images may have a good use, namely to renew the memory of things which have been done. Which thing, although not everywhere, yet in some places it happens conveniently, even as sometimes we speak some things by signs, and dumb men express many things by gestures. But whereas it is lawful to use this at some time and somewhere, do we therefore use it always and in all places?

Shall he be accounted a wise senator that in the senate house shows his judgment by pointing and nodding? And there is no doubt but we use water for the quenching of thirst, yet if you set the same before your guests at a banquet, you shall be called a fool and a covetous man. So in like manner images, although elsewhere they have their commodity, yet they must not be suffered in churches, where we may deal with God by far better ways and means, especially seeing that they cannot there be had without danger.

DOCUMENT 16

Gregory Martin, *A Discovery of the Manifold Corruptions of the Holy Scripture by the Heretics of Our Days*
(Rheims, 1582)

INTRODUCTION

Gregory Martin (c.1542–82) was a Catholic priest, theologian, and translator. Although his life is relatively unstudied, his works—particularly the Douai-Rheims translation of the Bible—continue to play a significant role in the history and life of the Roman Catholic Church. Before he went into exile (probably in 1569), Martin was a fellow at St. John's College, Oxford, where he became good friends with the future Catholic martyr Edmund Campion. After his patron Thomas Howard, duke of Norfolk, was arrested following his participation in the Northern Rebellion (a Catholic revolt against Elizabeth's reforms in 1569), Martin joined the ranks of the English College at Douai.[1]

It was in Douai that he wrote both his translation of the Latin Vulgate and, simultaneously, *A Discovery of the Manifold Corruptions of the Holy Scripture*. During his research and study for the translation, Martin seems to have compared English Protestant editions with both his own translation and with one another. *A Discovery* is an unprecedented assault upon the

---

1. Thomas McCoog, "Gregory Martin," ODNB.

legitimacy and veracity of Protestant translations, particularly in regards to how much they differ with one another and, more importantly, how much they vary from the original Greek and Hebrew. The importance of Martin's arguments can be seen in how much document 22 echoes not only Martin's logic but also his language and argumentative style.

In the text below, Martin reaffirms the traditional Catholic apologetic on religious images. Also, he reasserts that the having of images is not the same as the worshipping of them. Most importantly, Martin takes up the debate over words like *idolum*, but with much more concern for the linguistic minutiae and interpretative methodologies that had been employed in rendering these words into English. Particularly, Martin argues that the Protestant translators have no legitimate reason (or at least have not been forthcoming with their reasons) for translating the same Greek word one way in some passages and another way in others. He condemns their duplicity saying, "At the least you cannot deny but it was on purpose done, to make both seem all one." Martin sees the extent of this corruption in the translation of scripture, and he believes that mistranslation is the death knell of Protestant theological coherency. Unlike the Roman Catholic tradition, which is based upon the authority of the papal hierarchy and the church fathers, Protestantism was rooted in the individual's ability to interpret scripture (see also document 22), and without an assurance of accurate translation, most Protestants would be working with faulty texts and, ultimately, uncertain foundations for their faith.

TEXT[2]

Chap. 3 Heretical Translations Against Sacred Images

I beseech you what is the next and readiest and most proper English of *idolum, idolatra, idololatria*? (Or, in Greek, εἴδωλον, εἰδωλολάτρης, εἰδωλολατρεία). Is it not "idol," "idolater," "idolatry"? Are not these plain English words, and well known in our language? Why sought you further for other terms and words, if you had meant faithfully? What needed that circumstance of three words for one, "worshipper of images," and, "worshipping of images"? Whether (I pray you) is the more natural and convenient speech, either in our English tongue, or for the truth of the thing, to say as the Holy Scripture does, "Covetousness is idolatry," and consequently, "The covetous man is an

---

2. Earlier transcription in Rogers, ed., *English Recusant*, vol. CXXVII, 28–34; Martin, *A Discovery of Manifold Corruptions*, 32–51.

idolater": or as you translate, "Covetousness is worshipping of images," and, "The covetous man is a worshipper of images"?[3]

We say commonly in English, "Such a rich man makes his money his God." And the Apostle says in like manner of form, "Whose belly is their God" (Phil. 3.), and generally every creature is our idol, when we esteem it so exceedingly that we make it our God. But whoever heard in English, that our money, or belly, were our images, and that by esteeming of them too much, we become worshippers of images? Among yourselves are there not some even of your superintendents, of whom the Apostle speaks, that make an idol of their money and belly, by covetousness and belly cheer? Yet can we not call you therefore in any true sense, "worshippers of images," neither would you abide it. You see then that there is a great difference betwixt idol and image, idolatry and worshipping of images, and even so great difference is there between St. Paul's words and your translations.

Will you see more yet to this purpose? In the English Bible printed the year 1562 you read thus: "How agrees the Temple of God with images?" (2 Cor. 6.) Can we be ignorant of Satan's cogitations herein, that it was translated on purpose to delude the simple people and to make them believe that the Apostle speaks against sacred images in the churches, which were then in plucking down in England, when this your translation was first published in print? Whereas in very truth you know, that the Apostle here partly interprets himself to speak of mean, as of God's temples wherein he dwells, partly alludes to Solomon's temple, which did very well agree with images (for it had the cherubim, which were representations of angels, and the figures of oxen to bear up the lavatory) but with idols it could not agree, and therefore the apostle's words are these, "How agrees the Temple of God with idols?" (μὰτ των ειδώλων).

When Moses by God's appointment erected a brazen serpent and commanded the people that were stung with serpents to behold it, and thereby they were healed, this was an image only, and as an image was it erected and kept and used by God's commandment (Num. 21). But when it grew to be an idol (says St. Augustine), that is, when the people began to adore it as God, then King Hezekiah broke it into pieces to the great commendation of his piety and godly zeal (4 Kings 18).[4] So when the children of Israel in the absence of Moses made a calf, and said, "These are thy Gods of Israel that brought thee out of Egypt" (Exod. 32), was it but an image which they made? Was that so heinous a matter that God would so have punished them as he did? No, they made it an idol also, saying, "These are thy gods of

---

3. Col 3:5; Eph 5:5. Here, Martin is drawing from the Bishops Bible.
4. Augustine, *City of God*, X.8.

Israel." And therefore the Apostle says to the Corinthians, "Be not idolaters, as some of them" (1 Cor. 10). Which also you translate most falsely, "Be not worshippers of images, as some of them."

We see then that the Jews had images without sin, but not idols. Again for having idols they were accounted like unto the Gentiles, as the Psalm says, "They learned their works, and served their graven idols" (Ps. 165).[5] But they were not accounted like unto the Gentiles for having images, which they had in Solomon's temple, and in the brazen serpent. St. Jerome writes of the Ammonites and Moabites (who were Gentiles and idolaters) that coming into the temple of Jerusalem, and seeing the angelical images of the cherubim covering the propitiatory, they said (like to the Protestants) "Lo, even as the Gentiles, so Judah also has idols of their religion" (Ezech. 25).[6] These men did put no difference between their own idols, and the Jews' lawful images. And are not you ashamed to be like to these? They accused Solomon's temple of idols, because they saw there lawful images. You accuse the churches of God of idolatry, because you see there the sacred images of Christ and his saints.

But tell us yet I pray you, do the Holy Scriptures of either testament speak of all manner of images, or rather of the idols of the Gentiles? Your conscience knows that they speak directly against the idols and the idolatry that was among the pagans and infidels, from which as the Jews in the Old Testament, so the first Christians in the New Testament were to be prohibited. But will you have a demonstration that your own conscience condemns you herein, and that you apply all translation to your heresy? What caused you being otherwise in all places so ready to translate "images"; yet Isa. 31 and Zech. 13 to translate, "idols," in all your Bibles with full consent? Why in these places specially and so advisedly? No doubt because God says there, speaking of this time of the New Testament: "In that day every man shall cast out his idols of silver and idols of gold. And, I will destroy the names of the idols out of the earth, so that they shall no more be had in remembrance." In which places if you had translated "images," you had made the prophecy false, because images have not been destroyed out of the world, but are, and have been in Christian countries with honor and reverence even since Christ's time. Marry in the idols of the Gentiles we see it verified, which are destroyed in all the world so far as gentility is converted to Christ.

And what were the pagans' idols or their idolatry? St. Paul tells us, saying: "They changed the glory of the incorruptible God into the similitude of the image of a corruptible man, and of birds and beasts and creeping things:

---

5. This clearly is a typo. The correct scripture reference is Ps 106:35–36.
6. Hieronymus, *Commentariorum*, VI.235–36.

and they served (or worshipped) the creature more than the creator" (Rom 1). Does he charge them for making the image of man or beast? Yourselves have hangings and clothes full of such paintings and embroidering of imagery.[7] Wherewith then are they charged? With giving the glory of God to such creatures, which was to make them idols, and themselves idolaters.

The case being thus, why do you make it two distinct things in St. Paul, calling the pagans, idolaters, and the Christians doing the same, worshippers of images, and that in one sentence, whereas the Apostle uses but one and the selfsame Greek word in speaking both of pagans and Christians? It is a marvelous and willful corruption and well to be marked, and therefore I will put down the whole sentence, as it is in your English translation. "I wrote to you that you should not company with fornicators: and I meant not at all of the fornicators of this world, either of the covetous, or extortioners, either the idolaters etc. but that ye company not together, if any that is called a brother, be a fornicator, or covetous, or a worshipper of images, or an extortioner."[8] In the first, speaking of Pagans, your translator names "idolater" according to the text, but in the later part speaking of Christians, you translate the very selfsame Greek word εἰδωλολάτρης "worshipper of images." Why so? Forsooth to make the reader think that St. Paul speaks here, not only of pagan idolaters, but also of Catholic Christians that reverently kneel in prayer before the cross, the holy rood, the images of our Savior Christ and his saints, as though the apostle had commanded such to be avoided.

Where if you have yet the face to deny this your malicious and heretical intent, tell us, why all these other words are translated and repeated alike in both places, "covetous," "fornicators," "extortioners," both pagans and Christians, and only this word (idolaters) not so, but pagans, idolaters, and Christians, worshippers of images. At the least you cannot deny but it was on purpose done, to make both seem all one, yea and to signify that the Christians doing the foresaid reverence before sacred images (which you call worshipping of images) are more to be avoided than the pagan idolaters. Whereas the apostle speaking of pagans and Christians that committed one and the selfsame heinous sin whatsoever commands the Christian in that case to be avoided for his amendment, leaving the pagan to himself and to God, as having not to do to judge of him.

But to this the answer belike will be made, as one of them has already answered in the like case, that in the English Bible appointed to be read in

---

7. Recent studies of Protestant domestic furnishings have uncovered the truth in this statement. For further reading see Hamling and Williams, eds, *Art Re-formed*.

8. 1 Cor 5:9–10.

their churches it is otherwise, and even as we would have it corrected, and therefore (says he) "it had been good before we entered into such heinous accusations, to have examined our grounds that they had been true."[9] As though we accuse them not truly of false translation, unless it be false in that one Bible which for the present is read in their churches; or as though it pertained not to them how their other English Bibles be translated; or as though the people read not all indifferently without prohibition, and may be abused by every one of them; or as though the Bible, which now is read (as we think) in their churches, has not the like absurd translations, yea more absurd, even in this matter of images, as is before declared, or as though we must first learn what English translation is read in their church (which were hard to know, it changes so often) before we may be bold to accuse them of false translation; or as though it were not the same Bible that was for many years read in their churches, and is yet in ever man's hands, which has this absurd translation whereof we have last spoken.

Surely the 1562 Bible that we most accuse not only in this point, but also for sundry other most gross faults and heretical translations, spoken of in other places, is that Bible which was authorized (as it seems by Cranmer their Archbishop of Canterbury), and read all King Edward's time in their churches, and (as it seems by the late printing thereof again in 1562) a great part of this Queen's reign. And certain it is, that it was so long read in all their churches with this venomous and corrupt translation of and abandon the very sign and image of their salvation, the cross of Christ, the holy rood or crucifix representing the manner of his bitter Passion and death, the sacred images of the blessed Virgin Mary the Mother of God, and of St. John Evangelist, representing their standing by the cross at the very time of his passion (John 19:26). Insomuch that now by experience we see the foul inconvenience thereof, to wit, that all other images and pictures of infamous harlots and heretics, of heathen tyrants, and persecutors are lawful in England at this day, and their houses, parlors, and chambers are garnished with them. Only sacred images, and representations of the holy mystery of our redemption, are esteemed idolatrous and have been openly defaced in most spiteful manner and burned, to the great dishonor of our Savior Christ and his saints.

And as concerning the Bible that at this day is read in their churches, if it be that of the year 1577, it is worse sometime in this matter of images, than the other. For where the other reads, "Covetousness, which is worshipping of idols" (Col. 3:3), there is this later (whereunto they appeal) reads thus, "Covetousness, which is worshipping of images." And Eph. 5, it reads

9. Fulke, *Confutation*, 35.

as absurdly as the other, "A covetous man, which is a worshipper of images." Lo this is the English Bible which they refer us unto, as better translated, and as correcting the fault of the former. But because it is evident by these places, that this also is partly worse, and partly as ill as the other, therefore this great confuter of Mr. John Howlett flees once more, to the Geneva English Bible, saying, "Thus we read," and, "so we translate," to wit, "A covetous person, which is an idolater." Where shall we have these good fellows, and how shall we be sure that they will stand to any of their translations? From the first read in their churches, they flee to that which is now read, and from this again to the later Geneva English Bibles, neither read in their churches (as we suppose) nor of greatest authority among them. And we doubt not but they will as fast flee from this, to the former again, when this shall be proven in some places more false and absurd than the other.

. . .

But I beseech you sir, if the dictionaries tell you that εἴδωλον may by the original property of the word signify an image, (which no man denies) do they tell you also that you may commonly and ordinarily translate it so, as the common usual signification thereof? Or do they tell you that image and idol are so all one, that wherever you find this word "image," you may truly call it, "idol"? For these are the points that you should defend in your answer. For an example, do they teach you to translate in these places thus, "God has predestinated us to be made conformable to the idol of his Son" (*imagini*, Rom 8). And again, "As we have born the idol of the earthly" (Adam) "so let us bear the idol of the heavenly" (Christ; *imaginem*, 1 Corinthians 15). And again, "We are transformed into the same idol, even as of our Lord's spirit" (2 Corinthians 3). And again, "The Law having a shadow of the good things to come, not the very idol of the things" (Hebrews 10). And again, Christ "who is the idol of the invisible God"? (Colossians 1, 2 Corinthians 4). Is this (I pray you) a true translation? "Yea," say you, "according to the property of the word," but because the name of idols, in the English tongue, for the great dishonor done to God in worshiping of images, is become odious, no Christian man would say so.[10]

First note how foolishly and unadvisedly he speaks here, because he would confound images and idols, and make them falsely to signify one thing: when he says, the name of "idol" is become odious in the English tongue because of worshipping of "images," he should have said, "The dishonor done to God in worshipping idols, made the name of idols odious."

---

10. It is important to note here that all of the scriptural passages in this paragraph are hypothetical.

As in his own example of "tyrant," and king. He meant to tell us that "tyrant" sometimes was a usual name for very king, and because certain such tyrants abused their power, therefore the name of tyrant became odious. For he will not say (I trust) that for the fault of kings, the name of tyrant became odious. Likewise the Romans took away the name of Manlius for the crime of one Manlius, not for the crime of John of Nokes, or for any other name. The name of Judas is so odious that men now commonly are not so called. Why so? Because he that betrayed Christ was called Judas, not because he was also Iscariot. The very name of ministers is odious and contemptible, why? Because ministers are so lewd, wicked, and unlearned, not because some priests be naught. Even so, the name of idol grew to be odious, because of the idols of the Gentiles not because of holy images. For if the reverence done by Christians to holy images were evil, as it is not, it should in this case have made the name of images odious and not the name of idols. But God be thanked, the name of Images is no odious name among Catholic Christians, but only among heretics and iconoclasts, such as the second general Council of Nicea has condemned therefore with the sentence of anathema. No more than the cross is odious, which to all good Christians is honorable, because our Savior Christ died on a cross.

But to omit this man's extraordinary and unadvised speeches which be too many and too tedious (as when he says in the same sentence, "Howsoever the name 'idol' is grown odious in the English tongue," as though it were not also odious in the Latin and Greek tongues, but that in Latin and Greek a man might say according to his fond opinion, *Fecit hominem ad idolum suum*, and so in the other places where is *imago*) to omit these rash assertions I say, and to return to his other words where he says, that though the original property of the words has that signification, yet "no Christian man would say that God made man according to his idol, no more than a good subject would call his lawful prince a tyrant." Does he not here tell us that, which we would have, to wit, that we may not speak or translate according to the original property of the word, but according to the common usual and accustomed signification thereof? As we may not translate, *Phalaris tyrannus*, "Phalaris the king," as sometime *tyrannus* did signify, and in ancient authors does signify, but, Phalaris the tyrant, as now this word *tyrannus* is commonly taken and understood. Even so, we may not now translate, "My children keep yourselves from images" (*ab idolis*), as the word may and does sometime signify according to the original property thereof (ἀπὸ τῶν εἰδώλων, 1 John 5), but we must translate, "keep yourselves from idols," according to the common use and signification of the word in vulgar speech, and in the Holy Scriptures. Where the Greek word is so notoriously and usually peculiar to idols, and not unto images, that the holy fathers of the Second Nicene Council (which knew right well the signification of the Greek word, themselves being Grecians) do pronounce anathema to all such as interpret those places of the Holy Scripture that concern idols, of images or against sacred images, as now these Calvinists do, not only in their commentaries upon the Holy Scriptures, but even in their translations of the text.

This then being so, that words must be translated as their common use and signification requires, if you ask your old question, what great crime of corruption is committed in translating, "keep yourselves from images," the Greek being εἰδώλων?[11] You have answered yourself, that in so translating, idol and image are made to signify one thing, which may not be done, no more than tyrant and king can be made to signify all one. And how can you say then, that "this is no more absurdity, than instead of a Greek word, to use a Latin of the same signification." Are you not here contrary to yourself? Are idol and image, tyrant and king, of one signification? Said you not that in the English tongue, idol is grown to another signification than image, as tyrant is grown to another signification than king? Your false translations therefore that in so many places make idols and images all one, not only forcing the word in the Holy Scriptures, but disgracing the sentence thereby (as Ephesians 5 & Colossians 3) are they not in your own judgment very corrupt, and as your own consciences must confess, of a malicious intent corrupted, to disgrace thereby the Church's holy images by pretense of the Holy Scriptures that speak only of the pagans' idols.

. . .

Of this kind of falsification is that which is crept as a leprosy throughout all your Bibles, translating, *sculptile* and *conflatile*, "graven image," "molten image," namely in the first commandment, where you know in the Greek it is idol (εἰδώλων) and in the Hebrew (פֶּסֶל), such a word as signifies only a graven thing, not including this word "image." And you know that God commanded to make the images of Cherubim, and of oxen in the Temple, and of the brazen serpent in the desert, and therefore your wisdom might have considered that he forbade not all graven images, but such as the Gentiles made and worshipped as gods. And therefore *Non facies tibi sculptile* concurs with those words that God before, "Thou shalt have no other gods but me." For so to have an image as to make it a god, is to make it more than an image, and therefore, when it is an idol, as were the idols of the Gentiles, then it is forbidden by this commandment. Otherwise, when the cross stood many years upon the table in the Queen's chapel, was it against this

11. Fulke, *Confutation*, 35.

commandment? Or was it idolatry in the Queen's Majesty and her counsellors that appointed it there, being the supreme head of your church?[12] Or do the Lutherans your pew-fellows, at this day commit idolatry against this commandment, that have in their churches the crucifix, and the holy images of the Mother of God, and of St. John the Evangelist?[13] Or if the whole story of the Gospel concerning our Savior Christ, were drawn in pictures and images in your churches, as it is in many of ours, were it (trow you) against this commandment? Fie, for shame, that you should thus with intolerable impudence and deceit abuse and bewitch the ignorant people, against your own knowledge and conscience. For, wot[14] you not, that God many times expressly forbade the Jews both marriages and other conversation with the Gentiles, lest they might fall to worship their idols, as Solomon did (3 Reg 11) and as the Psalm reports of them (Ps 105:35)? This then is the meaning of the commandment, neither to make the idols of the Gentiles, nor any other like unto them, and to that end, as did Jeroboam in Dan and Bethel.

---

12. See the introduction to document 12.

13. Interestingly, the Protestant divine William Fulke will respond that "we will not accuse the Lutherans of idolatry, neither can we, because they worship no images" (Fulke, *A Defence*, 204–5). See also Koerner, *Reformation of the Image*; Heal, *Cult of the Virgin*, 116–47.

14. Know

PART 3

THE POST-REFORMATION

HISTORICAL OVERVIEW

The final part of this work represents the early seventeenth century, including the last few years of Elizabeth's reign (d.1603) and the reign of James I (1603–25). Since, by this time, iconoclasm had been a significant element of English religion for almost seventy years, it is easy to assume that iconography had disappeared from the churches if not from all public places. However, nothing could be further from the truth.

The ambiguity that characterized the Elizabethan reforms did not disappear, even with the increasing popularity of puritanism. At King James's first major church council, the Hampton Court Conference in 1604, the Thirty Nine Articles of 1563 were reaffirmed. While these articles said nothing about images directly, the articles describe the doctrine of the Second Book of Homilies (including the homily against idolatry) as "godly and wholesome," indirectly affirming the reformed iconoclastic sentiments set down in "An Homily Against Idolatry." In practice, images like some roodscreens, stained glass, and highway crosses survived the many waves of destruction; a few of these (which survived the subsequent iconoclasm of the English Civil War) can still be found in the more remote parish churches of England. Other images, like the popular Cheapside Cross in the center of London, continued to garner popular support as memorials and cultural features of the city.[15] Also, Protestantism was not without its own elements of visual religion, as we have seen already. Printed images in Bibles and other religious works continued to be proliferated. The Bible itself, as Ulinka Rublack suggests, became an object of religious devotion for some reformers (document 22).[16] Other material religious objects were being slowly restored by certain Protestant leaders like Lancelot Andrewes and Richard Neile, often referred to as avant-garde conformists.[17] Gifts to the parishes and cathedrals, like lavish altar cloths and ornate communion cups, in the late sixteenth and early seventeenth centuries, were evidence of the increasing influence of this type of conformism.[18]

While theologically James was a Calvinist, he found himself in opposition to the more outspoken Calvinist and puritan brands of the English clergy in the church conflicts of the early seventeenth century. The image debate absorbed less of the polemical rhetoric in James's England, while issues like Catholic loyalism and the monarch's religious authority took more of the limelight. However, the image debate did not disappear from religious debates; it was regularly returned to, often as a platform for addressing larger questions.[19] Among the most important issues for the image debate of this period was the distinction made by the Council of Trent in the 1560s between image-worship, which Trent condemned, and image reverence, which Trent affirmed (documents 18, 20). Equally important were the two distinct Protestant polemical discourses that opposed Catholic images. On the one hand, theologians like the Calvinist William Perkins maintained and developed the traditional Protestant attacks, emphasizing the tradition of image use within the Roman Catholic Church as idolatrous (document 17). On the other hand, avant-garde conformists and, later, Laudians advocated for a more conciliatory approach that conceded certain points of the Catholic defense, without completely capitulating (document 21).

15. Budd, "Rethinking Iconoclasm."
16. Rublack, *Reformation Europe*, 158–60.
17. Spraggon, *Puritan Iconoclasm*, 18–19.
18. Fincham and Tyacke, *Altars Restored*, 98–125.
19. Milton, *Catholic and Reformed*, 189–96.

DOCUMENT 17

William Perkins
Two Documents

INTRODUCTION

William Perkins (c.1558–1602) was perhaps the most popular Calvinist writer in late sixteenth- and early seventeenth-century England. Originally from Warwickshire, he studied at Christ's College, Cambridge, distinguishing himself in theology with a BA and MA. At Cambridge, Perkins fell in with the more moderate puritan theologians like Edward Dering and Laurence Chaderton. During his career as a university lecturer (from 1585 until his death), Perkins published dozens of devotionals, polemics, and theological treatises. As a testament to his popularity, his complete *oeuvre* began to be compiled and published only two years after his death.[1]

Like Dering and Chaderton, Perkins followed the theology of John Calvin, and his successor Theodore Beze, quite closely. Perkins, more so than his theological compatriots, was acutely mindful of the unity and stability of the English church, setting this priority above certain doctrinal particulars. W. B. Patterson recently explained that Perkins's theology, while robustly Calvinistic, was "adapted to the needs of the national church."[2] To that end, he did not tolerate reforming fervor to the point that it undermined the needs and demands of the Elizabethan religious compromise. He regularly addressed theological differences and staunchly defended conten-

---

1. Patterson, *William Perkins*; Michael Jinkins, "William Perkins," *ODNB*.
2. Patterson, *William Perkins*, 4.

tious positions like double predestination; however, these were ultimately secondary to the fellowship of English Protestants.

Perkins is the last major Elizabethan Protestant to take up the image debate.[3] In two books of popular theology, *A Reformed Catholic* and *A Golden Chain*, Perkins revisits and crystallizes many of the arguments that had been rehearsed elsewhere. Passages from both texts have been included here, as they each present a very different side of Perkins's thought and rhetorical style. At times in *A Reformed Catholic*, Perkins seems almost conciliatory. The subtitle is indicative of this attitude, and he offers a much more sophisticated understanding of image use (acknowledging three legitimate forms of honor and adoration) than many earlier Protestants (echoing the theology of Vermigli). However, this conciliation is little more than a façade.[4] In a very accessible style, with points and sub-points delineated, Perkins levels the typical Reformed assaults at the idolatry that he sees in Catholic image devotion. In *A Golden Chain*, Perkins is more direct with his reader, stripping away any rhetorical niceties, setting out (in almost a machine-gun style polemic) nine things that are forbidden in relation to, or stemming from, the first commandment. This lacks any effort to craft cunning arguments or careful rhetoric that may have appealed to the moderate Catholic or church papist. It at times is simply a list of scriptural references that demonstrate his point. At other times, Perkins seems almost to be raving against idolatry, connecting it to a variety of nefarious activities including: having "society with infidels," the corruption of government, and the evils of witchcraft.

TEXT: *A REFORMED CATHOLIC* (CAMBRIDGE, 1598)

The Ninth Point. Of Images[5]

Our consent.

Conclusion I. We acknowledge the civil use of images as freely and truly as the Church of Rome does. By civil use I understand that use which is made of them in the common societies of men, out of the appointed places of the solemn worship of God. And this to be lawful, it appears, because the arts of painting and engraving are the ordinance of God, and to be skillful

---

3. For writings and individuals in the image debate after 1625 see Spraggon, *Puritan Iconoclasm*.

4. Milton, *Catholic and Reformed*, 177.

5. Where appropriate, scriptural references that are mentioned within the original text have been placed in the footnotes for ease of reading. The excerpt from *A Reformed Catholic* comes from pages 170–84. Currently, Perkins's entire corpus of published works are being reprinted in a modern typeset by Reformation Heritage Books.

in them is the gift of God, as the example of Bezaleel and Aholiab declares.[6] This use of images may be in sundry things.

1. In the adorning and setting forth of buildings, thus Solomon beautified his throne with the image of lions. And the Lord commanded his temple to be adorned with the images of palm trees, of pomegranates, of bulls, cherubs, and such like.

2. It serves for the distinction of coins, according to the practice of emperors and princes of all nations. When Christ was asked, whether it was lawful to give tribute to Caesar or no? He called for a penny and said, "whose image or superscription is this." They said, "Caesar's." He then said, "give to Caesar the things that are Caesar's," not condemning but approving the stamp or image upon his coin.[7] And though the Jews were forbidden to make images in way of representation, or worship, of the true God, yet the Sycle of the sanctuary, which they used especially after the time of Moses, was stamped with the image of the almond tree and the pot of Manna.

3. Images serve to keep in memory friends deceased whom we reverence. And it is like, that hence came one occasion of the images that are now in use in the Roman Church. For in the days after the apostles, men used privately to keep the pictures of their friends departed, and this practice after crept into the open congregation, and at last, superstition getting head, images began to be worshipped.

Conclusion II. We hold the historical use of images to be good and lawful, and that is to represent to the eye the acts of histories, whether they be human or divine. And thus we think the histories of the Bible may be painted in private places.

Conclusion III. In one case is lawful to make an image to testify the presence or the effects of the majesty of God, namely when God himself gives any special commandment so to do. In this case, Moses made and erected a brazen serpent to be a type, sign, or image to represent Christ crucified.[8] And the cherubs over the mercy seat served to represent the majesty of God, to whom the angels are subject. And in the second commandment, it is not simply said, "You shall not make a graven image." But with limitation, "You shall not make to yourself," that is, on your own head upon you own will and pleasure.

6. Exod 35:30.
7. Matt 22:21.
8. John 3:14.

Conclusion IV. The right images of the New Testament, which we hold and acknowledge, are the doctrine and preaching of the Gospel, and all things that by the Word of God pertains thereto. Galatians 3, "Who has bewitched you that you should not obey the truth to whom Jesus Christ was before described in your sight and among you crucified." Hence, it follows that the preaching of the Word is as a most excellent picture in which Christ with his benefits are lively represented unto us. And we dissent not from Origen, who says, "We have no images framed by a base workmen, but such as are brought forth and framed by the Word of God, namely patterns of virtue and frames resembling Christians."[9] He means that Christians themselves are the images of Christians.

The difference.

Our dissent from them touching images stands in three points:

Objection I. The Church of Rome holds it lawful for them to make images to resemble God, though not in respect of his divine nature, yet in respect of some properties and actions. We on the contrary hold it unlawful for us to make any image, anyway, to represent the true God or to make an image of anything in way of religion, to worship God, much less the creature thereby. For the second commandment says plainly, "You shall not make to yourself any graven image or the likeness of anything in heaven, etc."[10] The papists say the commandment is meant of the images of false gods. But . . . it must be understood of the images of the true Jehovah, and it forbids us to resemble God, either in his nature, properties, or works or to use any resemblance of him for any sacred use, as to help the memory, when we are about to worship God. Thus much the Holy Ghost who is the best expounder of himself, teaches most plainly, "You saw no image at all (either of false or true god) and therefore you shall not make any likeness of anything."[11] And again the prophet Isaiah, reproving idolaters, asks to whom they will liken God, or what similitude will they set upon him. And verse 21, "Know you nothing? Have you not heard? Has it not been told you from the beginning?"[12] As if he should say, have you forgotten the second commandment that God gave unto your fathers? And thus he flatly reproves all them that resemble the true God in images. But they say further, that by images in the second commandment are meant idols, that is (say they) such things as men worship for gods.

---

9. Origen, *Contra Celsus*, in ANF, vol. IV, VIII.18.

10. Exod 20:4.

11. Deut 4:15, 16.

12. Isa 40:18, 21.

Answer: If it were so, we should confound the first and second commandments. For the first, "You shall have no other gods before my face," forbids all false gods, which man wickedly frames unto himself by giving his heart and the principal affections thereof to them, and therefore idols also are here forbidden when they are esteemed as gods. And the distinction they make that an image is the representation of true things, an idol of things supposed is false. Tertullian says that every form or representation is to be termed an idol. And Isidore says that the heathen used the names of image and idol indifferently in one and the same signification.[13] And St. Stephen in his apology calls the golden calf an idol.[14] Jerome says, that idols are images of dead men. Ancient divines accord with all this which I have said. Lactantius says, "Where images are for religion's sake, there is no religion." The Council of Elvira, "which is adored of the people."[15] Origen, "We suffer not any to worship Jesus at altars, images, and temples, because it is written, 'You shall have none other gods.'" And Epiphanius says, "It is against the authority of the scriptures to see the image of Christ or of any saints hanging in the church." In the Seventh Council of Constantinople these words of Epiphanius are cited against the Encratitae,[16] "Be mindful beloved children not to bring images into the Church, nor set them in the places where the saints are buried, but always carry God in your hearts, neither let them be suffered in a common house, for it is not meet that a Christian should be occupied by the eyes but by the meditation of the mind."[17]

Argument of the Papists.

The reasons which they use to defend their opinions are these.

Objection I.) In Solomon's temple were erected cherubim, which were images of angels on the mercy seat where God was worshipped, and thereby resembled the majesty of God, therefore it is lawful to make images to resemble God.

---

13. The passage from Tertullian likely comes from *The Apology*, where Tertullian writes "Every form or formling, therefore, claims to be called an idol," based upon his understanding of the Greek word *eidos* (Tertullian, *Apology*, in ANF, vol. III, 62); Seville, *Etymologies*, VIII.11–14, 184.

14. Acts 7:41.

15. Lactantius, *Divine Institutes*, II.19. This is a reference to the Synod of Elvira (305–306) held in present day Granada. It became an authoritative council for Protestant reformers on the matter of iconoclasm: Besançon, *The Forbidden Image*, 187. For more on the council see Hess, *The Early Development*, 40–42.

16. The Encratites were second century Christian ascetics.

17. Percival, ed., *The Seven Ecumenical Councils*, in NPNF, 2nd Series, vol. XIV, 549–51.

Answer. They were erected by special commandment from God, who prescribed the very form of them and they lace where they must be set, and thereby Moses had a warrant to make them, otherwise he had sinned. Let them show the like warrant for their images if they can. Secondly, the cherubim were placed in the holy of holies in the most inward place of the temple, and consequently were removed from the sight of the people, who only heard of them; and none but the high priest saw them, and that but once a year. And the cherubim without the veil, though they were to be seen, yet were they not to be worshipped.[18] Therefore, they serve nothing at all to justify the images of the Church of Rome.

Objection II.) God appeared in the form of a man to Abraham (Genesis) and to Daniel, who saw the Ancient of Days sitting on a throne.[19] Now, as God appeared, so may he be resembled, therefore (say they) it is lawful to resemble God in the form of a man or any like image in which he showed himself to men.

Answer. In this reason the proposition is false, for God may appear in whatever form it pleases his majesty; yet, it does not follow that man should therefore resemble God in those forms, man having no liberty to resemble him in any form at all, unless he be commanded so to do. Again, when God appeared in the form of a man, that form was a sign of God's presence only for the time when God appeared and no longer, as the bread and wine in the sacrament are signs of Christ's body and blood, not forever but for the time of administration. For afterward they become again as common bread and wine. And when the Holy Ghost appeared in the likeness of a dove, that likeness was a sign of his presence no longer than the Holy Ghost so appeared. And therefore he that would in these forms represent the Trinity does greatly dishonor God and does that for which he has no warrant.

Objection III.) Man is the image of God, but it is lawful to paint a man, and therefore to make the image of God.

Answer. A very cavil, for first a man cannot be painted, as he is the image of God, which stands in the spiritual gifts of righteousness and true holiness. Again, the image of man may be painted for civil or

---

18. Exod 20:4.
19. Gen 18:1–3; Dan 9.

William Perkins 153

historical use, but to paint any man for this end to represent God, or in the way of religion, that we may the better remember and worship God, it is unlawful. Other reasons which they use are of small moment and therefore I omit them.

II.) Difference. They teach and maintain that images of God and of saints may be worshipped with religious worship, especially the crucifix. For Thomas of Watering says, "Seeing the cross represents Christ, who died upon a cross, and is to be worshipped with divine honor, it follows that the cross is be worshipped so too."[20] We on the contrary hold they may not. Our principal ground is the second commandment, which contains two parts: the first forbids the making of images to resemble the true God, the second forbids the worshipping of them, or God in them. In these words, "You shall not bow down to them." Now, there can be no worship done to anything less than the bending of the knee. Again the brazen serpent was a type or image of Christ crucified appointed by God himself, yet when the people burned incense to it, Hezekiah broke it in pieces and is therefore commended.[21] And when the devil bade our Savior Christ but to bow down the knee unto him, and he would give him the whole world, Christ rejects his offer, saying, "You shall worship the Lord your God, and him only shall you serve."[22] Again, it is lawful for one man to worship another with civil worship, but to worship man with religious honor is unlawful. For all religious worship is prescribed in the first table, and the honor due to man is only prescribed in the second table, and the first commandment thereof, "Honor your father," which honor is therefore civil and not religious. Now the meanest man that can be is a more excellent image of God than all the images of God or of saints that are devised by men. Augustine, and long after him Gregory, in plain terms denies images to be adored.[23]

The papists defend their opinions by these reasons.

I.) Psalm 99:5 "Cast down yourselves before his footstool." *Answer.* The words are thus to be read, "Bow at his footstool," that is, at the Ark

---

20. Thomas of Watering is a snarky pun on Thomas Aquinas: Aquinas, *Summa Theologica*, III.25, 4.

21. John 3:14; 2 Kgs 18:4.

22. Matt 4:10.

23. Gregory the Great, "Epistle XIII," in NPNF, 2nd Series, vol. XIII, II.297–98.

and mercy seat, for there he has made a promise of his presence. The words therefore say not, "bow to the Ark," but to God at the Ark.

Objection. II. God said to Moses, "Stand afar off and put off your shoes, for the place is holy."[24] Now if holy places must be reverenced, then must more holy images, as the cross of Christ, and such like.

Answer. God commanded the ceremony of putting off the shoes, that he might thereby strike Moses with a religious reverence, not of the place but of his own majesty, whose presence made the place holy. Let them show the like warrant for images.

III. Objection. It is lawful to kneel down to a chair of estate in the absence of the king or queen, therefore much more to the images of God and of saints in heaven glorified, being absent from us.

Answer. To kneel to the chair of estate is no more but a civil testimony, or sign, of civil reverence, by which all good subjects when occasion is offered show their loyalty and subjection to their lawful princes. And this kneeling being on this manner, and to no other end, has sufficient warrant in the Word of God. But kneeling to the image of any departed saint is religious and consequently more than civil worship, as the papists themselves confess. The argument then proves nothing, unless they will keep themselves to one and the same kind of worship.

III. Difference. The papists also teach that God may be lawfully worshipped in images, in which he has appeared unto men, as the Father in the image of an old man, the Son in the image of man crucified, and the Holy Ghost in the likeness of a dove, etc. But we hold it unlawful to worship God in, by, or at any image, for this is the thing which (as I have proved before) the second commandment forbids. And the fact of the Israelites, in worshipping the golden calf is condemned as flat idolatry, albeit they worshipped not the calf but God in the calf, for verse 5, Aaron says, "Tomorrow shall be the solemnity of Jehovah," whereby he gives us to understand that the calf was but a sign of Jehovah whom they worshipped.[25]

Objection. It seems the Israelites worshipped the calf. For Aaron says, verse 4, "These be your gods, O Israel, that brought you out of Egypt."

---

24. Exod 3:5.
25. Exod 32:5.

Answer. Aaron's meaning is nothing else but that the golden calf was a sign of the presence of the true God. And the name of the thing signified is given to the sign, as upon a stage he is called a king that represents the king. And Augustine says, that "images are wont to be called by the names of things whereof they are images," as the counterfeit of Samuel is called Samuel.[26] And we must not esteem them all as madmen to think that calf made of their earrings, being but one or two days old, should be the God that brought them out of Egypt with a mighty hand many days before.

And these are the points of difference touching images, wherein we must stand at variance forever with the Church of Rome. For they err in the foundation of religion, making indeed an idol of the true God, and worshipping another Christ than we do, under new terms, maintaining the idolatry of the heathen. And therefore have we departed from them, and so must we still do, because they are idolaters, as I have proved.

TEXT: *A GOLDEN CHAIN* (CAMBRIDGE, 1597)[27]

The Negative Part. "You shall neither worship false gods, nor the true God with false worship."

Many things are here forbidden:

I. The representation of God by an image. For it is a lie. Habakkuk 2:18. "What profits the image? For the maker thereof has made it an image and a teacher of lies." Zechariah 10:2, "The idols have spoken vanity." Jeremiah 10:8, "The stock is a doctrine of vanity." The Elvira Council in the 39th canon has this edict, "We thought it not meet to have images in churches, unless that which is worshipped and adored, should be painted upon walls."[28]

...

The image also of the cross and Christ crucified ought to be abolished out of churches as the brazen serpent was, 2 Kings 18:4. Hezekiah is commended for breaking in pieces the brazen serpent to which

---

26. Augustine, *Responses*, II.iii.2 [quoted in O'Daly, *Augustine's Philosophy*, 113].
27. The following excerpts were taken from Perkins, *A Golden Chain*, 44–49.
28. Synod of Elvira, Canon 36.

the children of Israel did then burn incense . . . Some object to the figure or sign, which appeared to Constantine, wherein he should overcome, but it was not the sign of the cross (as the papists do triflingly imagine) but of Christ's name, for the thing was made of these two Greek letters (CHI RHO) conjoined together.[29]

Neither serve the cherubim, which Solomon placed in the temple, for the defense of images, for they were only in the holy of holiest, where the people could not see them. And they were types of the glory of the Messiah, unto whom the very angels were subject, which we have now verified in Christ.

If any man replies that they worship not the image, but God in the image, let him know that the creature cannot comprehend the image of the Creator. And, if it could, yet God would not be worshipped in it, because it is a dead thing, the work of man's hands not of God's, and therefore is more base than the smallest living creature of the which we may lawfully say it is the work of God.

. . .

II. The least approbation of idolatry. Hosea 13:2. "They say one to another while they sacrifice a man, let them kiss the calves." Now a kiss is an external sign of some allowance of a thing. Genesis 48:11.

Therefore it is unlawful to be present at Mass, or any idolatrous service, though our minds be absent. I Corinthians 6:20, "You are bought with a price, therefore glorify God in your body and in your spirits, which are God's." Romans 11:4, "What says the Scripture? I have reserved unto myself seven thousand men, which have not bowed the knee to Baal." Eusebius's third book, "The martyrs, when they were hauled unto to the temple of idols cried out, and with a loud voice in the middle of their tortures testified that they were not idolatrous sacrificers, but professed and constant Christians, rejoicing greatly that they might make such a confession."

That which may be objected of Naaman the Syrian, who worshipped in the temple of Rimmon, is thus answered, that he did it not with purpose to commit idolatry, but to perform that civil obeisance, which he was wont to exhibit to the king's majesty. 2 Kings 5:17, 18.

---

29. Eusebius, *Life of Constantine*, I.22, 25.

And for this cause are utterly forbidden all such processions, plays, and such feasts as are consecrated to the memorial and honor of idols.

All relics and monuments of idols, for these after the idols themselves are once abolished must be razed out of all memory. Exodus 23:13, "You shall make no mention of the name of other gods, neither shall it be heard out of your mouth." Isaiah 30:22, "And you shall pollute the covering of the images of silver, and the rich ornament of the images of gold, and cast them away as a menstruum cloth, and you shall say unto it, 'Get out.'"

III. Society with infidels is here unlawful, serving not only to maintain concord but also to join men in brotherly love. Of this society there are many branches.

The first is marriage with infidels. Genesis 6:2, "The sons of God saw the daughters of men that they were fair, and they took them as wives of all that they liked." Malachi 2:11, "Judah has transgressed and an abomination is committed in Israel, and in Jerusalem, for Judah has defiled the holiness of the Lord, which he loved, and has married the daughters of a strange god." Ezra 9:14, "Should we return to break your commandments and join in affinity with the people of such abomination?" 2 Kings 8:18, "He walked in the ways of the kings of Israel, as did the house of Ahab, for the daughter of Ahab was his wife and he did evil in the sight of the Lord." . . .

IV. Will worship, when God is worshipped with a naked and bare good intention, not warranted by the Word of God. Colossians 2:23, "Which things indeed have a show of wisdom in voluntary religion, and humbleness of mind, and in not sparing the body, neither have they it in estimation to satisfy the flesh." I Samuel 13:9, 10, "And Saul said, 'Bring a burnt offering to me and peace offerings,' and he offered a burnt offering. And as soon as he had made an end of offering the burnt offering, behold Samuel came and (verse 13) said to Saul, 'You have done foolishly, you have not kept the commandment of the Lord your God, which he commanded you.'" Hitherto may we add popish superstitions in sacrifices, meats, holidays, apparel, temporary and bed-ridden prayers, indulgences, austere life, whipping, ceremonies, gestures, gate, conversation, pilgrimage, building of altars, pictures, churches, and all other of that rabble.

...

Lastly, monastic vows, which: I.) are repugnant to the law of God, as that unchaste vow of single life and proud promise of poverty plainly evince, "for he that labors not must not eat," says Paul. II.) They are greater than man's nature can perform, as in a single life, to live perpetually chaste. III.) They disannul Christian liberty and make such things necessary as are indifferent. IV.) They renew Judaism. V.) They are idolatrous, because they make them parts of God's worship and esteem them as meritorious. VI.) Hypocrisy, which gives to God painted worship, that is, if you regard outward behavior, great sincerity, if the inward and hearty affection, none at all. Matthew 15:7, "Hypocrites, well has Isaiah prophesied of you, saying, 'This people comes near to me with their mouths and honors me with their lips, but their hearts are far from me.'" Psalm 10:4, "The wicked man is so proud that he seeks not for God."

...

V. Contempt, neglect, and intermission of God's service.[30] Revelation 3:15, 16, "I know your works, that you are neither cold nor hot. I would you were cold or hot. Therefore, because you are lukewarm, and neither cold nor hot, it will come to pass that I shall spew you out of my mouth."

VI. Corrupting of God's worship, and that order of government, which he has ordained for his Church, which is done when anything is added, detracted or, in any way against his prescript, mangled. Deuteronomy 12:32, "Everything which I command you, that do; neither add to it, nor detract from it." This condemns that popish elevation of bread in the Lord's Supper, and the administration of it alone to the people without wine, together with that fearful abomination of the Mass.

By this we may learn to reject all popish traditions, Matthew 15:9, "In vain do they worship me, teaching for doctrines men's precepts." Now it is manifest that all popish traditions, either on their own nature or other's abusing of them, serve as well to superstition

---

30. A typo in the original text designated this point as "VII" rather than "VI." The subsequent points follow this error. It has been corrected here.

and false worship, as to enrich that covetous and proud hierarchy. Whereas the scriptures contained in the Old and New Testaments are all-sufficient, not only to confirm doctrines, but also to reform manners. II Timothy 3:16, "The whole scripture is given by inspiration of God, and is profitable to teach, to improve, and to correct, and to instruct in righteousness, that the man of God may be absolute, being made perfect unto all good works."

The Romish hierarchy is here also condemned, from the paratour to the Pope. The government whereof is an express image of the old Roman Empire, whether we consider the regiment itself or the place of the Empire or the large circuit of that government. Revelation 13:15, "And it was permitted to him to give a spirit to the image of the beast, so that the image of the beast should speak and should cause that as many as would not worship the image of the beast should be killed."

VII. A religious reverence of the creature, as when we attribute more unto it than we ought. Revelation 22:8, "When I had heard and seen, I fell down to worship before the feet of the angel, which showed me these things. But he said unto me, 'See you do not, for I am your fellow servant.'" Acts 10:25, "As Peter came in, Cornelius met him, and fell down at his feet, and worshipped him. But Peter took him up saying, 'Stand up, for even I myself am a man.'"

If then it be so heinous a thing to reverence the creature, much more to pray unto it, whether it be saint or angel. Romans 10:14, "How shall they call upon him, in whom they have not believed." Matthew 4:10, "You shall worship the Lord your God, and him only shall you serve."

Neither may we pray unto Christ, as he is only man, but as he is God and man, for we direct not our prayers unto the humanity but to the deity to which the humanity is knit by a hypostatical union.

...

VIII. Worship of devils. Magic, which is a mischievous art, accomplishing wonders by Satan's assistance.[31] For it is appropriate to God

---

31. The association between Catholicism and witchcraft seems to have become increasingly popular as the sixteenth century wore on, particularly in the context of

to do miracles, for he alone both beyond and against the course of nature does wonderful things. Now the instruments which God uses in producing miracles are only they who do in the true Church of God make profession of faith.

Albeit the devils cannot work miracles, yet may they effect marvels, or wonders, and that, not by making a new thing, which before was not at all, but rather by moving, transporting, and applying natural things diversely, by causing a thin body as the air to be thick and foggy, and also by bewitching the senses of men.[32]

---

things like religious images. Stuart Clark explains that the comparison "arose from questioning the sense in which specific religious rituals could be said to be efficacious" (Clark, *Thinking with Demons*, 534).

32. This has been thoroughly analyzed in works too numerous to cite here. For an introduction to the figure of the Devil, demonic possession, and demonology in general in the early modern period see Johnstone, *The Devil* and Clark, *Vanities*, 123–53. Perkins's interest in witchcraft was developed in his treatise *A Discourse of the Damned Art of Witchcraft* (Cambridge, 1608).

DOCUMENT 18

William Bishop,
A Reformation of a Catholic Deformed
(English Secret Press, 1604)

INTRODUCTION

Well known for his election to the first titular English Catholic see, as the Bishop of Chalcedon in 1623, William Bishop (c.1554–1624) came from a landed and armigerous family with an estate in Brailes (Oxfordshire). Educated at Oxford, as well as the English Colleges in Rheims and Rome, Bishop eventually earned his doctorate in divinity at the Sorbonne. He was a prominent figure among English Catholic missionaries (being arrested by Protestant officials several times) and was outspokenly opposed to the encroachment of the Jesuits in English matters. In 1598, he lobbied the Pope on behalf of the secular clergy in contention with the Jesuits about the administrative and ecclesiastic framework of the English Catholic communities, and his appointment to the see of Chalcedon is evidence of the eventual secular victory over the Jesuits.[1]

Long before his election, Bishop wrote *A reformation of a Catholicke deformed* (c.1604) in the role of pastor and missionary, contending with William Perkins on several matters of faith and practice. Although it was a polemical pamphlet, Bishop's main motivation seems to have been to provide ammunition for other Catholics, as he explains that readers "shall find . . . the marrow and pith of many large volumes, contracted and drawn

1. Peter Holmes, "William Bishop," ODNB.

into a narrow room."[2] The final topic Bishop addressed was that of images. Although he is balanced and careful in his argument, Bishop is unforgiving with his attacks on Protestants. He refers to Perkins's woolly-headedness ("gone a wool gathering") and suggests the Calvinist theologian is skilled in deception, misleading his "simple" readers by intentionally misusing scriptures. Also, Bishop states that Protestants were like "Jews," the "barbarous Persian Xerxias," and "Mahomet" (Mohammed) in their iconoclasm.[3]

Such references, however, are tangential to his argument's structure which brings together traditional themes of the Catholic discourse, condenses them, and relates them to practical issues of worship and belief. Here, Bishop is adept at turning Protestant arguments and explanations against the reformers. Much like Roger Edgeworth in his rhetorical style, Bishop is willing to concede many points to the Protestants if the concession lends itself to a greater victory. For our purposes here, Bishop's argument has three key points. First, he reemphasizes the preeminence of scriptural and apostolic examples and tradition, although he is selective in this approach, silently passing over the miraculous and supernatural tales of images that were typical in Martiall's *A Treatise of the Cross*. Second, Bishop concedes the point that images cannot properly relate God's essence; however, he follows on by explaining that this is not their purpose. Instead, he argues that images used in devotion should be understood as visual metaphors that depict aspects of God's character and purposes in a comprehensible way. Essentially, images are another means by which God condescends to human limitation and frailty. Finally, Bishop latches on to the distinctions of worship that Perkins described. These distinctions, Bishop responds, confirm the essential Catholic defense of image devotion: that images should be reverenced with appropriate forms of reverence based upon what the image represents.

TEXT[4]

The Difference

Now to the points in controversy, which are three, as Master Perkins delivered. The first is in that the Church of Rome holds it lawful to make images

---

2. Bishop, *A reformation*, 2v.
3. Ibid., 49, 57.
4. Ibid., 45–57. Bishop's text is a typical academic polemic of the day, with large portions of Perkins's writings cut-and-pasted into the pages, in order to create the sense of an academic disputation. Most of these passages can be found in the previous document, so they have been deleted here in order to avoid repetition.

to resemble God, though not in respect of his divine nature, yet in respect of some properties and actions. We contrarily say Master Perkins holds it unlawful to make images any way to represent the true God. For the second commandment says plainly, "Thou shalt not make to thyself any graven image, nor the likeness of anything in heaven, etc."[5] The papists say that the commandment is meant of the images of false gods, but it must needs be understood by the image of the true Jehovah, and it forbids to resemble God, either in his nature or in his properties and works, for so says the Roman catechism upon the second commandment.

Answer

This passes all kinds of impudence to quote the Roman catechism in defense of that opinion which it does of set purpose disprove. It teaches indeed that the very nature and substance of God, which is wholly spiritual cannot be expressed and figured by corporal lineaments and colors and alleged the places produced by Master Perkins to prove that unlawful, yet by and by annexed these words: "Let no man therefore think it to be against religion, and the law of God, when any person of the most holy Trinity is portrayed in such sort as they have appeared, either in the Old or New Testament, etc. But let the pastor teach that not the nature of God but certain properties and actions appertaining to God are represented in such pictures."[6] If the man is not past grace, he will surely blush at such a foul error. His texts of scripture are taken out of the same place of the catechism and prove only that God's proper nature cannot nor may not be resembled in any corporal shape or likeness.

...

Having confuted the Protestants' arguments against the making image to represent some property or action of God, I now come unto Catholic proof of them. The first reason set down by Master Perkins I reserve to the next point. The second is, God appeared in the form of a man to Abraham and to Daniel, "Who saw the Ancient of Days sitting on a throne."[7] Now as God has appeared, so may he be portrayed and drawn. Master Perkins's answer is, not so unless it be expressly commanded by God.

---

5. Margin note: Exod 20.
6. Waterworth, ed., *The Council of Trent*, 234–35.
7. Margin note: Gen 18; Dan 9.

Reply

This first is flat against his own second conclusion, where he holds it lawful to present to the eye in pictures any histories of the Bible in private places. Both the foresaid apparitions be in the Old Testament and therefore may be painted in private places, which cannot be truly done without representing God in the same likeness as there he appeared. And what reason leads in words to represent those actions of God, the same serves to express them in lively colors. Not so says Master Perkins, because when God appeared in the form of a man, it was a sign of God's presence for that time only and for no longer, be it so it might notwithstanding be recorded in writing that the memory of such majesty joined with loving kindness might endure longer. And if it pleased God that this short presence of his should be written to be perpetually remembered, even so the same might be engraved in brass to recommend it to us so much the more effectually. For as the famous poet does by the light of nature sing:

> Segnius irritant animos demissa per aures,
> Quam quae sunt oculis subjecta fidelibus.
> Such worthy acts as by the ears are to the mind conveyed,
> Do move us less than that which is by faithful eye descried.[8]

This argument may be confirmed by the pictures of angels, of virtues, and other such like of spiritual or accidental nature, for if such things as have no bodily proportion or shape may notwithstanding be counterfeit and resembled in some qualities why may not some property or action of God be in like manner represented? That you (Reader) may understand the better what we mean, observe that pictures represent after three sorts. Some express to the quick, the very shape, proportion, and color of the pattern, as the lively picture of man or of any such corporal thing. Others represent things as they did appear and were acted, as if the painter should express the meeting of God with Abraham and his entertainment, he must then resemble God in the same likeness of a man in which he showed himself to Abraham.

Thirdly, an image of a spiritual thing may be drawn not to resemble nature of it, but to lead our understanding by such a similitude into some better knowledge of that thing, so are angels painted like godly young men with wings, to teach us that they are of an excellent, pure nature, ever flourishing and most ready to dispatch with all expedition any employment to which God sends them, and so may God the Father be portrayed, as a

---

8. This passage is from Horace's *The Art of Poetry*, lines 180–81 in Horace, *Satires, Epistles, The Art of Poetry*.

goodly, old grave man, sitting in his throne of majesty, attended upon by millions of angels (as he is described in Daniel 9) to instruct us how he is eternal, infinite, wise, and of most redoubtable majesty. In either of these two latter arts, we hold that God may be represented, and so in the seventh general council, the drawing of the Holy Ghost, in the form of a dove, as he appeared, Matthew 3, is approved.[9]

The first point then being obtained, that such images of God may be made, I come to the second: that all holy pictures may be placed in churches, which I proved by the argument that Master Perkins made for our first objection. In Solomon's temple were erected cherubim, which were images of angels on the mercyseat, where God was worshipped and upon the walls and the very doors of the same pictured. To this Master Perkins answered that they were erected by special commandment from God, who prescribed the very form of them, and the place where they should be set and thereby Moses had a warrant to make them. Let them show the like warrant for their images, if they can.

Secondly, (says he) the cherubs were placed in the most inward place of the temple and so were removed from the sight of the people, and the cherubs without the veil, though they were seen, yet they were not worshipped.

Reply

This man's wits were gone a wool-gathering, when proposing to himself the cherubs erected in Solomon's temple.... For if he had answered directly, he would not have had a word to say, for neither did God prescribe the form of them, nor give any special commandment to Solomon to make and erect any such cherubs, as he that reads the chapter may see, and there they were placed not only in the inward but also in the outward parts of the temple, upon the walls and very doors, that they might be seen by all the people. Which, Master Perkins finding, flitted from thence and did shy unto another, which because it spoke of cherubs, he thought would serve to blind his simple followers.

Moses indeed had an express precept for the making of them, as he had for the curtains and curtain-rods, and every particular belonging to the tabernacle. But Solomon without any special commandment out of his high and holy wisdom understood that he might most lawfully and laudably imitate that heavenly pattern of Moses. And as the building was far more sumptuous and stately, so in the number and quantity of pictures exceeded, which is a sufficient instruction and warrant for all men after his days to

---

9. Matt 3:16.

make and set images in the church. And this finally Master Perkins seems to grant, when he says that these cherubs without the veil were there to be seen, but not to be worshipped, so that we have gotten one step further, that images may not only be made but also set up in the churches.

...

Now I come unto a third point . . . that images may be not only made and set in churches but also worshipped.

Master Perkins holds the contrary, and his principal ground is the second commandment, which contains, says he, two parts. The first forbids the making of images to resemble God; the second, the worshipping of them or God in them, in these words: "Thou shalt not bow down to them."

Answer

If it be only forbidden to make the image of God, and to adore it, then the making and worshipping of the image of Christ, or of any other creature, is not there prohibited. And so this second commandment more than thrice alleged will not serve the turn against any other image but God only. And in plain reason, according also to Master Perkins's own confession, the commandments of the first table touches only our duty towards God, that we give him all his due honor and do not give any part thereof unto anything else whatsoever. Wherefore divine and godly worship is only there spoken of and not such worship as we give unto any creature, or to the picture of it. And consequently, there is nothing there against the worshipping of our holy images.

Observe that there is a sovereign worship due to God, as to the Creator and Governor of all the world, and to give this to any creature is idolatry. Another honor by infinite degrees inferior, yet absolute in itself, is ascribed unto angels and men as creatures endued with reason and made after the likeness of God, and to exhibit this to whom it is due is civility and not idolatry. This honor may be divided into two parts, because these creatures are like to God, as well in their natural powers and qualities as in their supernatural. And that honor which is given to man or angel in respect of any natural quality, may be called moral or civil. But that which is attributed unto them, in regard to their supernatural gifts may well be called religious and spiritual, because it is due unto them only for their spiritual and religious qualities.

There is a third kind of worship, yet meaner than the others, which is a kind of dependent and respective worship, as when a servant is honored or cherished, not for his own but for his master's sake. And this is that worship which we allow unto images, which for the saints' sake whom they represent, we do either reverently regard or take off our hat or bow our knee unto it.

. . .

The third reason proposed by Master Perkins in favor of the Catholics is: it is lawful to kneel down to a chair of estate, in the absence of the king. Therefore much more to the images of God and his saints in heaven glorifying, being absent from us.

To this he answers that it is be a civil worship to kneel to the chair of estate and that very commendable to show our loyalty unto our prince. But kneeling unto the images of saints is religious and therefore not alike.

Reply

He proposes that our argument to the halves, or else this answer had been prevented. For thus runs our reason, as the chair of estate is to be worshipped with civil reverence in respect of the temporal prince, whom it represents, even so the images of holy persons that reign now in heaven are to be worshipped with a holy and religious kind of curtesy. For as temporal honor is due unto a temporal prince, so religious and spiritual honor is due unto spiritual and most holy persons. And as a good subject testifies his loyalty and good affection towards his prince by honoring his regal throne, so does a good Christian give testament of his dutiful, both estimation and devotion toward those heavenly creatures, by giving honor unto their images. At least, why do not the Protestants exhibit civil reverence as well unto the representations of God's saints, as to the shadows of the secular majesty? Unless it be because they are fallen out with the saints of God, and are become adorers of sinful men.

Master Perkins makes a third point of difference, that we may not worship God in any such image, in which he has appeared unto men. In this we do not differ, unless he takes it otherwise then he delivered it. Those images we hold more reverend than any others, as representations nearer approaching unto the divinity, yet because they do not express the deity, God is not directly apprehended nor worshipped in them, but only by collection. For example, the form of a grave old man, in Daniel, does not represent God's person, but we gather by that ancient form God's eternity, whereby we arise to a more perfect conceit of God, whom we adore. Now, other images of Christ and his saints carry our minds directly upon their proper persons, whom in their images we adore and worship unto their degrees. But we worship images with far meaner reverence than any of the saints, in regard only that they represent such persons, and do induce us more to love and honor them, and stir up our dullness more often and ardently to honor God in the saints and the saints in their degrees, as also to imitate their holy example as has been said more than once, that all may understand how far off we are from giving God's honor unto either saint or image. But this point of difference is made to bring in a common argument of theirs, to wit, that the worshipping of the golden calf is condemned as flat idolatry. And yet the Israelites worshipped not the calf but God. The calf, to which we say, they did not worship the true God; the calf, but the gold of the Egyptians, which was taken by them to have the shape of a black calf, with white spots. See St. Augustine.[10] And therefore making the golden calf to represent this false god, and attributing their deliverance unto that supposed god and not unto the God of Israel, committed idolatry, which the text proves most manifest, "these be thy gods brought thee out of Egypt."[11]

---

10. Margin note: *De Civitate*. Augustine, *City of God*, XVIII.5.
11. Margin note: verse 4.

DOCUMENT 19

Robert Bellarmine,
An Ample Declaration
of the Christian Doctrine
(English Secret Press, 1604)

INTRODUCTION

Robert Bellarmine (c.1542–1621) was arguably the most important Roman Catholic theologian in the generation following the Council of Trent. Born to a poor family in Montepulciano, he secured a place at the University of Padua after joining the Jesuit Order. In his career, he was most well known as a Cardinal Inquisitor; however, it is as a systematic theologian (with the publication of his *Disputationes*, a definitive apology of papal authority) that Bellarmine has had a lasting impact upon the Catholic Church.

In English Catholic circles, Bellarmine was a key figure in the debates over James I's oath of loyalty.[1] Also, Bellarmine's influence in England can be seen in the multiple printings of several of his shorter works, including the English translation of his catechism *An Ample Declaration of the Christian Doctrine* (*Dichiarazione più copiosa della dottrina cristiana*). Published in English in 1604, the dialogue format of the *Declaration* was intended as a popular-level explanation of basic Catholic dogma. Although the text does not include anything original or unique to the image debate, it does offer an

---

1. Tutino, *Law and Conscience*, ch. 5.

important example of the kinds of literature that were being secreted to and from small communities of English Catholics still living in England.[2]

While *An Ample Declaration* is not theologically groundbreaking, it does key in upon a few important points. First, Bellarmine emphasizes, perhaps more than any other writer on the image debate, the majesty and authority of the Catholic Church ("there is no danger that she should be deceived"). Secondly, he raises the increasingly important point of physical demonstrations of reverence being offered to images of official status (e.g., kings, bishops, etc.).

TEXT[3]

Ch. 4 The Declaration of the Ten Commandments

Servant: Having now understood the creed and the Pater Noster with the Ave Maria, I desire that you would declare unto me the Ten Commandments of the law of God for that this is the third principal part of the Christian doctrine, as you told me in the beginning.

Master: You have reason to desire to learn and to understand well the ten commandments of the law of God, because that faith and hope without charity and without observing of the law are not sufficient to salvation.

S: What is the cause that, seeing in the world and in the Church there are so many laws and commandments, this law of the Commandments is preferred before all the rest?

M: Many reasons may be alleged concerning the excellency of this law. First, for that this law was made by God and written by himself, first of all in the hearts of men and afterwards in two tables of stone. Secondly, because this is most ancient law of all others and as the foundation of all the rest. Thirdly, because this is most universal law that is to be found, for it binds not only Christians but Jews also and Gentiles, as well the learned as the ignorant. Fourthly, because this law is immutable and cannot be taken away nor dispensed withal by any. Fifthly, because it is necessary to everyone to salvation, as our Lord has often taught us, in his Holy Gospel. Lastly, because it was promulgated with the greatest solemnity on Mount Sinai

---

2. For more on the English Catholic community at home see Questier, *Conversion, Politics and Religion*; Shagan, ed., *Catholics and the 'Protestant Nation'*; Questier, *Catholicism and Community*. Bellarmine's importance was so great that only Aquinas rivalled him in the minds of Protestant polemicists looking for an easy target at which to aim their accusations (Milton, *Catholic and Reformed*, 189–96).

3. Bellarmine, *An ample declaration*, 111–13, 124–30.

with the sound of angelic trumpets, with great thunder and lightning from heaven, in the presence of all the people of God.

S: Before you come to the declaration of the commandments in particular, it would be grateful to me to understand briefly the sum and order of them.

M: The end of all the commandments is the love of God and of our neighbor, for they all teach us not to offend God nor our neighbor, and for this cause they are divided into two parts and were written (as I have already said) in two tables of stone.

. . .

S: I desire to know how the honor which we give to saints and their relics and images is not against this commandment. For it seems that we adore all these things seeing we kneel unto them and pray unto them as we do unto God.

M: The Holy Church is the spouse of God and has the Holy Ghost for her master. And therefore there is no danger that she should be deceived or that she should do or teach others to do anything that were against the commandments of God. And to come to the particular, we honor and call upon saints as friends of God, who can help us with their merits and prayers before him, but we do not take them) for gods, neither adore them as God, neither is it important that we kneel, because this reverence is not proper to God alone, but is done also unto creatures of high dignity, as to the Pope, and in many places religious persons kneel unto their superiors. So that it is no marvel if that be done unto saints who reign with Christ in heaven, which is done unto some men on earth.

S: But what shall we say of the relics of saints, which understand nothing and yet we kneel and pray unto them?

M: We do not pray to the relics which we know well do not understand, but we honor the holy relics as those which have been the instruments of the holy souls to do many good works and shall again in their times be living bodies and are to us in the meantime dear pledges of the love which the saints did and do bare unto us. And therefore we do pray before the same relics unto the saints, desiring them by these dear pledges which we keep of them that they remember to help us as we remember to honor them.

S: The same perhaps may be said of images.

M: So it is, for the images of our Lord, of our Lady, and other saints are not taken by us for gods, and therefore they cannot be called idols, as those were of the Gentiles, but they are held as images, which make us to remember our Lord, our Lady, and other saints. So they serve such as cannot read in place of books.⁴ For that by images they learn many mysteries of our holy faith and the life and death of many saints. And the honor we do unto them, we do it not because they are figures of paper or of metal or because they are well-colored and well made, but because they represent unto us our Lord, our Lady, or other saints, and for that we know that the images do not live nor have sense, being made by the hands of men. We do not demand anything of them, but we pray before them unto those whom they represent unto us, to wit, our Lord, our Lady, or other saints.

S: If relics and images do not understand how then do they work so many miracles to such as recommend themselves unto them?

M: God works all the miracles, but he works them often by the intercession of saints and chiefly of our blessed Lady, and oftentimes he does them unto those who pray unto the saints before their relics or images, and sometimes he uses the relics and images, as instruments of such miracles to show unto us that our devotion towards the saints and towards their relics and images pleases him.⁵

S: When therefore it is said that one is recommended to such relics, or such images, and has received grace, it is to be understood that he is recommended to that saint to whom those relics or images pertain, and that God, by the intercession of that saint and by the means of those relics or images, has done him that grace.

M: So it is, and I am glad that you have well understood all that I have said unto you.

S: I would lastly know for what cause God the Father is painted like an old man and the Holy Ghost like a dove and the angels like young men with wings, seeing God and the angels are spirits and have no corporal figure, which can be drawn by painters as pictures of men may be.

M: When God the Father is painted in the form of an old man, and the Holy Ghost in the form of a dove, and the angels in the form of young men, that which they are in themselves is not painted, because as you have said they are spirits without bodies, but that form is painted in which they have sometimes appeared. And so, God the Father is painted like an old man because he appeared in that form in a vision to Daniel the prophet.⁶ And the Holy Ghost is painted in the form of a dove, because in that form he appeared upon Christ when he was baptized by St. John the Baptist. And the angels are painted in the form of young men for that they have sometimes so

---

4. The argument of laymen's books is one that predates the Reformation (Aston, *England's Iconoclasts*, 130–32; Wandel, *Voracious Idols*, 49–51).

5. This is essentially a restatement of the Council of Trent (Waterworth, ed., *The Council of Trent*, 234–35).

6. This is a reference to the phrase "Ancient of Days" in Dan 7:13.

appeared. Moreover, you are to know that many things are painted to make us understand, not what they are in themselves but what properties they have or what effect they use to work. So it may be said that God the Father is painted in the form of an old man to make us understand that he is most ancient, to wit, eternal and before all created things. And the Holy Ghost is painted in the likeness of a dove to signify the gifts of innocence, purity, and sanctity, which the Holy Ghost works in us. And the angles are painted like young men because they are always fair and full of strength, and with wings because they are ready to pass whither it pleases God to send them, and with white garments and with holy stoles, because they are pure and innocent and ministers of his divine majesty.

DOCUMENT 20

John Heigham,
The Touchstone of the Reformed Gospel
(St. Omer's Press, 1652)

INTRODUCTION

The details of John Heigham's life (c.1568—in or after 1634) are relatively unknown. As a Catholic merchant and printer, Heigham spent some time in Bridewell prison in the 1590s. Afterward, he fled to the English Catholic communities in Douai and St. Omer, becoming a prolific English Catholic printer in the early seventeenth century. Most of the works he printed were reprints of popular Catholic books, intended for a broad readership. Devotionals, primers, and popular polemics were his standard output, and he, at times, was a full-service agent for his English Catholic readership, serving as translator, printer, and bookseller. There is a strong possibility that by the early 1600s he was a smuggler of Catholic books into England, though we have very little detailed record of his whereabouts and activities.[1]

The Touch-stone of the Reformed Gospel, one of his few original works, was first printed in St. Omer (c.1623) under the title *The Gagge of the Reformed Gospel*, with the named author as Matthew Kellison, the president of the English College at Douai. It is unclear why Heigham misrepresented the author (other than for the potential financial benefit of having Kellison's name attached to it) or why the title was changed in subsequent editions. Nevertheless, the *Touch-stone* (or *Gagge*) proved to be an attractive polemic,

---

1. Allison, "John Heigham," 226–32; Paul Arblaster, "John Heigham" ODNB.

as the Protestant hierarchy quickly responded with a sharp polemic rebutting many of Heigham's points (see document 21).

In the text, Heigham argues that images in churches are not "specially" for worship, and that they can and should be used for other purposes (remembering, teaching, etc.). Also, he raises the similarity between images fashioned in words and images fashioned in stone, paint, etc., contesting that "words are signs" as much as images are. If we kneel at the name of Jesus or pay respect to the name of God in any way, that is essentially image worship. Finally, Heigham is so adamant that images are nothing in themselves that he challenges his readers with a unique offer. He writes, "I would before his face break a crucifix ... to satisfy him," the Protestant, that the honor given to the image is not idolatrous.

TEXT[2]

Ch. 49 That It is Not Lawful to Reverence Images

Contrary to the express words of their own Bible, "And he said, 'Draw not nigh hither, put off thy shoes from off thy feet, for the place whereon thou standest, is holy ground.'"[3] How clear a place is here produced against our reformers, wherein an insensible creature was commanded by God himself to be honored. For the refraining to tread upon it was the doing of honor to it. Therefore all dead images, representing unto us a holy thing, may be honored.

Psalm 99:5, "Adore ye the footstool of his feet." Which place is spoken literally of the Ark of the Testament, according to that of 1 Chronicles 28:2, "I had in my heart to build a house of rest for the Ark of the Covenant of the Lord, and for the foot-stool of our God." Now the principal reason why the Ark was worshipped was in regard of the images that were set upon it, which the Jews did worship, as St. Jerome witnessed in his epistle *Ad Marcellam*.[4]

Philippians 2:10, "That at the Name of Jesus, every knee should bow, of things in Heaven and things in Earth and things under the Earth." Now that is the name of Jesus, which either is pronounced in a book or painted and engraved in an image, but at any of these we are commanded to bow the knee.[5]

---

2. The text comes from Heigham, *The Touch-stone*, 123–33.

3. Exod 3:5. Heigham intentionally employs the King James Bible, here, to demonstrate his point.

4. Jerome, "Letter 46," *Letters of St. Jerome*, in NPNF, 2nd Series, vol. VI, 60–65.

5. Behind this reference, there is a larger conflict between Protestants and Catholics

Again, if images ought not to be worshipped we may not (whatsoever the Apostle says) bow our knee at the name of Jesus, seeing words (as Aristotle says, and as the truth is) are signs representative of the things they signify, and are the images of the ears, as the others are of the eyes.[6]

Numbers 21:8, "And the Lord said unto Moses, 'Make thee a fiery serpent, and set it up upon a pole, and it shall come to pass that everyone that is bit when he looks upon it shall live.'" Hence are evidently proved diverse things against our reformers. 1. That God commanded the making of this image. 2. The setting of it up for a sign. 3. He promised that the lookers thereon should assuredly receive succor and help. 4. He warrants the making, the setting up, the beholding, and the reverencing thereof to be exempted from breach of the first commandment, by working so many and so manifest miracles at and before the presence thereof. Therefore an image may be made, may be set up, may be looked on, and reverenced, as Doctor Sanders most learnedly concludes in his *Treatise on Images*.[7]

. . .

Their Third Objection

It is expressly forbidden by God himself to fall down before any image or to worship it.

Answer

Some of our reformers themselves do honor the sacrament of Christ's Supper, which they teach to be an image, or representation, of Christ's body and blood.[8] And seeing they believe no other substance to be in the sacrament, besides bread and wine, nor will give the honor of *latria* (as we give it)

---

over the use of the name of God (in the Tetragrammaton) and the name of Christ in the Holy Monogram (IHS). I have explored it in more detail in Davis, *Seeing Faith*, 99–101.

6. This is likely a reference to Aristotle's *On Interpretation*, sec. I.

7. See document 14.

8. This is an essential, albeit subtle, point that is part of the seventeenth-century polemic. Since the Reformed churches, including the Calvinist-influenced Anglican communion, designated communion as a sign or "token" of Christ's presence, then it is nothing more than an image, and to do it any religious reverence is to commit idolatry, according to the Protestant definition of idolatrous worship. For more on the development of English Protestant theology of the Eucharist in this regard see Wandel, *The Eucharist*, 40–48, 172–76.

thereunto, it follows invincibly that they do worship, or honor, some image. Now, as they would not for all this have us to judge, or call them idolaters, even so, let it please them (for their own sakes) to spare us. For as they do not place or stay this honor in the bread and wine, but from thence refer it to Christ himself, so do we transfer all our honor from all images unto the first form, or pattern, not suffering the same to rest or end in the image which we honor.

Their Fourth Objection

An image is a creature, and no God, and to set up a creature to be worshipped or adored is flat idolatry.

Answer

Images are set up in churches, not specially to the intent that the people should worship or adore them, but partly to stir up our minds to follow the example of those holy men, whose images we do there behold. So that the worship and reverence which is there given to images is given as it were by a consequence and rather because it may be lawfully given than because it is principally sought to be given. As for the idolatry which is objected, we are to understand that the word is compounded of *latria*, and *idolum*, and is as much to say as the giving of *latria* or of God's honor unto an idol. But our images are no idols, nor the honor we give unto them is that of *latria*. How then can it be said that images are set up to be used to idolatry?

Besides, for further eviction of a reformer, that should charge me with idolatry, for reverencing a picture or image, I would before his face break a crucifix, or tear a picture of a saint in pieces and throw the pieces into the fire, and this not out of any contempt or scorn of what the crucifix or picture represents, but to satisfy him, that I gave them only an inferior, relative kind of honor, and used them as helps to my memory. And then would show him the Council of Trent, session 25 in these words, "Images are not to be venerated for any virtue or divinity is believed to be in them, or for anything that is to be petitioned of them, or for any trust, or confidence, that is to be put in them, as the Gentiles did of old, who reposed their hope and trust in their idols, but because the honor that is exhibited to them is referred in the prototype represented by them, etc."[9] Thus for the council. And who can be

---

9. Waterworth, ed., *The Council of Trent*, 234–35.

so ignorant or malicious as to say this is idolatry? That no man has seen God in any form and that therefore his picture or image cannot be made.

Contrary to the express words of their own Bible, Genesis 3:8, where God appeared unto Adam, "walking in the garden of Paradise," in a corporal form. And Genesis 28:12–13, to Jacob, "standing above the ladder," whereon the angels ascended and descended.[10] For we must know that it is only the outward shape and form of the thing, which is expressed either in this or the like image and not the inward substance thereof, which is not possible for any painter or carver to express, which though in express not all that is therein, yet that which it expresses is a truth and that may God be expressed to us. Yea, why may not God be expressed by picture or image in the same form and manner, wherein he has manifested himself to mortal eyes?

Exodus 33:11. God appeared and spoke unto Moses face to face, as one man speaks to another. To the prophet, Isaiah 6:1–5, "sitting upon the throne." To Daniel 7:9, "Sitting, wearing garments, and having hair on his head like pure wool." How then can any wise man doubt, but that, that thing may be lawfully set forth, or expressed, in an outward image, which necessarily must be conceived by an inward?

I Kings 22:19, "I saw the Lord sitting on his throne and all the host of heaven, standing by him on his right and on his left." But perhaps they will say that God commands us to hear his Word and the histories which speak of his apparitions, but not to paint them. I answer that seeing we learn by our eyes, as well as by our ears, there is no reason why that may not be painted before our eyes, which may be preached to our ears. Again, seeing we may find the aforesaid visions and histories in the Bible, why may we not as well see them painted as written in a book of white paper?

---

10. It is possible that this is a reference to pictures of an anthropomorphic figure of God in the Bishops Bible, which contained several woodcuts of God, including one of Jacob's vision (Luborsky and Ingram, *A Guide to English Illustrated Books*, I.124).

Document 21

Richard Montagu,
A Gag for the New Gospel?
No, a New Gag for an Old Goose

(London, 1624)

INTRODUCTION

From a landowning family in Buckinghamshire, Richard Montagu or Montague (c.1577–1641) was educated at Eton College and the King's College, Cambridge. At King's, he became an expert in Greek Patristics, particularly in the works of Basil, John Chrysostom, and Gregory of Nazianzus. In the 1610s, he was one of King James I's main polemicists, writing theological treatises against Cardinal Caesar Baronius. By 1620, through a special dispensation from the king, he held a number of academic and clerical positions simultaneously, including: rector of both Stanford Rivers and Pentworth, canon of Windsor Cathedral, archdeacon of Hereford Cathedral, and fellow of Eton College.[1]

In the 1620s, Montagu became embroiled in the debates and conflicts between puritans and Arminians, having connections to church leaders like Bishops Richard Neile, William Laud, and Lancelot Andrewes, who were at the forefront of the movement of avant-garde conformity and anti-Calvinism.[2] Montagu's first foray into this internal Protestant conflict was a

1. John S. Macauley, "Richard Montague," ODNB.
2. Tyacke, *Aspects of English Protestantism*, 132–59; Tyacke, *Anti-Calvinists*; Lake, *Anglicans and Puritans*.

rebuttal of Heigham's polemic (document 20). In *A Gag for the New Gospel?* (1624), Montagu strikes an important theological note, being both an anti-Catholic response as well as a "clear assault" upon the Calvinist opinions that the pope was the antichrist and that Catholics were not part of the true Christian church.[3] Montagu writes, "Protestant or Papist, English or Roman Catholic, Christian if you be, though to all and any, I intend what I write."

Because of this, he is often read as a tempering and moderate voice in the oftentimes toxic rhetoric of early modern England.[4] Montagu, however, is not without a polemical edge, cutting at his Catholic counterpart with *ad hominem* attacks ("andabatarian fencer") and accusations of plagiarism. Nor is he easy to categorize. On the one hand, Montagu makes an alarming concession that "The pictures of Christ, the blessed Virgin, and Saints may be made, had in houses, set up in churches." Moreover, he reiterates throughout that they should receive a certain reverence, what the Catholics refer to as *dulia*. On the other hand, Montagu echoes Calvin et al. in his insistence that "live" images of humans and the natural world are preferable to stocks and stones. Also, he denounces the belief that the cross or any other image should receive the worship that is owed to God alone. Finally, he refutes Heigham's suggestion that words of God's name and images of God are essentially the same ("names pronounced are but transient, and names painted are not images").

TEXT[5]

Ch. 43 That It is Not Lawful to Make or to Have Images

Those that held it so unlawful mean that it is not lawful for men, of themselves, out of their own voluntary motion to make them. They never intended that God could not dispense with his own mandate or a man might not make them at his command. That text, Exod. 25:18, therefore does not contradict the opinion of those such proposers. For God there commands it to be done by special warrant, and in a retired and reserved place. So, this place, though express, is not to purpose. Nor that of 1 Kings 6:35, which was done by warrant of the former direction, and according to pattern in that direction Solomon did, as Moses was commanded, make cherubim in the holiest place.

---

3. Milton, *Catholic and Reformed*, 112.
4. Milton and Walsham, eds, "Richard Montagu," 69–102.
5. The excerpts here have been taken from Montagu, *A Gag*, 299–319.

But the truth is this andabatarian fencer fights with his own shadow.[6] No Protestant ever said that it was unlawful to make or to have images.[7] No Protestant but has, or has had in his house, closet, study, or the like, pictures and images, many or few. That which Protestants mislike and condemn in papists, is not the having, but adoring and worshipping of images; the giving them honor due unto God, as the ignorant do, that go to it bluntly and downright; the giving them the honor due unto the prototype, as the learned among them persuade unto: as much honor to a wooden crucifix as to Christ Jesus himself in Heaven, at the right hand of his Father. This they mislike.[8]

This is no divine ordinance, but a prohibition to do it, a curse upon the maker and adorer of it. St. Paul called among other things in the first tabernacle, those cherubim, we spoke of but now, divine ordinances, and so do we.[9] It is an impudent slander that Protestants call those cherubim idols. Those images which the Protestants call idols are images made, abused to adoration in the Church of Rome. Does he that calls the image of our Lady of Lauretto an idol call the picture of Baronius, or Bellarmine, idols?[10]

. . .

See more, you say, 1 Kings 7:36, 42, 44; Numb. 21:8, etc., and do so, reader, and you shall see so many testimonies of malice, of ignorance, of collusion. Never man thought, much less ever said, that painting and carving of pictures was idolatry, but lawful trades, excellent skills, sciences, not infused, but given by God to the use of man, the glory of God's name, the commendation of the parties therewithal endowed. Images have three uses assigned by your schools. Stay there, go no further, and we charge you not with idolatry. *Institutionem rudium, commonefactionem historiae, et excitationem devotionis*, you and we also give unto them.

See fathers that affirm the same. What do they affirm? This man cannot tell, for he knows not what, nor where they affirm. He sends us to Tertullian in his second book *De Pudicitia*. The poor ignorant that talks of fathers

6. A reference to John Heigham (although Montagu believes he is speaking of Matthew Kellison). An "andabatarian" fights blind or blindfolded.

7. Perhaps the exception to this may be more radical reformers like Andreas Karlstadt (Eire, *War Against the Idols*, 55–65) or puritans in the seventeenth century (Spraggon, *Puritan Iconoclasm*).

8. This is a reference to the Thomist tradition of giving the crucifix the worship and devotion due to Christ (Aquinas, *Summa Theologica*, III.25, 4).

9. Heb 9:5.

10. Interestingly, this argument will be turned around in document 20 to point out that Protestants make images of their own heroes of the faith.

knows not that there is but one book of Tertullian of that argument and title, and lo, he sends us to see the second book. It is well he told us not in what chapter we might find it. Such roters[11] as these are the men that talk of Fathers among their gossips and proselytes; and yet are so stupid as not to know what works a common Father has written.

. . .

But I can send him to Tertullian, to learn how like a woodcock he remembered those texts of Scripture, for the cherubim. *Sic et cherubim et seraphim aurea, in arcae figuratum exemplum, certe simplex ornamentum, accommodata suggestui, longe diversas habendo causas ab idolatriae conditione, ob quam similitudo prohibetur, non videntur similitudinum prohibitarum legi refragari, non in eo similitudinis statu deprehensa, ob quem similitudo prohibetur.*[12] This comes home to the reason why God ordained them, and answers your cavil to the full. As for your images, take this description in the like, *Igitur si statuas et imagines frigidas mortuorum suorum simillimas non adoramus, quas milui, et mures et araneae intelligunt, nonne laudem magis quam poenam merebatur repudium agniti erroris?*[13] He thought not then very honorably of images, whom we are bid go see, for I know not what, engraving on the chalices.

. . .

What Basil and Nazianzen could not do, Augustine supplies, who witnesses that "in his time Christ was to be seen painted in many places, between St. Peter and St. Paul."[14] So is he in many churches with us, between the blessed Virgin and St. John the Evangelist. So was the holy Virgin by St. Luke, you say. So let them be everywhere, if you please. Not the making of images is misliked, not the having of images is condemned, but the prophaning of them to unlawful uses, in worshipping and adoring them.

. . .

11. A reference to rote memorization.
12. Tertullian, *Against Marcion*, II.22 in ANF, vol. III, 314.
13. Tertullian, *Apology*, in ANF, vol. III, 28.
14. The previous section, which has been removed here, contains a wordy statement essentially claiming that neither Basil nor Naziazen make a definitive statement on Christian imagery. Eusebius, *The Church History*, in NPNF, 2nd Series, vol. I, VI.18; Augustine, *City of God*, XIV.28.

Ch. 45 That It is Not Lawful to Worship Images

Two several questions, as often confusedly propounded in one proposition, which are of different natures of unequal extents, of diverse and disparate approbation. The latter, that "it is not lawful to give any honor to any dead or insensible thing," is a false imputation cast upon us, a horrible lie against common sense, refelled[15] in ordinary practice of Protestants who give honor and respect, though not adoration to many dead and insensible things, as this fellow living in a Protestant state cannot choose but know unless with Bartimaeus "we were born blind" and withal have continued deaf from his mother's womb.[16]

This he cannot prove by express words that we deny nor yet any consequence thereupon. It is contrary he tells us for fashion sake unto the express words of our own Bible. What is distinct assertions, not of necessary consequences or dependence; and so, not necessarily inferred one upon the other. Besides, where is that express place of our Bible, which is contrary to the assertion? This place was forgotten through too much haste. I will supply the defect and design the place which the man intended when he passed over it.

Exod. 3:5, Joshua 5:15, "Take off your shoes from your feet, for the place whereon you stand is holy ground." This may prove that at some time by special precept, upon some occasion, some insensible thing may be honored, which no Protestant ever went about to deny; but, the inference they do, and most justly may, as having no reason of illation: "Therefore an image, representing unto us a holy thing, may be worshipped," say, and not honored. For, of honor, we contend not; our difference is about worship only.

But take it of honor, and see the handsome consequence. God said, "Some ground was holy," therefore all images may be worshipped. What an image of rye dough is this cods-head![17] To as good sense it might be spoken, Jerusalem was called the holy city; therefore, the Jews might worship images. Or, the Temple was a holy place. None but Israelites, and those also clean, might enter there. The priests and Levites washed their feet, being to do service there; all common people wiped the dust from their feet when they entered therein.[18] Therefore, Ahaz might erect his altars there. Manasseh prophaned it with idolatry. Antiochus set up the abomination of

---

15. Disproved
16. A reference to blind Bartimaeus: Mark 10:46–52.
17. A fool
18. Exod 30:18–21.

desolation there. Had not the beast cause to low[19] thus: "Lo how clear a place is commanded by God himself to be honored, for the refraining to tread upon it was the doing of honor to it?"[20]

Of honor be it, but not worship. Honor and worship differ more than *latria* and *dulia* do. Without sense, I grant, and life too. The Earth has neither life nor sense. The Earth was made to tread upon. . . . Honor was done, not worship, and not to the place, but to the holy place. The place was holy not in itself, not made so by man, but from the personal presence of the Most High. Make an image so holy, and then so honor it. This honor was not (you were asleep, man) in refraining to tread upon the earth. For, where did Moses and Joshua stand when they talked with God? In the air or nowhere? Or in the fifth imaginary body? But the honor was, in refraining to tread on it with their shoes, as when men come into the church, they uncover the head at their entrance into the church.

And for the honor in kind or correspondence, what similitude between that and yours, to an image? You fall down unto an image, at least, before it. You honor the image with the same honor that the representee is honored withal, at least accidentally in your relative worship. Did Moses and Joshua so honor the ground? Did they fall down unto it? Did they put their shoes off to it? For the ground's sake, and not rather for the presence of God there; whom, without any relative worship at all, they honored immediately in himself? Anything, I see, will serve a priest's turn. No matter what you prate, so that you prattle. Happy men that have so pliant proselytes that so easily believe whatsoever is told them, though it be a tale of a tub.[21]

There is a respect due to all the works of God, as good, as his, as arguing the art and excellency of the Maker. So all of them are honorable in their kinds. Do you therefore adore them? Make them images, as well you may, and far rather than a carved piece of wood? By them give relative honor unto God? This you cannot digest by any means, for, then your idolomania in images, with stocks and stones, were clean dashed. And yet, if dead and insensible things are to be honored, you cannot avoid the sequel, do you what you can: live things may be much more honored.

Upon the same ground, we are sent "to adore the footstool of his feet."[22] This is as common in your mouths for adoration, as ergo with boys in the schools, as if an image was God's footstool, and so must be worshipped.

---

19. The sound a cow makes

20. 2 Kgs 16; 21; 1 Macc 1:20–51.

21. A "tale of a tub" refers to any apocryphal tale; or, more derogatorily, it is a fantastical tale full of lies.

22. Ps 99:5.

Indeed, an image may be for him to trample and tread under foot, as he will do, in just anger, the image and the adorer of the image that gives his glory to a stock, a stone.

...

The Jews worshipped images upon the Ark. That is no warrant for you to do so; nor yet to take it as a precedent. They worshipped Balaam and the hosts of heaven, Milcom and Molech. Will you do the like? They burned their children in the valley of Hinnon. Would you be contented to be served so? I would I had the power to dress you so, to make you low a little louder, out of that bull. Such a wise collection as this, "Because there were images upon the Ark," and because the Jews worshipped those images, therefore the prophet took up that admonition, "Adore the footstool, etc."

...

From images, too, I cannot tell what to give unto it, but it is, the name of Jesus, somewhat strangely carried unto adoration. Phil. 2.10, "That at the name of Jesus every knee should bow, of things in Heaven, things in Earth, and of things under the earth." Upon which premises the conclusion is, therefore images are to be worshipped. So the name of Jesus is become an image. A strange kind of image to my understanding, that a man's name should be his images. *Imago* is quasi *imitago*, you say, which is not, says Sander, with Vasquez approbation, any similitude whatsoever, but only that which is expressed to represent the thing, as the picture of a long-eared beast does an ass. Jesus printed, or painted on a wall, is no image of our Savior, much less the word pronounced, conveyed to the ear, which at least is, if not the entire, yet principal meaning of St. Paul, "Names are notes of things."[23] But names pronounced are but transient, and names painted are not images. Your bottle-ale-wife called you so much, that a bottle is not the image of a bottle, and your baker, that his basket is no representation of himself. But to point. Your undertaking is for express words in our Bibles. What expressness in bowing the knee at the name unto an image made of what you will have it? Beside the name of Jesus is so far from being expressed to prove it, that it is not resolved what is meant by the name of Jesus here.

...

In the brazen serpent there is more resemblance. It may be warrant for making an image, no warrant for worshipping an image made, nor for

---

23. 1 Cor 3:5.

making ordinarily, because that was made by special direction to a special end, against a general practice, "You shall not make any graven image." God may so dispense with his own Law, where, when, in what sort, and to whom he will, but we cannot.

The first observation then, out of this text against the Protestant, that God commanded the making of his image, is idle. Never Protestant made question of it, nor of the second, that it was set up for a sign. Nor the third, that the lookers upon it should receive health. Nor the fourth, of exempting the practice commanded, from the breach of the first commandment. These they confess, they plead, and bid you show the like for your images, for making, erecting, beholding, reverencing any image of God, or saints in this sort, and they yield.

To conclude, no text of scripture expressly says, nor by consequence infers, that ever images were worshipped with countenance or commendation from God, or any holy man of scripture. St. Ambrose says no such thing as is pretended, that images lawfully may be worshipped. He says, "Whosoever crowns the emperor's statue, crowns the emperor, in other words, honors him," and whosoever dishonors the emperor's statue, dishonors him.[24] What then? Whosoever dishonors God's image, dishonors him. I grant. And what of that? Therefore, honor is to be given to some images. No man denies it. Therefore all images are to be worshipped. Away with that; no such consequence follows. Honor is one thing, *dulia*, if you will. *Latria* is another. First, what is God's image? Then, how far God's image? Then, what honor is due unto God's image? And lastly, whether the honor given is not more, or other, honor than is due unto an image?

St. Augustine in his third book of *De trinitate* names the brazen serpent expressly in the rank of such things, as *Honorem tanquam religiosa possunt habere*.[25] And so do we, and many things of that nature, as the sacraments of the church. . . . This place of St. Augustine is to no purpose, for there is not a word of images there.

St. Gregory is of later date than St. Augustine, and of less credit by much in controverted questions. Images in his time were much improved, and yet not unto adoration. Honor, reverence, and respect was given them, to be books for the simple and ignorant people, to be remembrances of things by representation. Hold you here, and we blame you not. As for Damascene, he was a child, in respect of those heroes of the church . . . yet he said no more (though what he said cannot be proved) than that the honoring of images was an apostolic tradition. You, or Damascene, prove this,

---

24. Ambrose, "Epistle XVII," NPNF, 2nd Series, vol. X, 411–17.
25. Augustine, *On the Trinity*, III.10.

and I yield. I marvel that none ever said so before Damascene, who yet had good occasion to avow it, if it had been so.[26]

...

Images and idols may be two things. These prophane and impious, never tolerable; those not unlawful, and sometimes profitable, especially resemblances of stories. Images were unlawful unto the Jews, even the very ordinary and civil use and making of them, except by special warrant, in some place, as in the temple upon the Ark. ... Unto Christians they are not unlawful for civil uses, nor utterly in all manner of religious employment. The pictures of Christ, the blessed Virgin, and saints may be made, had in houses, set up in churches.[27] The Protestants use them, they despise them not. Respect and honor may be given unto them. The Protestants do it and use them for aids in piety, in commemoration, and more effectual representing of the prototype. But *quatenus*?[28] In terms there is not much difference you say they must not have *latria*. So do we. You give them *dulia*. I quarrel not with the term, though resemblance, monuments of great men, friends, good men, saints, and Christ. If this you call *dulia*, we give it too. But whatsoever you say, howsoever you qualify the thing with gentle words, we say that in your practice you far exceed and give them that honor which is *latria*, part of divine respect and worship. We do not. Let practice and doctrine go together, we agree. So that the question is not: what may be given them? But, what is given them? You must then change the state, and prove that what you do is not any way, any jot or part of, divine honor, but merely civil respect, *dulia*. This you cannot do, so long as your people go to it with downright adoration, and your new schools defend that the same respect is due unto the representee, as must be given to the represented. So that the crucifix is to be reverenced with the self-same honor that Christ Jesus is. A blasphemy not heard of until Thomas Aquinas set it on foot.[29] Clear these enormities and others like these, then come and we may talk and soon agree concerning honor and respect unto relics and images of saints, or Christ. Until then, we cannot answer it unto our Maker, to give his honor unto a creature.

---

26. This is a general reference to the work of John of Damascus (Louth, ed., *Three Treatises*).

27. While the figure of the Virgin continued to play a role in Protestant faith, the reference to the saints here is quite unique in the context of religious imagery.

28. To what extent

29. Aquinas, *Summa Theologica*, III.25, 4.

DOCUMENT 22

Anonymous, "Controversii et compendium Becari" (1625)

INTRODUCTION

This anonymous letter from a Catholic to his Protestant cousin is a rare document in early modern England. While Protestants and Catholics communicated with one another, many even had amiable and friendly relationships, it is unique to find two people on opposing sides of the religious divide expressing their beliefs and opinions to one another in such a private context.[1]

The letter is dated May 1625 and is written by a single hand (both the text and the marginal notes). The letter contains several of the author's own deletions and additions to the text, and while it is not evident that this was a rough draft, there is no evidence that the letter was ever sealed or delivered.[2]

The Catholic author explains the use of religious images (particularly the cross), defending the tradition set out by the Second Council of Nicea (787). Writing to his Protestant "cosen," the author delivers a letter peppered with personal sentiments alongside a reiteration of many of the themes and arguments already seen in this collection.[3] Although it is short on

---

1. A more extensive introduction, along with speculations over the authorship, can be found in Davis, "'The meanes of justification,'" 288–311.

2. I am grateful to Heather Wolfe, Curator of Manuscripts at the Folger Shakespeare Library, for her insight and comments about the condition of the manuscript.

3. Aston, *England's Iconoclasts*, 173–94.

much personal detail, both author and reader clearly have a long-standing relationship, and their ongoing "correspondence" suggests an association that is friendly and familial.

The year 1625 was a pivotal one in English religion, as the death of King James ushered in the reign of his son Charles I. Also, in 1625, the plague returned to London wreaking havoc and highlighting the latent social and religious tensions within the capital. The Thirty Years War on the continent was tugging at English loyalties, which would soon draw the country into defending the Huguenot cause. Charles I's new Catholic wife Henrietta-Maria of France would arrive in London in June, inflaming worries about England's future religious views. Finally, an anti-Catholic pamphlet campaign, unleashed by puritans and Calvinists, had been in full swing since the early 1620s.[4] It is telling that even amid such turmoil, the role of images in worship continued to present important talking points that Catholics and Protestants believed to be critical dividing lines.

In the letter, the author challenges the justification of Protestant iconoclasm, employing various lines of argumentation, particularly the use of images in scripture and in the early Church. He nuances the traditional Catholic argument, avoiding sources that emphasize the miraculous tales of the cross (employing Ambrose rather than Eusebius to convey the story of St. Helen's finding of the true cross). Also, he explains that "neither do all Catholic doctors approve St. Thomas his doctrine" on the crucifix, which allows the author to argue that the Catholic Church is not dogmatic in its view of images. Secondly, the letter exposes certain Protestant duplicities (or inconsistencies) in attacking Catholic images on the one hand and producing images (e.g., the sign of the cross during baptisms, woodcuts, and engravings) on the other. Furthermore, while Catholic prostration before images and relics was condemned, Protestants bowed before images of the monarchy. Third, the letter attacks the linchpin doctrine of *sola scriptura*, arguing that the numerous linguistic mistranslations in Protestant Bibles amounted to a crisis of authority. If the Protestant scriptures are neither accurate nor always interpreted consistently, then what authority can they rely upon to provide absolute truth?

---

4. A great deal has been written on English religion and politics in the early seventeenth century, leading up to the Civil War. For a representative sample see Milton, *Catholic and Reformed*; Cogswell, *The Blessed Revolution*; Tyacke, *Anti-Calvinists*; Lake, *Anglicans and Puritans*.

Text

Dear Cousin,

I have your letter of the 14th of March and must entreat you that in this our paper correspondence, (which heretofore you seemed so earnestly to desire) I may not perceive your pen so passionate, your will so perverse, or your judgment and learning so shallow, as to use such discourteous terms in your writings as may seem to tax either me, or my Christian profession, with such heinous crimes as palpable idolatry which before you and I do part this time may perhaps with more show of probability light on your own shoulders, or on the prime professors of Protestant religion, if they stand to their grounds and erroneous principles, and not forsake them with shame and confusion.

You profess that you must importune me to satisfy you in one point of the Romish religion and the point (say you) is that which quite subverts religion, even palpable idolatry. I pardon this and the like your unmannerly language for this once, and taking no exception at your words will accept of your true meaning, which as I gather is to be satisfied of the practice of our Church, how it can be defended from error in these praises and prayers that in her hymns, and some part of her office, seem to you (if you understand either grammar or logic) as given and made to the very material cross it sees.

For answer (dear cousin) do but add the knowledge which I suppose you have in rhetoric, to your skill in the other to aforesaid, with some few scraps of true divinity; and, questionless, you may, without any of those tergiversations, or quaint evasions which you fear be easily satisfied, if you be really so desirous, and not disposed to cavil with disputes.

The *ara crucis* which you cite is not to be found in any Roman breviary, that ever I have read or met with. These other pieces of hymns and prayers, which you do authentically produce, are either *prosopopeias* made to the material cross in such manner as Moses spoke to the material heavens when he said *Audite caeli quae loquor*, etc., or if they be real prayers (as some of them are) they be (by the figure *metonymia*) directed to Christ represented and comprised under the name of the cross, in such likewise as the prophet Isaiah prayed to the true God that governs in heaven, and not to the material heavens, when he said even in prose *Rorate caeli desuper,* and *nubes pluant justum*.[5] Of when, though guided in his words by the Holy Ghost, you might have asked this same question you ask me. Why he spoke not more plainly?

---

5. Margin note: Isaiah 45; Isaiah 8. *Rorate coeli* was a popular phrase sung in the Mass. They are the opening words from Isa 45:1: "Drop down dew, ye heavens, from above, and let the clouds rain on the just."

As also you may ask St. Paul assisted in his writings by the same Holy Spirit, when he so often mentioned the name of the cross, when he thereby means signified Christ? As when he called the blessed blood that did redeem us, "The blood of the cross,"[6] and when he speaks of "The persecution of the cross,"[7] which materially taken, as it has no blood to shed, so can it not really suffer, being senseless of any persecution that enemies can raise against it. But a rabble of your own, Dr. Reynolds, will answer you for St. Paul, and tell you (if I be not much deceived) that (your example) after a figurative manner of speech by the cross meant Christ crucified.[8] Neither is any spark or special point of his puritanical conceits, but the approved canonical doctrine of your own Protestant congregation in her printed and public canons. The Holy Ghost (says the 30th canon) by the mouths of the apostles did honor the name of the cross so far, that under it they comprehended not only Christ crucified, but the force, effects, and merits of his death and passion, etc.[9] The honor and dignity of the name of the cross begat a reverent estimation, even in the apostles' times, of the sign of the cross. By this figurative comprehending of Christ under the name of the cross (whereof your own church acknowledges the Holy Ghost for author) you may, I know, easily understand the true sense as well of the prayers, as of the praises and speeches that seem by our Church to be uttered or ascribed to the material cross; especially if you be mindful of the other figure, aforesaid *prosopopeia*, when the speech cannot with propriety be applied to the person of Christ, in the cross represented. And if you take but pains to peruse and ponder the words which St. Ambrose uses to and of the cross you may easily perceive that the seeming praises and *prosopopeias* now used to the cross by the present Roman Church are no such profane novelties or palpable idolatries as Crashaw and others of your preachers have made you believe.[10] Where you may also observe that St. Ambrose says St. Helen, that she did wisely advance the cross to be on the heads of kings, that the cross in kings might be adored.[11] In whose Christian crowns was reverenced, as you may know, not that real cross whereon Christ did suffer to redeem us, but the sign of the cross, which your own canons do confess to have had reverent estimation

6. Margin note: Col 1:20; Phil 3:18.

7. Gal 6:13.

8. Rainolds, *De Romanae*, VIII.412–13.

9. The Church of England canons of 1604 affirmed the use of the cross and the sign of the cross in baptism: *Constitutio[ns]*, sigs. G1r–G1v.

10. It is unclear to which of William Crashaw's sermons the author is referring. But a good contender can be found in Crashaw, *The sermon*, 84.

11. Ambrose's "Oration on the Death of Theodosius I" can be found in Ambrose, *Ambrose of Milan*, 197–204.

even in the apostles' times. And shall now think you, the prating of your new preachers prevail so much with prudent men, as to persuade them, quite contrary to the confessed practice of those primitive times to become so profane as to allow this sacred sign no kind of reverence or honor at all? What kind of reverence, estimation, or honor is to be given to a cross representing Christ, or to his holy image is not so clearly defined by any decree, or canon of our Catholic Church, but that learned men are free to dispute the question. Neither do all Catholic doctors approve St. Thomas [Aquinas] his doctrine, or manner of speaking in this matter, as you must needs know, if you be so conversant in our schoolmen and controversial writers, as you pretend; yea, speaking absolutely and properly, most of them say with the seventh synod that *vera latria* is not to be given to the cross or image of Christ.[12] And those that (after a sort) would have *latria* given to the cross are far enough from honoring the same as they know God, or Christ our redeemer, for to Christ they give λατρεία as due to himself *ratione propriae excellentiae*, as to their supreme lord and mighty Creator; but to the cross being but a senseless creature, there give it not as due to itself or for it sees to rest their; but to be conveyed or transported through the cross to Christ their God and Creator, to whom it is wholly and only due, for his own most proper dignity. In such a sense as your parishioners[13] (if you be a Parson lawfully possessing an ecclesiastical benefice) may give the tithe (that is due only to you) to your man, who hath the office to gather them for you; of when you cannot with any reason complain, that in so doing they give your due to another; because they give it to him, but for your use; and not as having any tithe thereunto of his own. And (to give you an example in a higher key) so the very Crown of this realm which is the most supreme ensign of regal authorities, and due now, by right, only to our gracious King Charles (whom God long preserve) may notwithstanding, on the coronation day, without any prejudice to the right be given to the prelate whose office it is to crown his majesty, not to the end that the prelate may enjoy, or keep it for his own use; but to lay it on the sacred head of our foresaid sovereign to whom by right it only belongs.

And that even St. Thomas himself would have λατρεία (wherewith according to St. Thomas, Christ in his cross ought to be adored) a double respect, the one towards Christ; the other towards his cross, which art as it respects the cross, there will not have so much as to be named λατρεία, no more than the act of charity wherewith you relieve your neighbor's beast

---

12. Second Council of Nicea (or Seventh Ecumenical Synod), 787 AD.

13. Margin note: *si parvis liceat componere magna*. Translation: "if it is permissible for humble people to have an understanding of great things."

out of a ditch, or some other distress may be termed charity in respect of the beast or the act of villainy that kills a man willfully in the very church, which that very and prophanes, but must have some other name as the prophanation of the church or the like; and it to be called murder only in respect of the man willfully killed. So (say these men) the same act of *latria* that jointly honors Christ and his cross ought not to be called *latria* in respect of the cross, but as it respects Christ for whose sake and for whose dignity and title it is given to the cross, that does represent him.

All the seeming difficulty that can remain in this point is whether the nature of an image or any other dead and senseless thing (as the cross) represents unto us a living person be (according to the common concert of people) transform the honor that is given thereunto to the part it represents. In which point, omitting all other proofs, I appeal but to the practice of your own profession. The best noblemen of the land are bare (as you know) in the presence chamber at court, and how to the stool or chair of state as they bass by, doing reverence also to the royal sword or other ensigns of regal authority. I have seen with my eyes the lord deputy of Ireland Sir William FitzWilliams, being an earnest Protestant, bowing down to the ground to the picture of Queen Elizabeth, before he would turn his back to the same as he sat at his table.[14] And my own ears, in Westminster Hall, have heard it objected (as a heinous crime) Sir John Perrot at his arraignment that he called the royal sword, "A paltry sword."[15] Therefore the axiom of antiquity is current even according to your own principles and practice, that the honor or dishonor done to a picture or any other dead and senseless thing passes to the living party whose person it represented. Will you then have liberty and hold it lawful to honor the crown, sword, or stool of an earthly prince and bar us from honoring the king of heaven his crown of thorns or that gracious throne of our redeemer, the cross, being also the happy sword or instrument wherewith he conquered the kingdom of hell, and crushed the crooked serpent's crafty pate. Will you needs bow with reverence to the dead picture of a temporal Queen and rail at us for doing reverence to the image of Christ? Perhaps you will say that you give but civil reverence to those dead things, and that we to ours do give a respect that seems religious. At least that does convince all those to be rude and most uncivil that abuse or bow not with civil reverence to the cross and picture of Christ. But I reply besides that the foresaid difference of will and religious

---

14. The commentary on Fitzwilliam, here, is intriguing, since he was a prominent figure in Anglo-Irish politics, most significantly in his opposition to the Earl of Essex's campaign in Ulster, and he was well connected at the Elizabethan court: Mary Ann Lyons, "Sir William Fitzwilliam," *ODNB*.

15. The Perrot case has been studied in Turvey, *The Treason*.

proceeds from the diversity of the persons represented; for if there were any reverence or honor higher than civil due to an earthly prince, where he were in person present, the same might well be defended to be due unto him where he was but represented. And you yourselves do, I know, give your dead Bible a religious kind of reverence when you do solemnly kiss the book in swearing,[16] according to that exhortation of your great patriarch Martin Luther, of the scripture,

Hanc ne divinam Æneida tenta sed vestigia pronus adora.[17]

And you hope to be saved by the contents of that book or at least by your faith in Christ Jesus and yet use to pray neither to your faith nor to your book, therefore if I should grant that we do trust and hope for salvation by the cross as by the instrument of our redemption you may not well infer (as you seem to do) that then we may pray thereunto. And this much may suffice to have been said for a probable defense of that doctrine which you dislike in St. Thomas, though as yet it be not by the church so clearly defined.

What we firmly believe (as decided already) of honoring the image of Christ (and the like is to be understood of a cross that represents him). Bellarmine does thusly briefly deliver *Nos cum ecclesia asserimus imagines christi et sancto honorandas esse, modo tamen (ut in concilio Tridentino sess. 25 declaratur) in imaginibus non collecetur fiducia, nec ab eis aliquid petatur* (Then is it no point of the Roman profession to pray unto them) *nec in eis in esse credatur illa divinitas, sed solum honorentur propter eos quos nobis representant.*[18] Supposing with solid doctrine of Bellarmine's with his own declaration thereof (in that 21st chapter which you refer me unto) in these words, *Ad primam dico imagines sive honorentur proprie sine per se, sine per accidens, semper honorari propter prototypon, et semper honore earum transire ad exemplar.* And in the 19th chapter of the same second book acknowledging *imaginem non esse capacem honoris propter se et ideo imagines non honorari absolute sed relative ad prototypum.*[19] Supposing I say all this his solid doctrine I can see nothing in these two chapters of his (which you require me to read) so worthy of reprehension, or that should be enough

---

16. For Protestant veneration of scripture see Rublack, *Reformation Europe*, 158–60.

17. The author misquotes this phrase. The text—a supposed last phrase from Martin Luther on his deathbed—actually reads: *Hanc tu ne divinam. Aeneida tenta, sed vestigia pronus adora.* Translation: "Do not assail this divine *Aeneid*; rather adore the ground that it treads." For further reference to Luther's use of classical works and this quote see Michelet, *The Life of Luther,* 241.

18. Bellarmine, *Disputationes,* II.12.

19. Here, the author refers somewhat indirectly to the Council of Trent: Waterworth ed., *The Council of Trent,* 234–35.

(as you say) to make a modest papist blush. When you please to express the particulars I will press him again albeit I hold myself no more obliged to defend and maintain every point of Bellarmine's doctrine, than you to make good every particular passage in Luther or Calvin, which would puzzle you much to go about to perform. In the meantime tell me ingenuously, whether a modest Protestant has not more cause to blush on in your behalf of their brethren or fathers, the prelates of their church, who rudely suppressing and often irreligiously abusing the picture of Christ have the face not withstanding to permit their own practices or their brethren to set out in public view to be respected with such blasphemous praises annexed thereunto in print, of the persons represented as this that which follows in particular, expressed by a fair brazen stamp (like the face that did it) under the image or picture of Dr. Gervase Babington, Bishop of Worcester, and printed in the frontispiece or first leaf of his work AD 1622 and to be sold at the three pigeons[20] in Paul's churchyard.[21]

> *Non melior, non integrior, non cultor alter.*
> *Vir, Presul, Praeco, more, fide, arte fuit.*

What was there never better man, prelate, or preacher in this world then Bishop Babington? What was St. Paul? What was St. John Baptist? Nay what was our Savior Christ? Were not these prelates and preachers as really and truly men as Babington? Or shall we count them babies? I think your grammar and logic raked all together will scarce be able to excuse so gross a blasphemy, but that you must run to your rhetoric to maintain it as a lewd and lying hyperbole. It is time I end this my tedious discourse, but that I must first make good my promise against the professors of Protestant religion in England with this one argument.

It is palpable idolatry (if any idolatry can be palpable) to give the honor and adoration of true λατρεία to any idol for itself and to rest there.

But all the professors of Protestant religion in England do in that manner give true λατρεία to an idol (if their principles be true). Ergo if their principles be true, they commit most palpable idolatry.

---

20. The Three Pigeons was a bookshop in the churchyard of St. Paul's Cathedral.

21. The image and poem referenced here are on the frontispiece of Babington, *The Works*. The accompanying poem was written by the Bishop of Winchester Miles Smith, in memory of Babington. The translation reads, "No better, no more complete, no other honor. He was a skillful, faithful, and principled Man, Prelate, and Preacher." Similar images of other Protestant leaders are studied in: Aston, "Gods, Saints, and Reformers," 181–220; Phillips, *Reformation of Images*, 140–56.

All the foresaid professors do I know worship Christ Jesus with true λατρεία in the sense aforesaid. But Christ Jesus, according to their principles, is an idol.

Christ Jesus is an image, Colossians 1:15.

But according to protestant principles an image and an idol be *synonima*.²² Ergo, according to Protestant principles, Christ Jesus is an idol.

For the proof of the third minor I argue this. That all English translations of the Bible set forth by authority in the Church of England are the true Word of God is a principle with all the Protestants of England.

But in the same chapter and same verse, the self same world εἴδωλον is in some of their Bibles translated (images) in other some (idols).²³

Therefore according to the principles of English Protestants an image and an idol are *dynomina*.

Satisfy me dear Cousin in solving this argument without any of those quaint evasions or tergiversations ... or forego your protestant principles that all your English Bibles are the true Word of God, for there is no more reason to believe any one of them to be so which may not be alleged for all of them.

And tell me ingenuously whither your Bible makers or translators have not given more just cause to all modest Protestants to blush at this and the like corruption of God's own word, than ever Bellarmine gave (in the places you cite) to a modest papist (as you term a Roman Catholic) to blush for any shame? And moreover tell me I pray you sincerely, whether your own modesty in particular does not blush, as our countryman Dr. Morgan and his confederates most shamefully and vile ... corruption of the second chapter of St. James in so many a point of controversy as the means of justification? When they made St. James say that in Welsh, which he was never spoken by him in any other language before. *Onid trwy ffydd y cyfiawnwyd Abraham eyn tad ni*?²⁴ As if (faith) and (works) were words of the same signification. But god be thanked after that this corruption had passed current in your Church as God's own true word for so many years together, our finding fault therewith has prevailed so much at length with your late translators to move them to correct it, which hereafter may be a curb to bridle all your preach-

---

22. This is in reference to the earlier debate over the translation of the words *imago* and *idolum*, which Protestants often treated as the same, so that idol and image became interchangeable.

23. Margin note: [1 John 5.21. Bible {1562, 1577}]

24. Jas 2:21. The 1567 Welsh translation of the New Testament by William Salesbury reads: *Onid trwy weithredoedd i cyfiownwyd, Abraham yn tad ni* (*Testament Newydd*, sig. 2X6r). In English, the typical translation read: "Was not Abraham our father justified by works."

ers from carrying as such recognitions of our Catholic Bible, as are now and then necessary to reform such small errors and defects, as in process of time may creep into some copies through want of care in some negligent printers. But I pity much your case, who acknowledging upon Earth no infallible authorities to declare for certain what edition or translation of your Bible is authentically true—and to be taken for God's own word—are guided each one of you by his own private spirit, making of the one side the scripture to be the only rule of faith, to define and decide all controversies. Of the other side coining what scripture you please, partly by corrupting the words and partly by interpreting them according to everyone's private fancy. Supposing with slippery, and most uncertain, principles what means have you to convince an obstinate heretic, when he shall delude all that you can say against him with his own fantastical interpretation, what certainty have you (in your grounds) more than he in his, that you have the true sense of scripture, and not he? Or what certainty have you now of any true translation to guide you to god-ward, more than you had when King James came to the crown, who then confessed and acknowledged that he had never seen a true English Bible?

Consider dually (my dear cousin) that there is but one true Catholic faith: without the more it is impossible to please God: *quam nisi quisque fideliter firmiterque credidert, salvus esse non poterit. Quam nisi quisque integram inviolatamque servaverit, absque dubio in eternum peribit.*[25] Study then (dear cousin) and study hard, to find out more steady and certain grounds of faith, than those which yet you have, read our men's books as well as your own with great indifference, and pray to God most earnestly, that he will with the light of his special grace assist your industry. And if my poor endeavor may stand you instead in so good business, you shall be sure to find me ever ready, as one that desires your assured friend to continue, etc. and loving cousin.

May 3. 1625.

---

25. Margin note: [Eph 4.5; Heb 11.]. Both Latin lines are from the Athanasian Creed, parts 42 and 2, respectively (Burn, ed., *The Athanasian Creed*, 77, 98). Translation: "which except a man believe faithfully [truly and firmly], he cannot be saved. / Which faith except every one do keep whole and undefiled; without doubt he shall perish everlastingly."

Bibliography

PRIMARY SOURCES

Aquinas, Thomas. *The Summa Theologica*. Translated by Fathers of the English Dominican Province. New York: Benziger Brothers, 1947.
Ambrose. *Ambrose of Milan: Political Letters and Speeches*. Translated by J. H. W. G. Liebeschuetz. Liverpool: Liverpool University Press, 2005.
Aristotle. *Art of Rhetoric*. Translated by J. H. Freese. Loeb Classical Library, no. 193. Cambridge: Harvard University Press, 1926.
———. *Categories, On Interpretation, Prior Analytics*. Translated by H. P. Cooke and Hugh Tredennick. Loeb Classical Library, no. 325. Cambridge: Harvard University Press, 1938.
———. *Nichomachean Ethics*. Translated by H. Rackham. Loeb Classical Library, no. 73. Cambridge: Harvard University Press, 1926.
Augustine. *City of God against the Pagans*. Edited and translated by R. W. Dyson. Cambridge: Cambridge University Press, 1998.
———. *Responses to Miscellaneous Questions: Miscellany of Eighty-Three Questions*. Edited by Boniface Ramsey and Raymond F. Canning. New York: New City, 2008.
———. *Sancti Aurelii Augustini Opera Omnia Hipponensis Episcopi*. Paris: Apud Parent-Desbarres, 1836.
———. *The Trinity*. Translated by Edmund Hill, O. P. New York: New City, 2012.
Babington, Gervase. *The workes of the Right Reuerend Father in God, Geruase Babington, late Bishop of Worcester Containing comfortable notes vpon the five bookes of Moses*. London: Eld and Flesher, 1622.
Bellarmine, Robert. *An ample declaration of the Christian doctrine*. No loc: English Secret Press, 1604.
———. *Disputationes de controversiis Christianae fidei, adversus huius temporis haereticos, tribus tomis comprehensae*. Ingolstadt: Sartorius, 1586–93.
Bishop, William. *A reformation of a Catholike deformed*. No loc: English Secret Press, 1604.
Bishops Bible. *The holie bible*. London: Jugge, 1568.
Bonnet, Maximilian, and Richard A. Lipsius, eds. *Acta Apostolica Apocrypha*. Leipzig: Mendelssohn, 1891.
Brewer, J. S., J. Gairdner, and R. H. Brodie, eds. *Letters and Papers, Foreign and Domestic, of Reign of Henry VIII*. London: Her Majesty's Stationary Office, 1862–1932.
Bruce, John, ed. *The Works of Roger Hutchinson*. Cambridge: Cambridge University Press, 1842.

Bibliography

Bucer, Martin. *A treatise declarying and shewing diverse causes taken out of holy scriptures of the sentences of holy fathers and of the decrees of devout emperors, that pictures and other images which were wont to be worshipped are in no wise to be suffered in the temples or churches of Christian men.* London: n.p., 1535.

Bullinger, Henry. *The Decades of Henry Bullinger.* 4 vols. Translated by Thomas Harding. Cambridge: Cambridge University Press, 1852.

Calfhill, James. *An Answer to John Martiall's Treatise of the Cross.* Edited by Richard Gibbings. Cambridge: Cambridge University Press, 1841.

Calvin, John. *John Calvin's Sermons on the Ten Commandment.* Edited and translated by Benjamin Farley. Grand Rapids: Baker, 1980.

———. *Sermons on Deuteronomy.* Translated by Arthur Golding. Facsimile. Edinburgh: Banner of Truth Trust, 1987.

Calvin, John. *Institutes of the Christian Religion.* Translated by Henry Beveridge. Peabody, MA: Hendrickson, 2008.

Chrysostom, John. *Adversus Gentiles demonstratio, quod Christus sit deus,* in *Opera Omnia.* 5 vols. Basel: Froben, 1558. V. 1191–214.

Cicero, Marcus Tullius. *The Orations of Marcus Tullius Cicero,* vol. IV. Translated by C. D. Yonge. London: Bell and Sons, 1921.

Constitutio[ns] and canons ecclesiasticall treated vpon by the Bishop of London, president of the conuocation for the prouince of Canterbury, and the rest of the bishops and clergie of the said prouince. London: Barker, 1604.

Crashaw, William. *The sermon preached at the Crosse, Feb. xiiii. 1607. By W. Crashawe, Batchelour of Diuinitie, and preacher at the temple; iustified by the authour, both against Papist, and Brownist.* London: Lownes, 1609.

Crinitus, Petrus. *De honesta disciplina.* Basil: Petrus, 1532.

Elliott, J. K., ed. *The Apocryphal New Testament: A Collection of Apocryphal Christian Literature in an English Translation based on M. R. James.* Oxford: Oxford University Press, 1994.

Epiphanius. *The Panarion of Epiphanius of Salamis: Book I.* sects 1–46. Translated by Frank Williams. Leiden: Brill, 1987.

Erasmus, Desiderius. *Collected Works of Erasmus: Colloquies.* Translated and annotated by Craig R. Thompson. Toronto: University of Toronto Press, 1997.

Eusebius. *Ecclesiastical History,* vol. II. Translated by J. E. L. Oulton. Loeb Classical Library, no. 265. Cambridge: Harvard University Press, 1932.

———. *Life of Constantine.* Translated by Averil Cameron and Stuart G. Hall. Oxford: Oxford University Press, 1999.

Eutropius. *Abridgment of Roman History.* Translated by Rev. John Selby Watson. London: Bell and Sons, 1886.

Frere, W. H., and C. E. Douglas, eds. *Puritan Manifestoes: A Study in the Origin of the Puritan Revolt.* New York: Franklin, 1972.

Fulke, William. *A Brief Confutation of a Popish Discourse.* London: Dawson, 1581.

———. *A Defence of the Sincere and True Translations of the Holy Scriptures into the English Tongue: Against the Cavils of Gregory Martin.* Edited by Charles Henry Hartshorne. Cambridge: Parker Society, 1843.

Galen. *De differentiis frebrium lirri.* Lyons: Rovillium, 1570.

Geneva Bible. *The bible and holy scriptures conteyned in the olde and newe testament. According to the Ebrue and the Greke. With moste profitable annotations.* Geneva: Hall, 1560.

Griffiths, John, ed. *Two Books of Homilies*. 1858. Reprint. Vancouver, BC: Regent College, 2008.

Heigham, John. *The Touch-stone of the reformed Gospel*. Saint Omer, France: n.p., 1652.

Herodotus. *Histories*. Translated by Pamela Mensch and edited by James Romm. Indianapolis: Hackett, 2014.

Hess, Hamilton. *The Early Development of Canon Law and the Council of Serdica*. Oxford: Oxford University Press, 2002.

Hieronymus (Jerome). *Commentariorum Ezechielem Prophetam*. Patrologia Latina, vol. XXV. Edited by J. P. Migne. Paris: Garnier Fatres, 1866.

Hooper, John. *Early Writings of John Hooper*. Edited by Rev. Samuel Carr. Cambridge: Cambridge University Press, 1843.

Horace. *Satires, Epistles, Ars Poetica*. Translated by H. R. Fairclough. Loeb Classical Library, no. 194. Cambridge: Harvard University Press, 1929.

Jewel, John. *The Works of John Jewel*. 4 vols. Edited by John Ayre. Cambridge: Cambridge University Press, 1845–50.

John of Damascus. *Three Treatises on the Divine Images*. Edited and translated by Andrew Louth. Crestwood, NY: St. Vladimir's Seminary Press, 2003.

Lactantius. *Divine Institutes*. Translated by Anthony Bowen and Peter Garnsey. Liverpool: Liverpool University Press, 2003.

Lucretius. *On the Nature of Things*. Translated by Martin Ferguson Smith. Indianapolis: Hackett, 2001.

Luther, Martin. *Luther's Works, vol. 51: Sermons I*. Edited by John Doberstein. Minneapolis: Fortress, 1951.

Mela, Pomponius. *De situ orbis*. Edited by Charles-Pierre Fradin. Paris: La Librairie de Brissot-Thivars, 1827.

Montagu, Richard. *A Gagg for the New Gospell? No, A New Gagg for an Old Goose*. London: Snodham, 1624.

Pancoast, Henry Spackman, and John Spaeth, eds. *Early English Poems*. New York: Holt, 1910.

Paul the Deacon. *History of the Lombards*. Translated by William Dudley Foulke and edited by Edward Peters. Philadelphia: University of Pennsylvania Press, 2003.

Perkins, William. *A Golden Chain, or The Description of Theology Containing the Order of the Causes of Salvation and Damnation, according to God's Word*. Cambridge: Legat, 1600.

Philo. *On the Embassy to Gaius*. Translated by F. H. Colson. Loeb Classical Library, no. 379. Cambridge: Harvard University Press, 1962.

Platina, Bartholomeo. *Lives of the Popes: Antiquity*. Edited and translated by Anthony F. D'Elia. Cambridge: Harvard University Press, 2008.

Pliny the Elder. *Natural History, vol. I*. Translated by H. Rackham. Loeb Classical Library, no. 330. Cambridge: Harvard University Press, 1938.

Rainolds, John. *De Romanae Ecclesiae idolatria, in cultu sanctorum, reliquarum, imaginum, aquae, salis, olei, aliarumq[ue] rerum consecratarum, and sacramenti Eucharistiae*. Oxford: Barnes, 1596.

Sander, Nicholas. *Treatise on the Images of Christ*. Saint Omer, France: Boscard, 1624.

Seville, Isidore of. *The Etymologies of Isidore of Seville*. Edited and translated by Stephen A. Barney et al. Cambridge: Cambridge University Press, 2006.

Sider, Ronald J. *Karlstadt's Battle with Luther: Documents in a Liberal-Radical Debate*. Eugene, OR: Wipf & Stock, 2001.

Solinus, Gaius Julius. *De mirabilibus mundi*. Venice: de Pensis, 1498.
Strype, John. *Annals of the Reformation and Establishment of Religion*. London: Wyat, 1709.
Tacitus. *Agricola. Germania. Dialogue on Oratory*. Translated by M. Hutton and W. Peterson. Loeb Classical Library, no. 35. Cambridge: Harvard Classical Library, 1914.
Testament Newydd ein arglwydd Jesu Christ. Translated by William Salesbury and Richard Davies. London: Denham, 1567.
Tyndale, William. *An Answer to Sir Thomas More's Dialogue*. Edited by Henry Walter. Cambridge: Cambridge University Press, 1850.

SECONDARY SOURCES

Allison, A. F. "John Heigham of St. Omer. c. 1568–c. 1632." *Recusant History* 4 (1957) 226–32
Arnade, Peter. *Beggars, Iconoclasts, and Civic Patriots: The Political Culture of the Dutch Revolt*. Ithaca, NY: Cornell University Press, 2008.
Asselt, Willem van, et al., eds, *Iconoclasm and Iconoclash: Struggle for Religious Identity*. Leiden: Brill, 2007.
Aston, Margaret. *England's Iconoclasts: Laws Against Images*, vol. 1. Oxford: Clarendon, 1988.
Aston, Margaret. "Gods, Saints, and Reformers: Portraiture and Protestant England." In *Albion's Classicism: Visual Arts in Britain: 1550–1660*, edited by Lucy Ghent, 181–220. New Haven: Yale University Press, 1995.
———. *The King's Bedpost: Reformation and Iconography in a Tudor Group Portrait*. Cambridge: Cambridge University Press, 1991.
———. *Lollards and Reformers: Images and Literacy in Late Medieval Religion*. London: Hambledon, 1984.
Aston, Margaret, and Elizabeth Ingram. "The Iconography of the Actes and Monuments." In *John Foxe and the English Reformation*, edited by David Loades, 66–142. Aldershot, UK: Ashgate, 1997.
Barth, Karl, and Eduard Thurneysen. *Revolutionary Theology in the Making: Barth-Thurneysen Correspondence, 1914–25*. Richmond, VA: John Knox, 1964.
Belting, Hans. *Likeness and Presence: A History of the Image before the Era of Art*. Chicago: University of Chicago Press, 1994.
Bernard, George. *The King's Reformation: Henry VIII and the Remaking of the English Church*. New Haven: Yale University Press, 2007.
Besançon, Alain. *The Forbidden Image: An Intellectual History of Iconoclasm*. Chicago: University of Chicago Press, 1994.
Biel, Pamela. *Doorkeepers at the House of Righteousness: Heinrich Bullinger and the Zurich Clergy, 1535–1575*. New York: Lang, 1991.
Bouwsma, William J. *John Calvin: A Sixteenth-Century Portrait*. Oxford: Oxford University Press, 1989.
Brigden, Susan. *London and the Reformation*. Oxford: Oxford University Press, 1989.
Brown, Peter. *The Rise of Western Christendom*. 2nd ed. Oxford: Blackwell, 2003.
Brubaker, Leslie. *Inventing Byzantine Iconoclasm*. New York: Bloomsbury, 2012.

Brubaker, Leslie, and John Haldon, eds. *Byzantium in the Iconoclastic Era, 680–850: A History*. Cambridge: Cambridge University Press, 2011.
Bruce, F. F. *History of the Bible in English*. Cambridge: Lutterworth, 1961.
Budd, Joel. "Rethinking Iconoclasm in Early Modern England: The Case of the Cheapside Cross." *Journal of Early Modern History* 4 (2000) 379–404.
Burn, A. E., ed. *The Athanasian Creed*. London: Rivingtons, 1930.
Bush, M. L. *The Pilgrimage of Grace: A Study of the Rebel Armies of October 1536*. Manchester: Manchester University Press, 1996.
Butler, Alban, and Paul Burns, eds. *Butler's Lives of the Saints: New Full Edition*. Tunbridge Wells, UK: Burns and Oates, 2000.
Campi, Emidio, ed. *Peter Martyr Vermigli: Humanism, Republicanism, and Reformation*. Geneva: Droz, 2002.
Christensen, Carl C. *Art and the Reformation in Germany*. Athens, OH: Ohio University Press, 1979.
Clark, Stuart. *Thinking with Demons: The Idea of Witchcraft in Early Modern Europe*. Oxford: Oxford University Press, 1997.
———. *Vanities of the Eye: Vision in Early Modern Culture*. Oxford: Oxford University Press, 2007.
Cogswell, Thomas. *The Blessed Revolution: English Politics and the Coming of War, 1621–1624*. Cambridge: Cambridge University Press, 1989.
Collinson, Patrick. *The Birthpangs of Protestant England: Religious and Cultural Change in the Sixteenth and Seventeenth Centuries*. London: MacMillan, 1988.
———. *Elizabethans*. London: Bloomsbury, 2003.
———. "From Iconoclasm to Iconophobia." In *The Impact of the English Reformation, 1500–1640*, edited by Peter Marshall, 278–307. London: Arnold, 1997.
Craik, Henry, ed. *English Prose: Selections with Critical Introductions by Various Writers and General Introductions to Each Period*, vol. I. New York: MacMillan, 1916.
Crew, Phyllis Mack. *Calvinist Preaching and Iconoclasm in the Netherlands, 1544–1569*. Cambridge: Cambridge University Press, 1978.
Daniell, David. *William Tyndale: A Biography*. New Haven: Yale University Press, 1994.
Davis, David J. "'The meanes of justification': A Catholic Letter on the Image Debate in Reformation Britain." *Reformation and Renaissance Review* 14 (2013) 288–311.
———. *Seeing Faith, Printing Pictures: Religious Identity during the English Reformation*. Leiden: Brill, 2013.
Dewender, Thomas. "William of Ockham and Walter Burley on Signification and Imaginary Objects." In *Philosophy and Theology in the Long Middle Ages*, edited by Kenty Emery Jr. et al., 437–50. Leiden: Brill, 2011.
Dillenberger, John. *Images and Relics: Theological Perceptions and Visual Images in Sixteenth Century Europe*. Oxford: Oxford University Press, 1999.
Duffy, Eamon. *Stripping of the Altars: Traditional Religion in England, 1400–1580*. New Haven: Yale University Press, 1992.
———. *Voices of Morebath: Reformation and Rebellion in an English Village*. New Haven: Yale University Press, 2001.
Dyrness, William. *Reformed Theology and Visual Culture: The Protestant Imagination from Calvin to Edwards*. Cambridge: Cambridge University Press, 2004.
Eells, Hastings. *Martin Bucer*. New Haven: Yale University Press, 1931.
Eire, Carlos. *War Against the Idols: The Reformation of Worship from Erasmus to Calvin*. Cambridge: Cambridge University Press, 1986.

Bibliography

Ekonomou, Andrew J. *Byzantine Rome and the Greek Popes: Eastern Influences on Rome and the Papacy from Gregory the Great to Zacharias, AD 590–752.* Lanham, MD: Lexington, 2007.

Elizabeth Evenden, "The Fleeing Dutchmen? The Influence of Dutch Immigrants upon the Print Shop of John Day." In *John Foxe at Home and Abroad*, edited by David Loades, 63–77. Aldershot, UK: Ashgate, 2004.

Erler, Mary C. *Women, Reading, and Piety in Late Medieval England.* Cambridge: Cambridge University Press, 2006.

Evenden, Elizabeth. *Patents, Pictures, and Patronage: John Day and the Tudor Book Trade.* Aldershot, UK: Ashgate, 2008.

Fincham, Kenneth, and Nicholas Tyacke. *Altars Restored: The Changing Face of English Religious Worship, 1547–1700.* Oxford: Oxford University Press, 2007.

Fuller, Ross. *The Brotherhood of the Common Life and Its Influences.* Albany, NY: State University of New York Press, 1995.

Giakalis, Ambrosios. *Images of the Divine: The Theology of Icons at the Seventh Ecumenical Council.* Leiden: Brill, 2005.

Gombrich, Ernst. *Symbolic Images: Studies in the Art of the Renaissance.* London: Phaidon, 1972.

Gordon, Bruce, and Emidio Campi, eds. *Architect of Reformation: An Introduction to Heinrich Bullinger, 1504–1575.* Grand Rapids: Baker, 2004.

Hamling, Tara, and Richard Williams, eds. *Art Re-formed: Re-assessing the Impact of the Reformation on the Visual Arts.* Newcastle-upon-Tyne, UK: Cambridge Scholars, 2007.

Haugaard, William. *Elizabeth and the English Reformation: The Struggles for a Stable Settlement.* Cambridge: Cambridge University Press, 1968.

Heal, Bridget. *The Cult of the Virgin Mary in Early Modern Germany: Protestant and Catholic Piety, 1500–1648.* Cambridge: Cambridge University Press, 2007.

Hefele, Charles Joseph. *A History of the Councils of the Church: From the Original Documents*, vol. IV. Edinburgh: T. & T. Clark, 1895.

Hodnett, Edward. *Marcus Gheeraerts of Bruges, London, and Antwerp.* Utrecht: Haentjens Dekker & Gumbert, 1971.

Hunter, Michael, ed. *Printed Images in Early Modern Britain: Essays in Interpretation.* Aldershot, UK: Ashgate, 2010.

Jenkins, Gary W. *John Jewel and the English National Church: The Dilemmas of an Erastian Reformer.* Aldershot, UK: Ashgate, 2006.

———. "Peter Martyr and the Church of England after 1558." In *Peter Martyr and the European Reformations*, edited by Frank James, 47–69. Leiden: Brill, 2004.

Johnstone, Nathan. *The Devil and Demonism in Early Modern England.* Cambridge: Cambridge University Press, 2006.

Jones, E. A., and Alexandra Walsham, eds. *Syon Abbey and Its Books: Reading, Writing, and Religion, 1400–1700.* Woodbridge, UK: Boydell, 2010.

Kastan, David Scott. "'The noyse of the new Bible': Reform and Reaction in Henrician England." In *Religion and Culture in Renaissance England*, edited by Claire McEachern and Deborah Shuger, 46–68. Cambridge: Cambridge University Press, 1997.

King, John N. *Foxe's "Book of Martyrs" and Early Modern Print Culture.* Cambridge: Cambridge University Press, 2006.

———. *Tudor Royal Iconography: Literature and Art in the Age of Religious Crisis*. Princeton: Princeton University Press, 1989.

Kirby, Torrance. *The Zurich Connection and Tudor Political Theology*. Leiden: Brill, 2007.

Kitzinger, Ernst. *The Cult of Images in the Age before Iconoclasm*. Cambridge: Harvard University Press, 1954.

Koerner, Joseph. *The Reformation of the Image*. Chicago: University of Chicago Press, 2004.

Kolrud, Kristine and Marina Prusac, eds. *Iconoclasm from Antiquity to Modernity*. Aldershot, UK: Ashgate, 2014.

Lake, Peter. *Anglicans and Puritans? Presbyterianism and English Conformist Thought from Whitgift to Hooker*. London: Unwyn Hyman, 1988.

Lillback, Peter A. *The Binding of God: Calvin's Role in the Development of Covenant Theology*. Grand Rapids: Baker, 2001.

Louth, Andrew. *St. John of Damascus: Tradition and Originality in Byzantine Theology*. Oxford: Oxford University Press, 2002.

Luborsky, Ruth S., and Elizabeth Ingram. *A Guide to English Illustrated Books, 1536-1603*. 2 vols. Tempe, AZ: Medieval & Renaissance Texts & Studies, 1998.

MacCulloch, Diarmaid. *The Boy King: Edward VI and the Protestant Reformation*. Berkeley: University of California Press, 1999.

MacMullen, Ramsay. *Christianizing the Roman Empire: AD 100-400*. New Haven: Yale University Press, 1984.

Marshall, Peter. "(Re)defining the English Reformation." *Journal of British Studies* 48 (2009) 564–86.

———. *Religious Identities in Henry VIII's England*. Aldershot, UK: Ashgate, 2006.

Mayes, Robert J. H. "The Lord's Supper in the Theology of Cyprian of Carthage." *Concordia Theological Quarterly* 74 (2010) 307–24.

McCullough, Peter. *Sermons at Court: Politics and Religion in Elizabethan and Jacobean Preaching*. Cambridge: Cambridge University Press, 1998.

McGrath, Alister. *A Life of John Calvin: A Study in the Shaping of Western Culture*. Oxford: Blackwell, 1990.

McLelland, Joseph. "A Literary History of the Loci Communes." In *A Companion to Peter Martyr Vermigli*, edited by Torrance Kirby, Edmidio Campi, and Frank A. James III, 479–94. Leiden: Brill, 2009.

McNair, Philip. *Peter Martyr in Italy: An Anatomy of Apostasy*. Oxford: Clarendon, 1967.

McNeill, John T. *The History and Character of Calvinism*. Oxford: Oxford University Press, 1967.

Michalski, Sergiusz. *The Reformation and the Visual Arts: The Protestant Image Question in Western and Eastern Europe*. London: Routlege, 1993.

Michelet, Jules. *The Life of Luther: Gathered from His Own Writings*. Translated by G. H. Smith. New York: Bogue, 1846.

Milner, Matthew. *The Senses and the English Reformation*. Aldershot, UK: Ashgate, 2011.

Milton, Anthony, *Catholic and Reformed: The Roman and Protestant Churches in English Protestant Thought, 1600-1640*. Cambridge: Cambridge University Press, 1995.

Milton, Anthony, and Alexandra Walsham, eds, "Richard Montagu: 'Concerning Recusancie of Communion with the Church of England.'" In *From Cranmer to*

Davidson: A Church of England Miscellany, edited by Stephen Taylor, 69–102. Woodbridge, UK: Boydell, 1999.

Morton, Adam. "Images and the Senses in Post-Reformation England." *Reformation* 20 (2015) 77–100.

Naudé, Jacobus. "The Role of the Metatexts in the King James Version as a Means of Mediating Conflicting Theological Views." In *The King James Version at 400: Assessing Its Genius as Bible Translation and Its Literary Influence*, edited by David G. Burke, John F. Kutsko, and Philip H. Towner, 157–94. Atlanta: Society of Biblical Literature, 2013.

Newcombe, David Gordon. *John Hooper: Tudor Bishop and Martyr. c. 1495–1555*. Oxford: Davenant, 2009.

Noble, Thomas F. X. *Images, Iconoclasm, and the Carolingians*. Philadelphia: University of Pennsylvania Press, 2009.

O'Connell, Michael. *The Idolatrous Eye: Iconoclasm and Theater in Early Modern England*. Oxford: Oxford University Press, 2000.

O'Daly, Gerard. *Augustine's Philosophy of Mind*. London: Duckworth, 1987.

Oldridge, Darren. *The Devil in Early Modern England*. Stroud, UK: Sutton, 2000.

Overell, Ann. "Peter Martyr in England, 1547–1553: An Alternative View." *Sixteenth Century Journal* 15 (1987) 87–104.

Parker, T. H. L. *Calvin: An Introduction to His Thought*. Louisville: John Knox, 1995.

———. *Calvin's Doctrine of the Knowledge of God*. Grand Rapids: Eerdmans, 1959.

Parry, Kenneth. *Depicting the Word: Byzantine Iconophile Thought of the Eighth and Ninth Centuries*. Leiden: Brill, 1996.

Patterson, W. B. *William Perkins and the Making of a Protestant England*. Oxford: Oxford University Press, 2014.

Perry, S. G. F., ed. *The Second Synod of Ephesus*. Dartford, UK: Orient, 1881.

Pettegree, Andrew. *Emden and the Dutch Revolt: Exile and the Development of Reformed Protestantism*. Oxford: Oxford University Press, 1992.

———. *Reformation and the Culture of Persuasion*. Cambridge: Cambridge University Press, 2005.

Phillips, John. *The Reformation of Images: Destruction of Art in England, 1535–1660*. Berkeley: University of California Press, 1973.

Purvis, J. S., ed. *Tudor Parish Documents of the Diocese of York*. Cambridge: Cambridge University Press, 1948.

Questier, Michael. *Catholicism and Community in Early Modern England: Politics, Aristocracy, Patronage and Religion, 1550–1640*. Cambridge: Cambridge University Press, 2006.

———. *Conversion, Politics and Religion in England, 1580–1620*. Cambridge: Cambridge University Press, 1996.

Rose, Els. *Ritual Memory: The Apocryphal Acts and Liturgical Commemoration in the Early Medieval West, c. 500–1215*. Leiden: Brill, 2009.

Rublack, Ulinka. *Reformation Europe*. Cambridge: Cambridge University Press, 2005.

Ryrie, Alec. *Being Protestant in Reformation Britain*. Oxford: Oxford University Press, 2013.

———. *The Gospel and Henry VIII: Evangelicals in the Early English Reformation*. Cambridge: Cambridge University Press, 2003.

Schaefer, J. O. "Saint Luke as Painter: From Saint to Artisan to Artist." In *Artistes, artisans, et production artistique au Moyen Âge*, edited by X. Barral i Alter, 413–27. Paris: Picard, 1986.

Scribner, Robert. *For the Sake of the Simple Folk: Popular Propaganda for the German Reformation*. Oxford: Clarendon, 1994.

Selderhuis, Herman J. *John Calvin: A Pilgrim's Life*. Downers Grove IL: IVP, 2009.

———. *Marriage and Divorce in the Thought of Martin Bucer*. Translated by John Vriend and Lyle D. Bierma. Kirksville, MO: Thomas Jefferson University Press, 1999.

Shagan, Ethan. ed., *Catholics and the 'Protestant Nation': Religious Politics and Identity in Early Modern England*. Manchester: Manchester University Press, 2006.

———. *Popular Politics and the English Reformation*. Cambridge: Cambridge University Press, 2002.

Shuger, Deborah. *The Renaissance Bible: Scholarship, Sacrifice, and Subjectivity*. Berkeley: University of California Press, 1998.

Spraggon, Julie. *Puritan Iconoclasm during the English Civil War*. Woodbridge, UK: Boydell, 2003.

Stronks, Els. *Negotiating Differences: Word, Image, and Religion in the Dutch Republic*. Leiden: Brill, 2011.

Turvey, Roger. *The Treason and Trial of John Perrot*. Cardiff: University of Wales Press, 2005.

Tutino, Stefania. *Law and Conscience: Catholicism in Early Modern England, 1570 –1625*. Aldershot, UK: Ashgate, 2007.

Tyacke, Nicholas. *Anti-Calvinists: The Rise of English Arminianism, 1590–1640*. Oxford: Clarendon, 1987.

———. *Aspects of English Protestantism, 1530–1700*. Manchester: Manchester University Press, 2001.

Vanhaelen, Angela. *The Wake of Iconoclasm: Painting the Church in the Dutch Republic*. University Park, PA: Pennsylvania State University Press, 2012.

Veech, Thomas. *Dr. Nicholas Sanders and the English Reformation, 1530–1581*. Louvain: Bureaux du Recueil, 1935.

Wabuda, Susan. *Preaching During the English Reformation*. Cambridge: Cambridge University Press, 2002.

Walsham, Alexandra. "Angels and Idols in England's Long Reformation." In *Angels in the Early Modern World. Cambridge*, edited by Alexandra Walsham and Peter Marshall, 134–67. Cambridge: Cambridge University Press, 2006.

———. *Church Papists: Catholicism, Conformity and Confessional Polemic in Early Modern England*. Woodbridge, UK: Boydell, 1993.

———. "Invisible Helpers: Angelic Intervention in Post-Reformation England." *Past and Present* 208 (2010) 77–130.

Wandel, Lee Palmer. *The Eucharist in the Reformation: Incarnation and Liturgy*. Cambridge: Cambridge University Press, 2006.

———. *Voracious Idols and Violent Hands: Iconoclasm in Reformation Zurich, Strasbourg, and Basel*. Cambridge: Cambridge University Press, 1995.

Waterworth, James, ed. *The Council of Trent: The Canons and Decrees of the Sacred and Oecumenical Council of Trent*. London: Dolman, 1848.

Watson, Rowan. "Some Non-Textual Use of Books." In *A Companion to the History of the Book*, edited by Simon Eliot and Jonathan Rose, 480–92. Malden, MA: Wiley-Blackwell, 2007.

Watt, Tessa. *Cheap Print and Popular Piety, 1550–1640*. Cambridge: Cambridge University Press, 1991.

Webster, Thomas. *Godly Clergy in Early Stuart England: The Caroline Puritan Movement, 1620–1643*. Cambridge: Cambridge University Press, 2003.

Werrell, Ralph S. *The Theology of William Tyndale*. Cambridge: James Clarke, 2006.

Wizeman, William. *The Theology and Spirituality of Mary Tudor's Church*. Aldershot, UK: Ashgate, 2006.

Wooding, Lucy. "From Tudor Humanism to Reformation Preaching." In *The Oxford Handbook of the Early Modern Sermon*, edited by Hugh Adlington, Peter McCullough, and Emma Rhatigan, 329–47. Oxford: Oxford University Press, 20011.

Woolgar, C. M. *The Senses in Late Medieval England*. New Haven: Yale University Press, 2006.

Wright, D. F., ed. *Martin Bucer: Reforming Church and Community*. Cambridge: Cambridge University Press, 1994.

Zachman, Randall. *Image and Word in the Theology of John Calvin*. Notre Dame: University of Notre Dame Press, 2009.

General Index

Aaron, high priest of Israel, 67, 154–55
Abgarus, 122
Abraham, 31–32, 83–84, 133, 152, 163–64, 196
adiaphora, 9, 16
Agatha, Saint, 28
altars, 1, 3, 6, 17–18, 20, 72–73, 77, 80, 85, 103–4, 113, 130, 132, 146, 151, 157, 183
Ambrose, Saint, 22, 90, 114, 186, 189, 191
Andrew, Saint, 102, 107
anti-Catholicism, 5, 74, 80, 180, 189
Aquinas, Thomas. *See* Thomas Aquinas
Aristotle, 57, 59, 120, 176
Ark of the Covenant, 33, 53, 84, 126, 153–54, 175, 185, 187
Aston, Margaret, 2–3, 6–7, 10, 15, 17–18, 20, 24–25, 51, 57, 64–65, 72, 74, 79–80, 89–91, 93, 114–15, 172, 188, 195
Athanasius, 9, 41, 90, 114, 197
Augustine of Hippo, 9, 22, 68, 90, 98, 104–6, 108, 114, 122, 124, 129–32, 137, 153, 155, 168, 182, 186

Babington, Gervase, 195
Basil, Saint, 179, 182
Bellarmine, Robert, 169–73, 181, 194, 196
Beze, Theodore, 6, 147
Bishop, William, 12, 161–68
Bishops Bible, 6, 74, 77–78, 137, 178
Bonner, Edmund, 18
Brotherhood of the Common Life, 20
Bucer, Martin, 10–11, 35–42, 64–65, 118
Bullinger, Heinrich, 82–83
Byzantine iconoclasm, 2, 91, 9–94, 122

Calvin, John, 4, 11, 36, 47–55, 64–65, 91, 119, 147, 180, 195
Cheapside Cross, 11, 145
Chrysostom, John, 9, 62, 105–6, 108, 179
churches
    Bow Street, 72
    Bremgarten, 82
    Ipswich, 11
    St. Margaret Pattens, 16
    St. Peter's (Lille), 98
    St. Peter's (Rome), 93
    St. Paul's, 195
    Sudbury, 15
Clark, Stuart, 54, 160
Collinson, Patrick, 4, 16, 90
Constantine I, emperor, 92–93, 126, 131, 156
Constantinople, Seventh Council of, 151
Cranach, Lucas, 5, 74
Cranmer, Thomas, 44, 64, 72, 118, 140
Cromwell, Thomas, 44

General Index

cross (crosses), 1–2, 4–5, 8, 11, 15–16, 22, 25–28, 39–40, 53, 57, 65, 72–73, 80, 83, 90, 98–109, 113, 127, 139–40, 142–43, 145, 153–56, 162, 180, 188–94
crucifix, 54, 61, 72–73, 80, 100, 104, 140, 144, 153, 175, 177, 181, 187, 189
Cyril, Saint, 90, 108

Daniel (prophet), 8, 125, 152, 163, 165, 167, 172, 178
Douai-Rheims Bible, 135
Duffy, Eamon, 7, 15–16, 28
dulia, 8–9, 95, 119, 129, 180, 184, 186–87
Dyrness, William, 25, 36, 132

Edgeworth, Roger, 18, 56–63, 162
eidolon, 9, 120
eikon, 9
Eire, Carlos, 1, 3–4, 51, 79–80, 114, 181
Elvira, Council of, 151, 155
Epiphanius, 90, 122, 130, 151
Erasmus, Desiderius, 20, 25, 95
Eusebius of Caesarea, 9, 90, 114, 122, 156, 182, 189
Ezekiel (prophet), 74–75, 77–78, 88, 125

Geneva Bible, 6, 74–75, 77–78
Gheeraerts, Marcus, 79–80
Gombrich, Ernst, 115
Great Bible, 43–44
Gregory the Great, 9, 51, 91–92, 97, 153

Hampton Court Conference, 145
Harding, Thomas, 83, 114
Heigham, John, 174–78, 180–81
Helen, Saint, 189, 191
Herodotus, 68
Hezekiah, king of Israel, 70, 113, 137, 153, 155
Hooper, John, 17, 64–70
Horace, 95, 164

iconoclasm, 1–9, 11, 15–18, 65, 71–73, 79, 83, 90–91, 109–10, 112–13, 119, 131–32, 138, 145, 151, 162, 189
idols, 2, 4, 8–10, 25, 48, 50–52, 55, 57, 60–62, 80, 84–85, 87–88, 90, 93–94, 101, 107, 112–14, 120, 126, 131–32, 137–44, 150–51, 155–57, 171, 177, 181, 187, 196
image devotion / worship:
  decking / adorning, 89, 91–92
  kissing, 194
  kneeling / bowing, 6, 10, 25, 27, 37, 54, 67, 69, 88, 95, 139, 153–54, 166–67, 171, 175–76, 185, 193
images of:
  angels / cherubim, 8, 53, 111, 114, 119, 123, 127, 132–33, 137–38, 143, 149, 151–52, 156, 164–66, 172, 178, 180–82
  Christ, 5, 26, 36, 40–41, 44, 48, 54–55, 58, 83, 87, 100, 103, 109, 111–13, 116, 119, 122, 127–28, 130, 132–33, 138–39, 141, 149, 151, 153, 155, 166–67, 180, 182, 187, 192–96
  God the Father, 5, 78, 124, 164, 172–73
  Trinity, 8, 111, 124, 152, 163
  Virgin, 5, 16, 80, 103, 122, 140, 180, 187
Isaiah (prophet), 8, 33, 34, 50, 66, 70, 74–75, 77–78, 124–25, 150, 157–58, 178, 190

Jeremiah (prophet), 50–51, 70, 155
Jerome, Saint, 9, 90, 108, 123, 130, 138, 151, 175
John of Damascus, 9, 98, 122, 187
Josiah, king of Israel, 2, 17

Karlstadt, Andreas, 4, 53, 83, 96, 181
King, John N., 6, 44, 77
Koerner, Joseph, 6, 36, 53, 75, 80, 144

latria, 8–9, 95, 119, 129, 176–77, 184, 186–87, 192–93
laymen's books, 9–10, 39, 51, 133, 172

General Index

Lollards, 3, 6, 15, 58
Lord's Supper, Eucharist, communion, 40–41, 52, 55, 146, 158, 176
Lucretius, 124
Luther, Martin, 3, 5–6, 15, 19, 24–25, 35–36, 43, 53–54, 58, 72, 74–75, 80, 83, 96, 111, 144, 194–95

Martiall, John, 9, 71, 98–110, 162
Martin, Gregory, 57, 71, 135–44
Michalski, Sergiusz, 3–4, 36, 65, 82,
miracles, 1, 39, 67, 99, 101, 107, 160, 172, 176
Montagu, Richard, 12, 119, 179–87
More, Thomas, 10, 19, 24, 110
Moses, 22, 33, 47, 49, 53, 58, 62, 66, 70, 74, 83–84, 117, 125, 132–33, 137, 149, 152, 154, 165, 176, 178, 180, 184, 190

names of God:
    Tetragrammaton, 6, 176
    Holy Monogram, 176
Nazianzus, 9, 179
Nicea, Second Council of, 91, 97, 103, 125, 142, 188, 192
Nowell, Alexander, 98, 100

Origen, 9, 42, 90, 150–51
Orleans, Synod of, 103

Paul, Saint, 22–23, 30–32, 34, 41, 58, 61–62, 67, 74, 86, 95, 107, 123, 129, 131–32, 137–39, 158, 181–82, 185, 191, 195
Perkins, William, 8, 12, 119, 146–67
Perrot, John, 193
Pettegree, Andrew, 5, 112
Peter, Saint, 74, 93, 95, 98, 131, 159, 182
Philip, Saint, 100, 102
Philo, 121
Pilgrimage of Grace, 16
pilgrimages, 1, 7, 28–29, 67, 88, 94, 157

Pliny, 62
Pole, Reginald, 18

Ryckes, John, 19–23, 25
Ryrie, Alec, 11, 56

Sander, Nicholas, 10, 71, 109–17, 185
Satan, the Devil, devils, 42, 51, 54, 69, 95–96, 101, 130, 153, 160
Scribner, Robert, 5–6, 80, 132
Second Helvetic Creed, 65
Solinus, 62
Solis, Virgil, 78
Spraggon, Julie, 17, 71, 148, 181
statues, 1, 7–9, 17–18, 25, 79, 186
Stephen, Saint, 25, 29, 34, 74, 151
superstition, 13, 17, 25, 41–42, 52, 54–55, 67, 88, 84, 96, 102, 108, 122, 149, 158

Tacitus, 86
Temple (Jerusalem), 29–30, 33–34, 48, 53, 85, 91, 113–14, 121, 132, 137–38, 143, 149, 151, 156, 165, 183, 187
Tertullian, 9, 90, 98, 108, 120, 122, 128, 151, 181–82
Thomas Aquinas, 153, 170, 181, 187, 192
Tours, Council of, 103
Trent, Council of, 2, 109, 146, 163, 169, 172, 177, 194
Tyndale, William, 11, 15, 24–35

Vermigli, Peter, 54, 118–34, 148
vestments, 11, 17–18, 22, 44, 64, 72, 85, 103

Wandel, Lee Palmer, 1, 3, 10, 51, 172, 176
Walsham, Alexandra, 19, 73, 127, 180
witchcraft, 148, 159–60

Zwingli, Ulrich, 36, 64, 83, 118

www.ingramcontent.com/pod-product-compliance
Lightning Source LLC
Chambersburg PA
CBHW051522230426
43668CB00012B/1704